"For all the genuine horror and revulsion they inspire in us, there's no point in denying that serial killers exert a dark attraction. They appeal not just to our morbid interest but also to our need to comprehend an ultimate human mystery: how people who seem so ordinary, so much like the rest of us, can possess the hearts and minds of monsters."
  —From *THE A TO Z ENCYCLOPEDIA OF SERIAL KILLERS*
  by Harold Schechter and David Everitt

"A grisly tome. . . . Schechter knows his subject matter."
  —*Rocky Mountain News* (Denver)

"The ultimate reference on this fascinating phenomenon."
  —*PI Magazine*

"Harold Schechter combines the graphic style of a horror novelist with a keen eye for bizarre material. . . . One of the few names that guarantee quality."
  —John Marr, *The Bay Guardian* (San Francisco)

More praise for Harold Schechter's true-crime works

"Must reading for crime buffs . . . gruesome, awesome, compelling reporting."
  —Ann Rule, *New York Times* bestselling author of *Worth More Dead*

"Meticulously researched, brilliantly detailed, and above all, riveting."
  —Caleb Carr, bestselling author of *The Alienist*

The
A *to* Z
Encyclopedia
of
Serial Killers

Harold Schechter
and David Everitt

Revised and Updated

POCKET BOOKS
NEW YORK   LONDON   TORONTO   SYDNEY

POCKET BOOKS, a division of Simon & Schuster, Inc.
1230 Avenue of the Americas, New York, NY 10020

ISBN-13: 978-1-4165-2174-7
ISBN-10:   1-4165-2174-7

This Pocket Books trade paperback edition July 2006

10   9   8   7   6   5

POCKET and colophon are registered trademarks of
Simon & Schuster, Inc.

Manufactured in the United States of America

For information regarding special discounts for bulk purchases,
please contact Simon & Schuster Special Sales at 1-800-456-6798
or business@simonandschuster.com.

The
A to Z Encyclopedia
of Serial Killers

Preface
to the
Second Edition

In the decade since our book first appeared, the phenomenon it explores—the brand of compulsive, sexually sadistic homicide we now call serial murder—continues to maintain a tight grip on the public imagination. Indeed, the serial killer has become such a pervasive part of our popular culture that a comprehensive list of all the movies, TV shows, and bestselling thrillers that feature such villains would now require a volume of its own.

Even the horrific events of September 11, 2001, haven't managed to stem the tide of serial killer entertainments. Though we now face far graver threats to our national well-being than psychopathic sex-killers, we continue to crave stories about the latter. At the time we wrote the introduction to the first edition, for example, David Fincher's *Se7en* was America's number-one film. At the present moment (we are writing this in the spring of 2005), the same director is in the midst of shooting *Zodiac,* about the search for the notorious serial murderer who terrorized the San Francisco area in the late 1960s. *Plus ça change.*

In the news, real-life serial killers also continue to command widespread media attention. The savage exploits of Angel Maturino Resendez—aka the "Railroad Killer"—held the country in thrall in the summer of 1999. Two years later, Gary Ridgway's arrest for the infamous "Green River" killings was front-page news across the country. So was the apprehension, in early

2005, of Dennis Rader, the seemingly ordinary city worker and churchgoer who confessed to being the notorious murderer known as "BTK."

That such long-unresolved cases as Green River and BTK have finally been closed in recent years represents one main reason for the existence of this new edition of *The A to Z Encyclopedia of Serial Killers*. A great deal has happened since the book first came out in 1995. Major new cases have occurred (like that of Dr. Harold Shipman, now regarded as the most prolific serial killer in modern history). There have been important new developments in old cases (including a supposed "final" solution of the most legendary serial murders of all, those committed by Jack the Ripper).

Significant shifts have taken place in our understanding of the subject (it is clear, for example, that both female and African-American serial killers are far more common than previously thought). We have even managed to trace a different—and significantly older—origin for the phrase "serial killer" itself.

In revising our book, then, we have tried to make it as up-to-date as possible. But *The A to Z Encyclopedia* was never meant to be simply a reference tool. It always aimed to be something else: a book which acknowledged that the subject of serial murder exerts a dark but undeniable attraction—the kind of "dreadful pleasure" that, as children, we derive from immersing ourselves in the fairy-tale world of demons and witches and flesh-eating ogres.

There's little point in denying the fact that, for whatever reasons—anxiety management, morbid curiosity, latent sadism—people enjoy reading about monsters. Like the first edition of our book, this revision is meant to both enlighten and entertain. It is offered, in short, not only in the spirit of serious scholarship but in frank recognition of what Joseph Conrad calls "the fascination of the abomination."

Preface
to the
First Edition

We are writing this preface in the fall of 1995, when the number-one film at the box office is *Se7en*, a dark, intensely creepy thriller about a serial murderer who contrives to kill his victims in accordance with the seven deadly sins (lust, greed, gluttony, sloth, pride, anger, and envy). The American public's long-standing interest in psychopathic butchers—the same morbid fascination that, back in 1991, made Jeffrey Dahmer a *People* magazine cover boy and Jonathan Demme's *The Silence of the Lambs* an Oscar-winning blockbuster—is still going strong.

Indeed, what was initially a fringe phenomenon—an obsession with blood-crazed psychokillers that was more or less limited to diehard splatter-movie fans—has become so mainstream that publications as traditionally staid (if not stuffy) as *The New York Review of Books* and *The New Yorker* have jumped on the bandwagon of late. The former ran a major essay on serial killers by novelist Joyce Carol Oates, while the latter did an extended, pre-execution profile of John Wayne Gacy that included exclusive excerpts from the unpublished writings of "America's most notorious killer."

Moralizing critics have been quick to condemn this phenomenon (labeled "serial chic") as still another nasty symptom of societal rot, along with gangsta rap and ads for Calvin Klein underwear. We would point out that in considering the significance of pop phenomena it is always useful to put things in a broader cultural context. For better or worse, human beings have always been intrigued by anything that is monstrous, aberrant, or criminal. And grisly murder has been the subject of story and song, of art high and low, for centuries. True-crime books have been around since at least the 1600s, when John Reynolds's *God's Revenge Against Murder and Adultery* was one of the most popular works in England. During the late eighteenth century, the British public devoured the true-crime accounts in *The Newgate Calendar,* while Victorian readers thrilled to the gory details of murders, mutilations, and torture dished out by *The Illustrated Police News,* the most popular periodical of its day.

In our own country, the media frenzy set off by the atrocities of Dr. H. H. Holmes, "America's first serial killer," was akin to the hysteria generated by the O.J. trial a century later. In 1895, Chicagoans lined up around the block when an enterprising showman opened an H. H. Holmes "Murder Museum," complete with gruesome mock-ups of the "arch-fiend's" crimes. And the exploitation of mayhem and murder has not been restricted to schlockmeisters. Serious artists from Cézanne to Francis Bacon—as well as novelists from Dostoevsky to Dreiser—have made violent crime the subject of their work.

In short, we don't see America's fascination with serial killers as an aberration but rather as a contemporary manifestation of an age-old human reality. Moreover—insofar as telling stories or swapping jokes or watching movies about fearful things represents a method of coping—this fascination is not at all unhealthy. In late-twentieth-century America, the serial killer has come to embody a host of gnawing anxieties: anxieties about runaway crime and sexual violence and the breakdown of civil conduct. If we are haunted to the point of obsession by the figure of the psychopathic killer, it is not because we revel in the sadistic and ghastly (though there is some of that, too, built into the archaic depths of the psyche) but rather because, like children who love to hear spooky stories at bedtime, reading or hearing about serial killers is a way of gaining a sense of control over our fears.

Though there have been plenty of books about serial murder in the past few years, *The A to Z Encyclopedia of Serial Killers* is the first to deal with the phenomenon in all its aspects: historical, biographical, criminological, psychological, and cultural. The entries cover every topic we could conceive of, from **Ads** and **Animal Torture** to **Zombies** and **Zoophilia.** Readers will notice that some words within each entry are boldfaced; these are key names and concepts that are treated in separate entries of their own.

For all the genuine horror and revulsion they inspire in us, there's no point in denying that serial killers exert a dark attraction. They appeal not just to our morbid interest but also to our need to comprehend an ultimate human mystery: how people who seem so ordinary, so much like the rest of us, can possess the hearts and minds of monsters.

In recognition of the need to confront and explore that "mystery of iniquity" (as Herman Melville describes it), we offer the following pages.

ADS

Back in the old days, desperate singles in search of a mate might turn to a professional matchmaker. Nowadays, they are more likely to look in the personals section of the classified ads or subscribe to an **Internet** dating service. Of course, when it comes to getting anything that people are peddling in newspapers or online—whether it's a used car or themselves—it pays to take heed of the old warning: Buyer Beware! Those Handsome SWMs and Sensual DWFs who make themselves look and sound so attractive in their digital photos and printed descriptions might turn out to be very different when you meet them in person.

Occasionally, in fact, they might turn out to be serial killers.

Using classifieds as a way of snaring potential victims is a ploy that dates back at least as far as the early 1900s. That's when the infamous American **Black Widow,** Belle Gunness, lured a string of unwary bachelors into her clutches by placing matrimonial ads in newspapers across the country: "Rich, good-looking widow, young, owner of a large farm, wishes to get in touch with a gentleman of wealth with cultured tastes." There was a certain amount of misrepresentation in this classified, since Gunness was actually fat, fiftyish, and bulldog-ugly. She wasn't lying about being a rich widow, though, since she had murdered at least fourteen husbands after separating them from their life savings.

In France, Gunness's near contemporary, Henri Landru, known as the "Bluebeard of Paris," also found his lover-victims through the newspapers. Some of the classifieds were matrimonial ads in which Landru presented himself as a wealthy widower searching for a mate. In others, he pretended to be a used-furniture dealer looking for merchandise. In either case, if the person who responded was a lonely woman of means, Landru would turn up the charm. The results were always the same. The woman's money would end up in his bank account. The woman herself would end up as a pile of ashes in the stove of his country villa.

In the late 1950s, a sexual psychopath and bondage nut named Harvey Murray Glatman (see **Photographs**) was able to procure victims by posing as a professional photographer and placing ads for female models. After luring an unwary woman into his "studio," Glatman would rape her, truss her up, take pictures of her while she screamed in terror, then strangle her. (Glatman's case served as the real-life basis for Mary Higgins Clark's bestselling novel *Loves Music, Loves to Dance,* which—as the title suggests—deals with the sometimes perilous world of the personals.)

In more recent times, a vicious sociopath named Harvey Louis Carignan lured young women to their deaths by advertising for employees at the Seattle gas station he managed. Carignan's MO earned him the nickname the "Want-Ad Killer" (the title of Ann Rule's 1983 bestselling true-crime book on the subject). At roughly the same time, an Alaskan baker named Robert Hansen—who was ultimately convicted of four savage sex killings, though he was allegedly responsible for seventeen—used the personals page of his local newspaper to attract several of his victims. Hansen, who was married with children, would send his family off on a vacation, then take out a classified, seeking women to "join me in finding what's around the next bend." After snaring a victim, he would fly her out to the wilderness in his private plane. Then, after raping her at knifepoint, he would strip off her clothing, give her a head start, and (in a sick, real-life duplication of Richard Connell's famous short story "The Most Dangerous Game") stalk her like an animal.

Even scarier was the wizened cannibal and child killer Albert **Fish,** who regularly scoured the classifieds in his endless search for victims. In 1928,

Albert Fish; from
52 Famous Murderers
trading cards
(Courtesy of Roger Worsham)

Albert Fish

Fish came across a Situation Wanted ad placed by a young man named Edward Budd, who was looking for a summer job in the country. Masquerading as the owner of a big Long Island farm, the monstrous old man visited the Budd household, intending to lure the youth to an abandoned house and torture him to death. Fish altered his plans when he laid eyes on Edward's little sister, a beautiful twelve-year-old girl named Grace. It was the little girl who ended up dead, dismembered, and cannibalized—and all because her brother's innocent ad brought a monster to their door.

Arguably the most bizarre advertising gambit in the annals of psychopathic sex crime occurred in 2002, when a forty-one-year-old German computer technician, Armin Meiwes, posted an Internet ad that read: "Wanted: Well-Built Man for Slaughter and Consumption." Though it is impossible to conceive of a less enticing come-on, it caught the fancy of a forty-two-year-old microchip designer named Bernd-Jürgen Brandes, who showed up at Meiwes's door, eager to be butchered. With the victim's enthusiastic cooperation, Meiwes cut off Brandes's penis, cooked it, then served it up for the two of them to eat together. He then stabbed Brandes through the neck, chopped up the corpse, froze certain parts for future consumption, and buried the rest (see **Cannibalism**).

To describe Herr Meiwes as "disturbed" is clearly an understatement.

It must be acknowledged, however, that—in contrast to such wolves-in-sheep's-clothing as Robert Hansen and Albert Fish—at least he wasn't guilty of false advertising.

Advertising for Victims

In the 1989 film *Sea of Love,* a serial killer with a seductive line goes trolling for male victims in the classifieds. When a sucker bites, the killer reels him in, then leaves him facedown on the mattress, a bullet in the back of his skull.

As he did nine years earlier in *Cruising,* Al Pacino plays a homicide detective who goes undercover to catch the killer. By placing his own ad in the papers, he turns himself into live bait. In the process he plunges into a turbulent affair with Ellen Barkin—who may or may not be the killer.

A riveting thriller, *Sea of Love* is especially good at conveying the dangerous undercurrents that run beneath the surface of big-city singles life, where lonely people looking for a good catch sometimes end up with a barracuda.

ALLIGATORS

When it comes to getting rid of human remains, most serial killers prefer to keep things simple, relying on such standbys as shallow graves, basement crawl spaces, river bottoms, and remote, densely wooded areas (see **Disposal**). Occasionally, however, a serial killer may resort to more exotic expedients.

Back in the 1930s, for example, a hard-drinking reprobate named Joe Ball ran a seedy roadhouse called (ironically enough) the Sociable Inn on Highway 181 outside Elmsdorf, Texas. Ball installed a cement pond and stocked it with a brood of five full-grown alligators. To keep his pets fat and happy, Ball fed them a diet of horse meat, live dogs, and human body parts—the remains of various female employees he murdered and dismembered. The exact number of his victims is unknown, since Ball went to his death without confessing. When two sheriffs who were investigating the disappearance of a pretty young waitress named Hazel Brown showed up to question the brutish barkeep, he whipped out a pistol from the drawer beneath his cash register and fired a bullet into his heart.

(Tobe Hooper, the auteur who directed the original *Texas Chainsaw Massacre,* used Ball's crimes as the basis for his uninspired follow-up, *Eaten Alive,* a 1977 dud about a psychopathic, scythe-wielding hotel keeper whose guests have an unfortunate tendency to end up in the reptile-infested swamp behind his establishment.)

The alligator's first cousin—the West African crocodile—has also been exploited for this nefarious purpose. In the 1920s, Carl **Panzram**—arguably the most unregenerate murderer in the annals of American crime—journeyed to Portuguese West Africa as a merchant seaman. Making his way down the coast, he hired a canoe and the services of a half-dozen locals to help him hunt crocodiles. Panzram ended up shooting all six of the Africans in the back and feeding their corpses to the ravenous reptiles.

Crocodilians haven't been the only creatures whose indiscriminate eating habits have come in handy to homicidal maniacs. In turn-of-the-century California, a farmer named Joseph Briggen fed his prize hogs the body parts of butchered farm hands. Briggen's porkers invariably fetched

Carl Panzram; from
52 Famous Murderers
trading cards
(Courtesy of Roger Worsham)

Carl Panzram

top dollar at local auctions. When people asked for the secret of his success, he would just smile and reply, "It's all in the feeding."

Another Canadian pig farmer, Robert Pickton—alleged to be that country's worst serial killer—apparently relied on the same porcine method of corpse disposal. Arrested in 2002, Pickton, as of January 24, 2004, has been implicated in the murders of up to thirty-one women.

> **"I have no desire whatever to reform myself. My only desire is to reform people who try to reform me, and I believe the only way to reform people is to kill 'em. My motto is: Rob 'em all, rape 'em all, and kill 'em all."**
>
> **CARL PANZRAM**

ANIMAL TORTURE

Childhood cruelty toward small, living creatures isn't necessarily a sign of psychopathology. Lots of little boys who enjoy pulling the wings off of flies grow up to be lawyers or dentists. The sadistic behavior of budding serial killers is something else entirely. After all, it's one thing to chop an earthworm in two because you want to watch the separate halves squirm; it's quite another to eviscerate your neighbor's pet kitten because you enjoy listening to its agonized howls.

The case histories of serial killers are rife with instances of juvenile animal torture. As a boy, for example, Henry Lee **Lucas** enjoyed trapping small animals, torturing them to death, then having sex with the remains. The earliest sexual activity of the appalling Peter **Kürten**—the "Monster of Düsseldorf"—also combined sadism with bestiality. At thirteen, Kürten discovered the pleasures of stabbing sheep to death while having intercourse with them.

Instead of more conventional items, like baseball cards and comic books, little Jeffrey **Dahmer** collected roadkill. According to neighbors, he also liked to nail bullfrogs to trees and cut open live fish to see how their innards worked. One of the favorite childhood pastimes of **Moors Murderer** Ian Brady (see **Killer Couples**) was tossing alley cats out of tenement windows and watching them splat on the pavement. Cats, in fact, are a favorite target of youthful sociopaths. Edmund **Kemper** was only ten when he buried the family cat alive, then dug up the corpse and decapitated it. And former FBI Special Agent Robert K. Ressler—the man credited with coining the term "serial killer"—mentions one sadistic murderer who was nicknamed "Doc" as a child because he liked to slit open the stomachs of cats and see how far they could run before they died.

Animal torture is, in fact, such a common denominator in the childhoods of serial killers that it is considered one of the three major warning signals of future psychopathic behavior, along with unnaturally prolonged bed-wetting and juvenile pyromania (see **Triad**).

The vast majority of little boys who get their kicks from dismembering daddy longlegs or dropping firecrackers into anthills lose their stomach for sadism at an early age. The case is very different with incipient serial killers. Fixated at a shockingly primitive stage of emotional development, they never lose their craving for cruelty and domination. Quite the contrary: it continues to grow in them like a cancer. Eventually—when dogs, cats, and other small, four-legged creatures can no longer satisfy it—they turn their terrifying attentions to a larger, two-legged breed: human beings.

ARISTOCRATS

For the most part, the only truly remarkable thing about modern-day serial killers is their grotesque psychopathology. Otherwise, they tend to be absolute nobodies. It is precisely for this reason that they are able to get away with murder for so long. No one looking at, say, Joel Rifkin—the Long Island landscape gardener who slaughtered a string of prostitutes and stored their bodies in the suburban home he shared with his adoptive parents—would ever suspect that this utterly nondescript individual was capable of such atrocities.

For many serial killers, in fact, the notoriety they achieve through their crimes is, if not their main motivation, then certainly an important fringe benefit. Murder becomes their single claim to fame—the only way they have of getting their names in the paper, of proving to the world (and to them-selves) that they are "important" people.

In centuries past, the situation was frequently different. Far from being nonentities, the most notorious serial killers of medieval times were peo-ple of great prominence and power. The most infamous of these was the fifteenth-century nobleman Gilles de Rais. Heir to one of the great fortunes of France, Gilles fought alongside Joan of Arc during the Hundred Years War. For his courage in battle, he was named marshal of France, his country's highest military honor.

Following Joan's execution in 1431, however, Gilles returned to his an-cestral estate in Brittany and plunged into a life of unspeakable depravity. During a nine-year reign of terror, he preyed on the children of local peas-ants. Unlike today's low-born serial killers, the aristocratic Gilles didn't have to exert himself to snare his victims; his servants did it for him. Whisked back to his horror castle, the children (most of them boys) were tortured and dismembered for the delectation of the "Bestial Baron," who liked to cap off his pleasure by violating their corpses. Executed in 1440, he is widely regarded as the model for the fairy-tale monster **Bluebeard.**

A female counterpart of Gilles was the Transylvanian noblewoman Elizabeth Bathory, a vampiric beauty who believed she could preserve her youth by bathing in the blood of virgins. According to conservative esti-mates, Bathory butchered and drained the blood of at least forty young women before her arrest in 1610.

Her tally was topped by her near contemporary, the French noblewoman Marie Madeleine d'Aubray, marquise de Brinvilliers. Having run through a fortune, this profligate beauty decided to knock off her father in order to get her hands on his estate. In her efforts to concoct an indetectable poison, she volunteered her services at the Hôtel Dieu—Paris's public hospital—and began trying out different formulas on her patients, ultimately dispatching at least fifty of them. In 1676, she was beheaded for her crimes.

Closer to our own time, some **Jack the Ripper** buffs (or "Ripperologists," as they prefer to be called) speculate that the legendary "Butcher of Whitechapel" was actually Albert Victor, Duke of Clarence, Queen Victoria's grandson and heir to the throne of England. As tantalizing as this theory sounds, it is almost certainly a complete fantasy, akin to the wilder Kennedy assassination scenarios. The unglamorous truth is that Jack was probably nothing more than a knife-wielding nobody—just like the scores of hideously sick nonentities who have followed in his bloody footsteps.

ART

Serial killer art can be divided into two major categories: (1) works of art *about* serial killers, and (2) works of art *by* serial killers.

To start with the latter: the best known of all serial killer artists was John Wayne **Gacy**, who began dabbling in oil painting while in prison. Though Gacy painted everything from Disney characters to Michelangelo's *Pietà*, his trademark subject was Pogo the Clown—the persona he adopted during his prearrest years, when he would occasionally don circus makeup and entertain the kids at the local hospital. Gacy's amateurish oils could be had for a pittance a decade ago, but their value increased as they became trendy collectibles among certain celebrities, like film director John Waters and actor Johnny Depp. Since Gacy's execution, the price for his paintings has shot even higher. While some of his oils are explicitly creepy (like his so-called Skull Clown paintings), even his most "innocent"—like his depictions of Disney's Seven Dwarves—have an ineffable malevolence to them.

Pogo the Clown; painting by
John Wayne Gacy
(Courtesy of Mike Ferris)

For a while, Gacy's exclusive art dealer was the Louisiana funeral director and serial killer enthusiast Rick Staton (see **The Collector**). Under Staton's encouragement, a number of other notorious murderers have taken up prison arts and crafts. Staton—who started a company called Grindhouse Graphics to market this work and has staged a number of Death Row Art Shows in New Orleans—has represented a wide range of quasicreative killers, including Richard "Night Stalker" **Ramirez** (who does crude but intensely spooky ballpoint doodles); Charles **Manson** (who specializes in animals sculpted from his old socks); and Elmer Wayne Henley. Henley—who, along with his buddy Dean Corll, was responsible for the torture-murder of as many as thirty-two young men—likes to paint koala bears.

As devoted as he is to promoting the work of these people, even Staton concedes that they possess no artistic talent. There are a couple of exceptions, however. Lawrence Bittaker—who mutilated and murdered five teenage girls—produces some truly original pop-up greeting cards. The most gifted of the bunch, however, is William Heirens, the notorious "Lipstick Killer," who has been in prison since 1946 and who paints exquisitely detailed watercolors.

As far as serious art goes (i.e., art about, not by, serial killers), painters have been dealing with horrific sex crimes since at least the nineteenth century. The Victorian artist Walter Sickert, for example, did such disturbing pictures of murdered prostitutes that crime writer Patricia Cornwell has accused him of being **Jack the Ripper.** Scholars have also discovered that, in addition to the post-Impressionist landscapes and still lifes he's best known for, Paul Cézanne did a whole series of paintings and drawings depicting grisly sex crimes.

Throughout the twentieth century, hideous murder often appears as a subject of serious art. In *The Threatened Assassin,* a 1926 painting by Surrealist René Magritte, a bowler-hatted man wields a clublike human limb while a nude woman lies bleeding in the background. Even more unsettling is Frida Kahlo's 1935 *A Few Small Nips,* in which a gore-drenched killer, clutching a knife, stands at the bedside of his savaged girlfriend. In 1966, the German postmodern painter Gerhard Richter caused an uproar when he displayed his *Eight Student Nurses,* realistic portraits of Richard **Speck**'s victims, based on their yearbook photos. That controversy was minor, however, compared to the outcry provoked in 1997, when a highly publicized British art show included Marcus Harvey's *Myra*—an enormous portrait of the notorious **Moors Murderer** created from the handprints of children.

Of all serial murder paintings produced in the twentieth century, probably the greatest are those by Otto Dix, the famous German Expressionist who was obsessed with images of sadistic sexual mutilation and produced a series of extraordinary canvases on the subject. His contemporary George Grosz (who posed as Jack the Ripper in a famous photographic self-portrait) also created a number of works about sex-related killings, including the harrowing *Murder on Acker Street,* which depicts a cretinous killer scrubbing his hands after decapitating a woman, whose horribly mangled corpse occupies the center of the picture. (If you're interested in a brilliant study of sexual murder in Weimar Germany—which reproduces several dozen works by Dix and Grosz—check out the 1995 book *Lustmord* by Harvard professor Maria Tartar.)

The spiritual heir of Dix and Grosz is Joe Coleman, America's preeminent painters of serial killers (see **The Apocalyptic Art of Joe Coleman**). Coleman's work has inspired a number of younger artists, including the young Brooklyn painter Michael Rose, whose subjects range from religious martyrdoms to grisly accidents to the atrocities of Albert Fish. Another Brooklyn artist, Chris Pelletiere, has done a series of stunning portraits of some of America's most notorious killers, including Charles Starkweather, Henry Lee **Lucas,** and Ed **Gein.**

Finally, there is the well-known Pop surrealist Peter Saul. Now in his sixties, Saul has been offending sensibilities for the past three decades with canvases like *Donald Duck Descending a Staircase, Puppy in an Electric Chair,* and *Bathroom Sex Murder.* Rendered in a garish, cartoony style, Saul's recent paintings of serial killers—which include grotesque depictions of John Wayne **Gacy**'s execution and Jeffrey **Dahmer**'s eating habits—are among his most electrifying works.

═══ **The Apocalyptic Art of Joe Coleman** ═══

America's premier painter of serial killers, Joe Coleman is also the only significant artist ever to perform as a geek. Indeed, one of his most powerful self-portraits—*Portrait of Professor Momboozoo*—shows the crucified Cole-

Joe Coleman in his "odditorium"   *(Photo by Steve Bonge)*

man with a bitten-off rat's head jutting from his mouth. Like so much of Coleman's work, it's an astounding image, one that sums up three of the major themes of his art: horror, sideshow sensationalism, and (insofar as devouring the body and blood of a rodent represents a grotesque parody of the Last Supper) religious obsession.

Coleman was born on 11/22/55—a date (as he likes to point out) full of doubles, prefiguring his own fascination with linked dualities: sinner and saint, heaven and hell, corruption and purity, killer and victim. Growing up across from a cemetery and steeped in Catholicism, he developed an early fascination with death and disease, suffering and sacrifice. His childhood imagination was also shaped by two books: the Bible (particularly its juicier stories of sex and violence) and a volume on Hieronymus Bosch, whose teeming, demonic dreamscapes made a profound impression on Coleman's budding artistic sensibility.

Indeed, though Coleman is often classified under the ever-so-slightly disparaging category of "naive" or "outsider" artist, his work falls into a mainstream tradition that extends from such medieval painters as Bosch and Breughel to modern German Expressionists like Dix and Grosz. It's also true, however, that—as accomplished and sophisticated as Coleman's paintings are—there is, in his densely textured, meticulously detailed style, a distinctly folk-art quality. He is, in short, a complete original, an all-American delineator of the darkest recesses of the soul. If Bosch had coupled with Grandma Moses, their unholy offspring would have been Joe Coleman.

In the festering landscape of Coleman's art, legendary serial killers like Carl **Panzram** and Charles **Manson** become mad visionaries, driven by a savage need to rip away the comforting illusions of conventional society and expose the terrible realities of existence: random horror, inexorable death. Coleman is quick to point out that his paintings are self-portraits, and the same ferocious drive is evident everywhere in his work. He uses his paintbrush like a vivisectionist's scalpel, to penetrate to the bloody innards, the guts of existence. Beneath our skins, his art seems to say, we are nothing but blood, shit, and phlegm, with a latent tumor undoubtedly lurking somewhere in our cells. But there is another element, too, one that redeems his work from sheer morbidity: the belief, or at least the hope, that if he penetrates far enough, he will discover something much deeper—the soul.

As one critic has commented, Joe Coleman has put the *pain* back in painting. But his work blazes with power and meaning. For those unfamiliar with it, we strongly recommend his book *Cosmic Retribution* (Fantagraphic Books, 1992)—the only art volume (so far as we know) with an enthusiastic jacket blurb by Charles Manson. More recent examples of his paintings can be found in *Original Sin* (Heck Editions, 1997) and *The Book of Joe* (La Luz de Jesus Press, 2003).

> "My earliest drawings were of the crucifixion of Christ. That's one thing that's going to turn little boys on—that your religion has to do with a guy getting nailed to a fucking cross and all this blood spurting out and all these saints being set on fire. That's the kind of religion I like."
>
> **JOE COLEMAN**

AXE MURDERERS

Though the figure of the axe-wielding maniac is a staple of horror movies and campfire tales, he is largely a figment of the popular imagination. In reality, serial killers rarely rely on axes.

The most famous axe in American criminal history, of course, was the one that belonged to Miss Lizzie Borden, who, according to folklore, used it to give her sleeping stepmother "forty whacks" in the face (and when she saw what she had done, she gave her father forty-one). Lizzie, however, was no serial killer but a chubby, thirty-two-year-old spinster with long-simmering resentments who apparently went berserk one sweltering day in August 1892. In short, her crimes (assuming she committed them, which seems fairly certain, in spite of her acquittal) were a one-shot deal—a lifetime's worth of stifled emotions exploding in a single savage deed.

Another fatal female who was handy with an axe was the notorious Belle Gunness (see **Black Widows**), who murdered at least fourteen of her husbands and suitors. Some apparently were poisoned, others were dispatched in their sleep with a hatchet. Though the fat, ferocious Gunness cut a more frightful figure than the ladylike Miss Lizzie, she was no wild-eyed thrill killer. Rather, she was a cold-blooded mercenary, killing to collect on her spouses' life-insurance policies or inherit their savings.

Closer than either of these lethal ladies to the popular stereotype of the axe-wielding psycho was a hard-bitten drifter named Jake Bird. Roaming around Tacoma in 1947, Bird hacked a mother and daughter to pieces with an axe he found in their woodshed. Alerted by the victims' dying shrieks, neighbors summoned the police, who managed to subdue Bird after a violent struggle. Bird pled innocent until forensic analysis established that the stains on his trousers were human blood and brain tissue. Before his execution in 1949, he confessed to no fewer than forty-four murders throughout the United States, a number of them committed with his weapon of choice—the axe.

The most fear-provoking axe killer in the annals of American crime, however—one who kept a whole city in a state of panic for over two years—was a maniac whose identity remains unknown. This is the shadowy figure known as the "Axeman of New Orleans."

On the night of May 23, 1918, a New Orleans couple named Maggio was butchered in bed by an intruder who smashed their skulls with an axe blade,

Lizzie Borden; from
52 Famous Murderers
trading cards
(Courtesy of Roger Worsham)

then slit their throats with a razor, nearly severing the woman's head. Thus began the reign of terror of the so-called Axeman, a real-life boogeyman who haunted the city for two and half years. His MO was always the same. Prowling through the darkness, he would target a house, chisel out a back-door panel, slip inside, and find his way to the bedroom. There, he would creep toward his slumbering victims, raise his weapon, and attack with demoniacal fury. Altogether, he murdered seven people and savagely wounded another eight.

Panic gripped the city, particularly since the police were helpless to locate the killer. Hysterical citizens pointed fingers at various suspects, including a supposed German spy named Louis Besumer and a father and son named Jordano, who were actually convicted on "eyewitness testimony" that later proved to be fabricated. Since many of the victims were Italian grocers, there was also a theory (wholly unsubstantiated) that the killer was a Mafia enforcer. To cope with their fears, citizens resorted to morbid humor, throwing raucous New Orleans-style "Axeman parties" and singing along to a popular tune called "The Mysterious Axeman's Jazz."

Though the killer was never identified, some people believe that he was an ex-con named Joseph Mumfre, who was shot down by a woman named

Pepitone, the widow of the Axeman's last victim. Mrs. Pepitone claimed that she had seen Mumfre flee the murder scene. Whether Mumfre was really the Axeman remains a matter of dispute, but one fact is certain: the killings stopped with his death.

Hatchet Man

Frailty, a creepily effective chiller released in 2002, stars Bill Paxton (who also directed) as a Texas widower whose fatherly devotion to his two young sons is somewhat undercut by his rampaging religious mania. Dad (the only name he's given in the film) believes that God has chosen him to hunt down and destroy demons-in-human-form, using a very large axe as his weapon of divine retribution.

Complications arise when Dad comes to believe that his own twelve-year-old son, Fenton, is a demon in disguise. Reluctant to dismember his child, Dad settles for locking the boy in a dungeon until he repents. Thanks to this act of paternal solicitude, Fenton manages to make it to manhood. In the grown-up form of Matthew McConaughey, Fenton shows up years later at FBI headquarters to tell his story to an agent named Doyle (Powers Boothe), who is investigating an unsolved serial murder case known as the "God's Hand" killings.

Solid acting, surprising plot twists—and the scariest axe-wielding father to appear in movies since Jack Nicholson went off the deep end in Stanley Kubrick's *The Shining*—make *Frailty* a highly satisfying little horror film.

BATHTUBS

Exploring the spooky labyrinth of Buffalo Bill's basement at the climax of Thomas Harris's *The Silence of the Lambs,* Clarice Starling happens on a ghastly sight: a "big bathtub . . . almost filled with hard red-purple plaster. A hand and wrist stuck up from the plaster, the hand turned dark and shrivelled, the fingernails painted pink." Clarice has stumbled onto one of the monster's former victims, who has been turned into some sort of grotesque tableau.

Like the rest of us, of course, real-life serial killers require an occasional bath and so can't clog up their tubs with decomposed corpses encased in red-purple plaster of Paris. Some, however, have put their tubs to specialized uses.

For obvious reasons, bathtubs make a handy place to dismember corpses. After picking up a female hitchhiker in January 1973, for example, Edmund **Kemper** shot her in the head, then drove the body back home, hid it in his bedroom closet, and went to sleep. The next morning, after his mother left for work, he removed the corpse, had sex with it, then placed it in his bathtub and dismembered it with a Buck knife and an axe.

Dennis **Nilsen**'s tub, on the other hand, was used for a more traditional purpose. He liked to bathe his lovers in it. Of course, they were dead at the time. Like Jeffrey **Dahmer,** this British serial killer murdered his homosexual pickups partly because he was desperate for companionship. Turning them into corpses was his way of ensuring that they wouldn't leave in the morning. After strangling a victim, Nilsen would engage in a regular ritual, tenderly cleaning the corpse in his tub, then lovingly arranging it in front of the TV or stereo or perhaps at the dining room table, so he could enjoy its company until it became too decomposed to bear.

And then there is the occasional serial killer who turns his tub into a killing device, like the British **Bluebeard** George Joseph Smith, the notorious "Brides in the Bath" murderer, who drowned three of his seven wives for their insurance money.

Of course, the most famous of these bathroom fixtures is the shower-tub combo where Janet Leigh meets her brutal end at the hands of Anthony Perkins as Norman Bates. Thanks to Hitchcock's *Psycho,* countless unclad starlets have been butchered by maniacs while soaping up in the shower or relaxing in a bubble bath. Every now and then, a knife-wielding psycho will even pop out of a tub as in *Fatal Attraction.* But on the whole, these are perils that hardly ever occur outside the movies. For the most part, bathtubs are perfectly safe—as long as you don't slip on the soap.

BED-WETTING

See **Triad.**

David Berkowitz

It was the era of New York disco fever—of platform shoes, leisure suits, dancing to the Bee Gees while a mirrored globe spun and flashed overhead. But for a little more than a year, between 1976 and 1977, the disco beat turned into a pulse of fear as a gun-wielding madman prowled the city streets at night. His weapon was a .44 revolver—and at first the tabloids tagged him the ".44-Caliber Killer."

The terror began on July 29, 1976, when two young women were shot in

5. DAVID BERKOWITZ:
"Son of Sam"

David Berkowitz; from
Bloody Visions trading cards

a parked car in the Bronx. Young people in cars—often dating couples—
would continue to be the killer's targets of choice. On one occasion, however, he gunned down a pair of young women sitting on a stoop. On another,
he shot a woman as she walked home from school. Frantically she tried
protecting her face with a book—but to no avail. The killer simply raised the
muzzle of his weapon to the makeshift shield and blasted her in the head.
Before his rampage was over, a total of six young New Yorkers were dead,
seven more severely wounded.

At the scene of one double murder, police found a long, ranting
note from the killer. "I am the 'Son of Sam.' I am a little brat," he wrote.
From that point on, the killer would be known by his bizarre new
nickname.

For months, while the city was gripped by panic, police made no head-
way. When a break finally came, it happened as a result of a thirty-five-dollar
parking ticket. On July 31, 1977, when a couple was shot along the Brooklyn shore, a witness noticed someone driving away from the scene in a car
that had just been ticketed. Tracing the summons through their computer,
the police came up with the name and address of David Berkowitz, a pudgy-
faced postal worker living in Yonkers.

When police picked him up, they found an arsenal in the trunk of

Berkowitz's car. Son of Sam had been planning an apocalyptic act of carnage—a kamikaze assault on a Long Island disco.

Under arrest, Berkowitz explained the meaning of his bizarre moniker. "Sam" turned out to be the name of a neighbor, Sam Carr, who—in Berkowitz's profoundly warped mind—was actually a "high demon" who transmitted his orders to kill through his pet dog, a black Labrador retriever. Insane as this story was, Berkowitz was found mentally fit to stand trial. He was eventually sentenced to three hundred years in the pen, where he has recently undergone a religious conversion and become a jailhouse televangelist, preaching the gospel on public-access TV.

> "I didn't want to hurt them,
> I only wanted to kill them."
>
> **DAVID BERKOWITZ**

BLACK WIDOWS

Classic serial sex murder—in which a sadistic sociopath is driven to stalk, slay, and commit unspeakable acts on a succession of strangers—is an outrage perpetrated almost exclusively by men. As two-fisted culture critic Camille Paglia puts it, "There are no female **Jack the Rippers**" (see **Women**). On the other hand, women who murder a whole string of their mates, often for mercenary reasons, are relatively common in the annals of crime. These female counterparts of the male **Bluebeard**-type killer are known (in homage to the deadly arachnid that devours its mates after sex) as "Black Widows."

The most infamous of this breed was the legendary Belle Gunness, née Brynhild Storset, who came to this country from a small fishing village in Norway in 1881. Like other nineteenth-century immigrants, the enterprising young woman found America to be a land of plenty, where she could put her God-given talents to the most profitable use. As it happened, Belle's particular talent was serial murder. After a fire destroyed her Indiana farm in 1908, searchers found the decomposed remains of at least a dozen people on her property, some interred in the basement of the gutted house, others buried in the muck of the hog pen or planted in her garden. Most of her victims were either prospective husbands or hired hands who doubled as lovers. Their deaths allowed Gunness to cash in on their insurance policies and loot their bank accounts. Like the sow that devours its farrow, she also murdered two of her own infant children after insuring their lives. Gunness has gained legendary status not only because of the enormity of her crimes but also because she disappeared without a trace, slipping (like **Jack the Ripper**) into the realm of folklore and myth.

Other notorious Black Widows followed Gunness's avaricious pattern. In the mid-nineteenth century, America's "Queen Poisoner," Lydia Sherman, bumped off one husband after another in order to inherit their savings. Reluctant to split her new bounty with anyone else, she also poisoned her children, dispatching more than one of her victims with arsenic-spiked hot chocolate. In a strikingly similar fashion, her British con-

Mary Ann Cotton; from
Bloody Visions **trading cards**

*(© & ™ 1995 M. H. Price and
Shel-Tone Publications. All
rights reserved.)*

temporary Mary Ann Cotton liquidated a whole string of spouses and children. Their deaths were attributed to "gastric fever"—until a postmortem on her final victim, her seven-year-old stepson, turned up traces of arsenic in his stomach.

Not all Black Widows, however, are motivated by greed. The matronly multicide Nannie Doss—dubbed the "Giggling Granny" by the press because she chuckled with amusement while confessing her crimes—became incensed when police accused her of killing four husbands for their insurance policies (which were, in fact, pretty paltry). An avid reader of true-romance fiction, Nanny insisted that she had murdered for love, not money. "I was searching for the perfect mate, the real romance of life." When a husband didn't measure up, she simply dispatched him (slipping liquid rat poison into his corn whiskey or stewed prunes), then went in search of another Prince Charming. Of course, her explanation was not entirely convincing, since her victims also included her mother, two sisters, two children, one grandson, and her nephew. Nannie Doss was sentenced to life in prison, where she died of leukemia in 1965 after writing her memoirs for *Life* magazine. She murdered neither for love nor for money. She killed because she enjoyed it.

BLASPHEMY

For the most part, this is an outrage perpetrated by devil-worshipping cultists who delight in blaspheming the orthodox rituals of Christianity (see **Satanism**). The central ceremony of satanic worship, for example, is the so-called Black Mass, an obscene travesty of the Catholic mass involving baby sacrifice, orgiastic sex, and other abominations.

There is, however, at least one serial killer who added blasphemy to his staggering list of outrages. After murdering his final victim—an eighty-eight-year-old grandmother named Kate Rich—Henry Lee **Lucas** carved an upside-down cross between the old woman's breasts. Then he raped her corpse.

ROBERT BLOCH

Say the word *psycho* to most people and they will immediately visualize scenes from the classic horror film: Janet Leigh getting slashed to pieces in a shower, Martin Balsam being set upon by an old biddy with a butcher knife, Anthony Perkins smiling insanely while a fly buzzes around his padded cell. But while it was Alfred Hitchcock's genius that made *Psycho* into a masterpiece, it was another imagination that first dreamed up Norman Bates and his motel from hell. It belonged to Robert Bloch, one of the most prolific and influential horror writers of the century.

Born in Chicago in 1917, Bloch began publishing stories in the pulps while still a teenager. He received encouragement from his pen pal and muse, horrormeister H. P. Lovecraft (who named a character after Bloch in his story "The Haunter of the Dark"). After working as an advertising copywriter in Milwaukee, Bloch quit to become a full-time writer in the early 1950s. He specialized in tales whose macabre twist endings make them read like extended sick jokes. Psychopathic killers figure prominently in his fiction. One of his best-known stories is titled, "Yours Truly, Jack the Ripper."

In 1957, Bloch—who had relocated to Los Angeles to write screenplays—moved back to Wisconsin so that his ailing wife could be close to her parents. He was living in the town of Weyauwega, less than thirty miles from Plainfield, where police broke into the tumbledown farmhouse of a middle-aged bachelor named Edward **Gein** and discovered a collection of horrors that sent shock waves around the nation. Fascinated by the incredible circumstances of the Gein affair—particularly by the fact (as he later put it) "that a killer with perverted appetites could flourish almost openly in a small rural community where everybody prides himself on knowing everybody else's business"—Bloch hit on the idea for a horror novel. The result was his 1959 thriller, *Psycho,* about the schizophrenic mama's boy, Norman Bates—a monster who (like Dracula and King Kong) has become a permanent icon of our pop mythology.

Bloch wrote hundreds of short stories and more than twenty novels, in addition to dozens of screenplays and television scripts. However, when he died, on September 23, 1994, the headlines of his obituaries invariably identified him (as he predicted they would) as the "Author of *Psycho.*" As interpreted by Hitchcock, this pioneering piece of serial-killer literature set the pattern for all cinematic slasher fantasies of the past forty-six years. In spite of his lifelong obsession with psychopathic killers, Bloch himself was the gentlest of men, who had little use for the kind of graphically gory horror movies his own work had inspired. When asked his opinion of films like *The Texas Chainsaw Massacre*, the man who gave birth to Norman Bates admitted, "I'm quite squeamish about them."

BLUEBEARDS

Reputedly modeled on the fifteenth-century monster Gilles de Rais (see **Aristocrats**), the folktale character Bluebeard is a sinister nobleman who murders a succession of wives and stores their corpses in a locked room in his castle. In real life, the term is used to describe a specific type of serial killer who, like his fictional couterpart, knocks off one wife after another.

There are two major differences between a Bluebeard killer and a psycho like Ted **Bundy.** The latter preys on strangers, whereas the Bluebeard type restricts himself to the women who are unlucky (or foolish) enough to wed him. Their motivations differ, too. Bundy and his ilk are driven by sexual sadism; they are lust murderers. By contrast, the cardinal sin that motivates the Bluebeard isn't lust but greed. For the most part, this kind of serial killer dispatches his victims for profit.

The most infamous Bluebeard of the twentieth century was a short, balding, red-bearded Frenchman named Henri Landru (the real-life inspiration for Charlie Chaplin's black comedy *Monsieur Verdoux*). In spite of his unsightly appearance, Landru possessed an urbane charm that made him appealing to women. It didn't hurt, of course, that there were so many vulnerable women around—lonely widows of the millions of young soldiers who had perished on the battlefields of World War I. An accomplished swindler who had already been convicted seven times for fraud, Landru found his victims by running matrimonial **Ads** in the newspapers. When a suitable (i.e., wealthy, gullible) prospect responded, Landru would woo her, wed her, assume control of her assets, then kill her and incinerate the corpse in a small outdoor oven on his country estate outside Paris. He was guillotined in 1922, convicted of eleven murders—ten women, plus one victim's teenaged son.

Even more prolific was a German named Johann Hoch, who emigrated to America in the late 1800s. In sheer numerical terms, Hoch holds some

Victorian engraving, showing Bluebeard's collection of chopped-off female heads.

sort of connubial record among Bluebeards, having married no fewer than fifty-five women, at least fifteen of whom he dispatched. Like Landru, he never confessed, insisting on his innocence even as the hangman's noose tightened around his neck.

Another notorious Bluebeard from across the sea was the Englishman George Joseph Smith, who became known as the "Brides in the Bath" murderer for his habit of drowning his wives in the tub in order to collect on their life insurance. Like Landru and Hoch, Smith vehemently proclaimed his innocence, leaping up during his trial and shouting, "I am not a murderer, though I may be a bit peculiar!" The jury didn't buy it, at least the first part. He was hanged on Friday, August 13, 1915.

Though the killer who snares his female victims with his suave, attentive manners seems quintessentially European, our own country has produced its share of Bluebeards. Born and bred in Kansas, Alfred Cline looked like a Presbyterian minister—one of the reasons, no doubt, that he was able to win the trust of so many well-to-do widows, eight of whom he married and murdered between 1930 and 1945. Even Cline's favorite killing device—a poisoned glass of buttermilk—was as American as could be.

Then there was Herman Drenth, who dispatched an indeterminate number of victims in his homemade gas chamber outside Clarksburg, West Virginia. He was hanged for five murders in 1932. Unlike most Bluebeards, Drenth was an admitted sadist, deriving not only financial profit but also sexual pleasure from his crimes. Watching his victims die, he told police, "Beat any cathouse I was ever in."

> **"I may be a bit peculiar."**
>
> **GEORGE JOSEPH SMITH,**
> *the "Brides in the Bath" murderer*

BOARD GAMES

Though it seemed unlikely to become the next Trivial Pursuit, a board game called Serial Killer set off a firestorm of outrage when it was put on the market a few years ago. The brainchild of a Seattle child-care worker named Tobias Allen, Serial Killer consisted of a game board printed with a map of the United States, four serial-killer playing pieces, "crime cards," "outcome cards," and two dozen plastic "victims" (in the possibly ill-advised form of dead babies).

With the roll of a die, each player would move along the map and draw a crime card. Each card would involve either a "high-risk" or a "low-risk" crime, and the player would collect victims accordingly. As Allen explained, "A high-risk crime might be breaking into the house of a prominent citizen and killing him. A low-risk crime would be murdering a prostitute or a street person. Whoever has the highest body count at the end of the game wins."

Game cards from Serial Killer board game *(Courtesy of Tobias Allen)*

Though Allen intended the game as "a bit of a spoof on the way we glorify mass destruction," many people failed to see the humor. A number of Canadian politicians mobilized to ban the game's sale in their country. The fact that it came packaged in a plastic body bag apparently didn't help.

"A quiet dorm could turn into a house of horrors when you visit! This campus is crawling with cops, though—so beware!"

Crime card from Serial Killer board game

BODY PARTS

See **Trophies.**

BTK

The insatiable urge to kill is not a passing fancy. On the contrary, it is more like an addiction. And for serial murderers, like heroin junkies, it is very hard, if not impossible, to kick the habit.

True, there have been rare occasions when a string of savage murders comes to a sudden, mysterious halt: the Jack the Ripper case, for example, or the original Zodiac killings. Few experts believe, however, that those two psychopaths simply decided to quit committing random murder and return to their day jobs. It is far more likely that they were either locked away on some unrelated charge or died, either of natural causes or by suicide.

There's an exception to every rule, however, as the case of the so-called BTK murders proves. Twenty-eight years after that madman's last reported homicide, police finally arrested a suspect. His name was Dennis Rader, a colorless bureaucrat who—after allegedly terrorizing the city of Wichita, Kansas, in the 1970s with a series of horrific murders—somehow managed to set his homicidal impulses aside and retreat into a life of bland Midwestern normality.

The nightmarish case began in January 1974, when the killer murdered a husband and wife and two of their children. He went on to kill three more people, all young women, over the next three years. All the victims were bound and strangled and forced to endure prolonged suffering. As the murderer explained in one of the anonymous letters he sent to the media, his method was "Bind them, Torture them, Kill them." He also supplied his own catchy moniker, as if to make it easier for the media to promote him. Using the acronym for his murder method, he called himself the "BTK Strangler."

Always a hog for attention, the killer could get a bit peevish if he didn't receive the response he thought he deserved. Once, he stewed for a week waiting for a newspaper to acknowledge his note, then wrote a TV station to complain: "How many do I have to kill before I get my name in the paper or some national attention?"

While all this was going on, Dennis Rader was working in his quiet, fussy way, first at a residential security system company, then as a municipal codes enforcer who harried citizens for failing to leash their dogs or for letting their grass grow too high (see **Civil Servants**). In his spare time, he volunteered at his local Lutheran church and led a Boy Scout troop. As a troop leader, the alleged binder and torturer was especially keen on teaching boys how to tie a proper knot.

After the BTK murders seemed to stop at the end of 1977, experts like legendary FBI profiler Robert Ressler concluded that the culprit was out of commission in some way. Events of 2004 proved that, in the BTK case at least, this bit of conventional wisdom did not apply.

In March 2004 the killer sent another package to the media that included photocopies of a woman's driver's license and of some photos of the woman's dead body (see **Xerox**). Her name was Vicki Wegerle, and she was murdered in 1986. Until this latest message, the police had no idea that Wegerle was another BTK victim.

Other messages followed, and eventually one of them provided the po-

Mug shot of Dennis Rader, aka "BTK"

lice with the lead they needed to crack the case. It contained a computer disk that was electronically traced back to a computer in Wichita's Christ Lutheran Church. Before long, the police narrowed their search to Rader, the church's balding, fifty-nine-year-old deacon. In all, prosecutors charged Rader with ten murders, the latest committed in 1991, five years after the Wegerle killing.

On June 27, 2005—exactly four months after his arrest—Rader, dressed in a beige sports coat and blue tie, stood in a Wichita courtroom and pled guilty to all ten murders. Speaking in a flat, dispassionate voice—as if he were "reading out of a phonebook," according to one observer—he offered graphic details of his enormities, explaining how he had trolled for victims, then stalked them, killed them, and—in several cases—masturbated over their bodies.

When the judge asked him about his motivation, the onetime Boy Scout leader and church president calmly replied that he was simply acting out his sexual fantasies.

Ted Bundy

He was a genuine Jekyll and Hyde—a clean-cut Joe College type, so attractive and charming that young women, meeting him for the first time, would climb into his car without hesitation. Once there, however, they found themselves face-to-face with a monster: an implacable lust murderer who tortured and killed with maniacal glee.

Ted Bundy's bestial alter ego first came roaring to the surface during his student days at the University of Washington. In 1974, he killed seven women in as many months and inflicted permanent brain damage on another, using a metal rod to fracture her skull, then ramming it into her vagina. From Seattle, he moved to Salt Lake City, enrolling in the University of Utah school of law. Before long, he had established himself as an up-and-coming young Republican with bright political prospects. At the same time, however, the creature that lurked beneath this brilliant facade continued to lust after blood. Young women began disappearing from the Salt Lake area—including a police chief's teenage daughter, whose nude and mutilated remains were eventually found in a canyon.

Bundy also made occasional forays into Colorado, where at least five

8. THEODORE BUNDY:
The Beast,
Subdued

FLA DOC
A069 D 063

Ted Bundy; from
Bloody Visions trading cards

other young women vanished and died. In 1976, he was finally arrested but managed to escape twice, once by climbing through a courthouse window, the second time by sawing a hole in the ceiling of his cell.

In January 1978 he turned up in Tallahassee, Florida. By now, the monster inside him—his evil Mr. Hyde—was taking control. No longer did Bundy bother to coax young women into his car. Instead, he simply slipped into their rooms at night and pounced with demoniacal fury. In one case, he nearly chewed off the nipple of a victim, then bit her buttocks so savagely that he left teeth marks in her flesh. Those marks were his undoing. After Florida police arrested him in February—for driving a stolen vehicle—they were able to match photographs of the bite marks with impressions of Bundy's teeth.

At his trial, the erstwhile law student acted as his own attorney. He failed to impress either the judge or the jury—though he *was* able to delay his execution for ten years following his conviction. In a desperate effort to fend off death, he also began cooperating with authorities. Interviewed by agents of the **FBI**'s Behavioral Science Unit, he offered invaluable insights into the psychology of serial killers. He also confessed to twenty-eight murders (though he is suspected of more, perhaps as many as one hundred).

Ultimately, the legal process caught up with him. He was electrocuted in February 1989. Outside the prison walls, hundreds of people toasted his death with champagne.

"We serial killers are your sons, we are your husbands, we are everywhere. And there will be more of your children dead tomorrow."

TED BUNDY

CALENDARS

As everyone knows, there's a "theme" calendar available for enthusiasts of every stripe, from cat fanciers to Tolkien fanatics to connoisseurs of fine art. To satisfy the demand of hardcore horror fans (or "gorehounds" as they

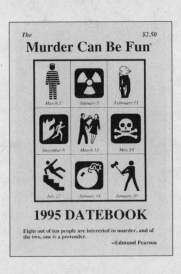

Murder Can Be Fun Datebook

(Courtesy of John Marr)

Film Threat magazine's 1990 "Mass Murderer" calendar; art by
Glenn L. Barr *(Courtesy of Chris Gore, © 1989 Film Threat, Inc.)*

fondly refer to themselves), crime enthusiast John Marr—publisher of the popular "zine" *Murder Can Be Fun*—offered a handsome yearly datebook, the perfect gift for those discriminating people who like to keep track of such important anniversaries as the date of David **Berkowitz**'s second "Son of Sam" killing (October 23) and Gary Gilmore's execution (December 4). A tour de force of research, Marr's macabre desk calendar managed to come up with a different depressing event for every single day of the year.

Calendar of an Organized Psychotic

Several years ago, a sick but amusing item concocted by some cleverly macabre wit made the rounds—one of those anonymous laugh getters that get passed from hand to hand (or faxed from machine to machine). It pretended to be the monthly calendar of the world's most anally retentive psychokiller. As an example of hilariously black humor, it remains, in our opinion, unsurpassed. We don't know the name of the demented genius who produced it, but here it is:

CALENDAR OF AN ORGANIZED PSYCHOTIC August

Sunday	Monday	Tuesday	Wednesday	Thursday	Friday	Saturday
				1 SET FIRE TO CATHOLIC SCHOOL	**2** BUY S+M MAGAZINES AND CUT OUT ALL THE FACES IN THE PICTURES.	**3** GO FLASHING IN PARK
4 CALL MOM AND MAKE HER CRY THREATEN TO KILL DAD.	**5** MASTURBATE ALL DAY	**6** GRAPPLE WITH SELF-HATRED AND ATTEMPT SUICIDE	**7** STARE AT WALL AND ATTEMPT TO STOP BREATHING	**8** ROCK BACK AND FORTH ALL DAY	**9** DROOL AND HYPERVENTILATE	**10** 3 P.M. MEETING WITH PAROLE OFFICER— KILL HIM
			C A T A T O N I A			
11 STEAL CAR DESTRUCTIVE RAMPAGE! RAPE WEEK	**12** RAPE 2 PROSTITUTES	**13** RAPE TEENAGE GIRL + GET CAUGHT	**14** GET RAPED IN JAIL BY SADIST GUARDS	**15** ESCAPE JAIL AND RAPE EX-WIFE	**16** PARTICIPATE IN GANG RAPE OF BAGLADY	**17** RAPE YOUNG FILIPINO BOY
18 AND ON THE SEVENTH DAY HE RESTED.	**19** GO TO CLINIC FOR AIDS TEST. WRITE TO PRESIDENT + PREDICT HIS DEATH.	**20** TERRORIZE LAUNDROMATS! SCRATCH BUTT IN PUBLIC	**21** PANHANDLE ALL DAY, THEN ROB 7-11 WITH TOY GUN.	**22** AIDS TEST RESULT— CROSS FINGERS, KILL ANIMAL FOR GOOD LUCK	**23** IF HAVE AIDS, COMMIT SUICIDE. IF NOT, CELEBRATE AT GAY BAR	**24** SLASH THROATS OF 3 DRUNKS IN ALLEY
25 ATTEMPT SUICIDE AGAIN— GO TO HOSPITAL	**26** IN HOSPITAL STEAL DRUGS + TAKE THEM ALL. VOMIT ON NURSE	**27** BUY HIGH-POWERED RIFLE. MUTILATE LEFT ARM WITH POCKET KNIFE	**28** TAKE POTSHOTS AT CARS ON FREEWAY	**29** SPEND ALL DAY TYPING HYSTERICAL TRACT ABOUT REVELATIONS, SPERM + GRAVITY.	**30** TORTURE NEIGHBOR-HOOD CATS WITH CATTLE PROD	**31** DRINK VIRGIN'S BLOOD TO PURIFY BODY. HIJACK PLANE TO GALAPAGOS ISLANDS

Several years ago, the cult magazine *Film Threat* put out a slick Mass Murderer calendar, featuring witty caricatures of America's most infamous psychos (Ed **Gein**, Albert **Fish**, Ted **Bundy**, John Wayne **Gacy**, and eight more) by artist Glenn L. Barr. Unfortunately, the magazine no longer produces this item, and original copies of the rare, out-of-print 1990 edition have become coveted **Collectibles** among serial-killer buffs.

CANNIBALISM

Ever since the Stone Age, human beings have indulged in cannibalism, either for dietary or ritual reasons. The prehistoric hominids known as *Homo erectus* enjoyed supping on the brains of their fellow cavemen. Aborigines throughout the world, from New Zealand to North America, routinely devoured the hearts of enemy warriors as a way of absorbing their courage. Ceremonial cannibalism was a central feature of the Aztec religion. And Fijians consumed human flesh (which they called *puaka balava* or "long pig") just because they liked its taste.

In the Judeo-Christian tradition, however, cannibalism is regarded with such intense abhorrence that when faced with a choice between eating other humans or starving to death, some people have opted for the latter. (This was the case, for example, with several survivors of the famous 1972 plane crash that stranded a party of young Uruguayans in the high Andes.) As a result, of all the horrors associated with serial killers, cannibalism strikes many people as the worst. When Thomas Harris, author of *The Silence of the Lambs,* set out to create the most monstrous serial killer imaginable, the result was Dr. Lecter, aka "Hannibal the Cannibal," whose idea of a gourmet meal is human liver with fava beans and a nice Chianti on the side.

In point of fact, however, real-life cannibal killers are relatively few and far between. For reasons that can only be surmised, Germany has produced a disproportionately high percentage of twentieth-century people eaters. During the social chaos of the 1920s, the hideously depraved Fritz **Haarmann** slaughtered as many as fifty young boys, dined on their flesh, then sold the leftovers as black-market beef. His equally degenerate countryman Georg Grossmann also supplemented his income by peddling human flesh, though his preferred victims were plump young females, whose meat he made into sausages. Yet another postwar German cannibal was Karl Denke, an innkeeper who killed and consumed at least thirty of his lodgers.

At about the same time in America, the sadomasochistic madman Albert **Fish** was roaming the country, preying on small boys and girls. He was finally executed for the abduction-murder of a pretty twelve-year-old named Grace Budd, parts of whose body he made into a stew. In recent years, the "Milwaukee Monster," Jeffrey **Dahmer**, has served as a grotesque reminder

Albert Fish murdering
Grace Budd; painting by
Michael Rose

that the forbidden urge to consume human flesh may still lurk beneath the surface of supposedly civilized life.

Appalling as they were, Dahmer's crimes were outstripped by the Russian "Mad Beast," Andrei **Chikatilo**, who—with a confirmed body count of fifty-two victims—holds the record as the worst serial killer of modern times. Among his countless atrocities, Chikatilo devoured the genitals of some of his victims—a practice that left him (according to his captors) with a telltale case of bizarre halitosis.

A cannibalistic contemporary of Chikatilo and Dahmer was Arthur Shawcross, whose wildly sadistic tendencies first found free play in the jungles of Vietnam, where (according to his own account) he raped, slaughtered, and cannibalized two peasant women during an army combat mission. Shawcross's subsequent career of psychopathic violence included the murder of a ten-year-old boy whose genitals he devoured, and the strangulation of a string of prostitutes whose bodies he dumped in the woods in upstate New York. Occasionally, he would sneak back to the body weeks after the murder, then cut out and eat pieces of the decomposing corpse (a particularly abhorrent form of cannibalism technically known as *necrophagy*).

During the past twenty-five years or so, there have been a number of appalling cannibal killers who might well have become full-fledged serial murderers if they hadn't been arrested after committing a single atrocity. These include Albert Fentress, a former schoolteacher in Poughkeepsie, New York, who, in the summer of 1979, lured an eighteen-year-old boy into his basement, cut off and ate the victim's penis, then shot him to death; Issei Sagawa, a Japanese national living in Paris who, in 1981, killed his girlfriend, had sex with her corpse, then dismembered and ate parts of her body; Daniel Rakowitz, who likewise murdered and dismembered his girlfriend, then boiled her into a soup which he allegedly served to homeless people on New York's Lower East Side in 1989; and Peter Bryan, a British schizophrenic arrested in 2004 after killing a friend and frying his brain for consumption.

Most bizarre of all is undoubtedly Armin Meiwes, a middle-aged German computer technician who, in 2001, advertised for a victim willing to be slaughtered and consumed (see **Ads**). When a forty-three-year-old man named Bernd-Jürgen Brandes showed up in response to this Internet posting, Meiwes—with Brandes's full approval—sliced off the latter's penis. The two men then shared a meal of the severed organ. Brandes was then stabbed to death, dismembered, and frozen for future consumption.

Meiwes was arrested shortly thereafter. Since Germany has no laws against cannibalism, he was charged with murder "for sexual satisfaction" and "disturbing the peace of the dead." His attorney at his 2004 trial attempted to argue that since Brandes consented (indeed, eagerly cooperated) in his own death, the case should be classified as a mercy killing. The court was not convinced. Meiwes was convicted of manslaughter and sentenced to eight and a half years in prison, though in April 2005, prosecutors— objecting to the leniency of the sentence—won an appeal for a retrial.

Despite Meiwes's claim that he had gotten his cannibalistic urges out of his system—"I had my big kick and I don't need to do it again," he declared—there is reason to doubt his word. Certainly, if he had chosen to indulge his unnatural appetites a second time, he would have had a varied menu to choose from. At his trial, a state police inspector testified that Meiwes's computer files showed that his ad had drawn responses from 204 applicants looking to be his next meal.

In the realm of serial-killer cinema, cannibalism features prominently in Tobe Hooper's splatter classic *The Texas Chainsaw Massacre,* about a family of deranged good ol' boys who turn unwary teens into barbeque. Like *Psycho* and *The Silence of the Lambs,* Hooper's movie was inspired by the crimes of Edward **Gein**. Ostensibly, investigators found unmistakable signs of cannibalism in Gein's horror house—a human heart in a frying pan, a refrigerator stocked with paper-wrapped body parts. This allegation, however, was just one of many hysterical rumors that floated around in the wake of his crimes. Though Ghoulish Gein committed all sorts of unspeakable acts, cannibalism was apparently not one of them. He did, however, enjoy eating baked beans from a bowl made out of a human cranium.

> **"With every piece of flesh I ate I remembered him. It was like taking communion."**
>
> **ARMIN MEIWES,**
> *testifying at his trial*

CARDS, COMICS, AND COLLECTIBLES

Some years ago, a company called Eclipse Enterprises started marketing a set of true-crime trading cards, featuring full-color portraits of America's most infamous serial killers (among other notable lawbreakers). Predictably enough, a coast-to-coast chorus of outraged voices immediately denounced these collectibles as dangerously immoral, and at least one locality—Nassau County in Long Island, New York—passed a law forbidding their sale to minors.

Of course, what these right-minded folk failed to realize is that American children have always gotten a charge out of all that is violent, gross, and offensive to adult sensibilities. At least as far back as the 1940s, there were trading cards depicting famous gangsters. Members of the boomer generation can fondly recollect the famous Civil War series of bubble-gum cards that depicted such educational scenes as soldiers getting impaled on one another's bayonets and having their limbs blown off by cannon fire. Another kiddie classic, the legendary Mars Attacks trading cards, featured explicit

Cover of Jeffrey Dahmer comic book from Boneyard Press
(Courtesy of Hart D. Fisher)

Cover of Richard Speck comic
book from Boneyard Press
(Courtesy of Hart D. Fisher)

images of humans having their bodies destroyed by the flesh-dissolving rays
of alien invaders.

By contrast, Eclipse's true-crime series was positively tasteful, consisting
of nothing but rather handsomely painted full-face portraits. Take our word
for it—in terms of sheer repulsiveness, the Garbage Pail Kids were infinitely
more objectionable.

Why kids (particularly little boys) should get such a kick out of all kinds
of gross-out merchandise, from rubber vomit to Gummi worms, is a question we'll leave to child psychologists (though we suspect that managing
anxieties by creating games around them has something to do with it). But
the notion that a three-by-five illustration of Jeffrey **Dahmer**'s face might
cause "juvenile crime and impair ethical development" seems highly dubious, to say the least.

As it happened, a federal magistrate concurred with that opinion and
ruled that Nassau County's ban on these trading cards was unconstitutional.
By that time, however, the point was somewhat moot, since Eclipse Enterprises had already gone out business.

Trading cards haven't been the only controversial collectibles. Serial-killer enthusiasts who covet a lock of Charles **Manson**'s hair or an original John Wayne **Gacy** artwork or an autographed letter from Ted **Bundy** now routinely buy, sell, and swap their macabre mementos over the **Internet.** This practice has led at least one critic—Andy Kahan of the Mayor's Crime Victims Assistance Office in Houston, Texas—to launch a widely publicized campaign against the trade in what he has memorably labeled "murderabilia."

The notion that collecting crime relics is a symptom of America's "cultural rot" is, however, simply mistaken. From seventeenth-century Englishmen (and women) who would dip their handkerchiefs in the blood of beheaded criminals, to eighteenth-century Frenchmen who treated their children to working, scale-model guillotines, to God-fearing Americans in the early twentieth century who purchased graphic postcards of Southern lynchings, there have always been people drawn to grisly souvenirs. And after all, how much difference is there between collectors of "murderabilia" and the many people who scour the flea markets for Nazi memorabilia? There's no point in denying the fact that, for countless ordinary law-abiding folk, evil exerts a dark fascination.

Still, the thought that serial murderers are being "glamorized" by these hobbyists is deeply offensive to many people—particularly to those whose family members have fallen victim to a psychokiller. Some years ago, rela-

Cover of Ed Gein comic book
by Pat Gabriele
(*Courtesy of Hart D. Fisher*)

Charles Manson T-shirt collection *(Courtesy of Damon Fox)*

THE SERIAL KILLER COLLECTION!

ED GEIN   CHARLES MANSON   JEFFREY DAHMER

Beautiful air-brushed, extra large scale artwork completely takes up the entire front of the shirt. Each is individually hand made with super stunning black & white portraits in L and XL on high quality shirts

HIGH QUALITY 100% COTTON!   *Only* $39.95 *ea.*   HIGH QUALITY 100% COTTON!

A FOXX ENTERTAINMENT EXCLUSIVE!

Serial-killer fashions *(Courtesy of Damon Fox)*

tives of some of Jeffrey Dahmer's victims sued a company called Boneyard Press of Champaign, Illinois, for publishing a Dahmer comic book. The same company also put out comics about Richard **Speck** and Ed **Gein.** Gein's story was also told in an earlier "underground" comic, *Weird Trips No. 2*, which featured a memorable cover illustration of ol' Eddie in his kitchen by artist William Stout.

While some of these comics have been attacked for being exploitative, a number of more recent graphic novels have won praise for their artistry and intelligence. One of the most highly regarded is *From Hell.* This eight-part saga about **Jack the Ripper,** illustrated by Eddie Campbell and written by Alan Moore, was the basis for the stylish 2001 film starring Johnny Depp (see **Movies**). Rick Geary, a brilliant comic book illustrator whose work has appeared everywhere from the *National Lampoon* to *Rolling Stone* to the *New York Times Book Review,* has done a series of critically acclaimed graphic novels called "A Treasury of Victorian Murder," whose subjects include Lizzie Borden, Jack the Ripper, and H. H. **Holmes.**

The Collector

In the realm of coveted collectibles, serial-killer memorabilia doesn't quite rank with early American coins, rare commemorative stamps, and Golden Age superhero comics. Still, there are some serious collectors out there— people who would regard an original Ed **Gein** autograph as more valuable than a Mickey Mantle rookie card.

One of the most prominent of these is Rick Staton, an affable Louisiana funeral director, who—like so many members of the baby boom generation—developed an early taste for the macabre from his childhood exposure to creature-feature television shows, Roger Corman horror movies, and *Famous Monsters of Filmland* magazine.

In 1990, Staton—who until that time had collected nothing more controversial than grade-B movie posters—heard that John Wayne **Gacy** had taken up oil painting in prison. Staton struck up a correspondence with Gacy and eventually became his art dealer, selling original Gacy paintings (mostly of clowns) to a roster of clients that included celebrity collectors like Johnny Depp, John Waters, and Iggy Pop.

Before long, Staton had also contacted other infamous killers—including Charles **Manson,** Richard **Speck,** Richard **Ramirez,** and Henry Lee **Lucas**—who were soon turning out everything from crude ballpoint doodles to oil-painted seascapes, which Staton sold through a mail-order business called Grindhouse Graphics (see **Art**).

Rick Staton   *(Photo by Arbie Goings, Jr.)*

In the meantime, Staton assembled his own personal collection of serial-killer artifacts and memorabilia, which currently includes such unique items as a bird painting on canvas by Speck; Polaroid photos of Lucas and David **Berkowitz;** Ted **Bundy**'s autograph; the high school diploma of **Hillside Strangler** Kenneth Bianchi; cards and letters from Jeffrey **Dahmer,** Edmund **Kemper,** and a host of other notorious killers; charcoal rubbings of Gein's grave marker; soil from Gary **Heidnik**'s front yard; and many works by Gacy, including a unique painting of Michelangelo's *Pietà.*

Though Staton understands that his interests are bound to raise eyebrows, he makes no bones about his hobby (so to speak). Straightforward and self-aware, he knows that monsters have always exerted a fascination for people—partly because, in confronting them, we are facing and coping with our own deepest fears and forbidden desires.

Staton and his buddy Tobias Allen (creator of the infamous Serial Killer **Board Game**) are the focus of Julian Hobbs's fascinating documentary

Collectors (2000), which uses their obsession with convicted sex-killer-turned-sensitive-artist Elmer Wayne Henley to explore the phenomenon of serial-killer fandom.

CAUSES

What turns a person into a serial killer? There's no shortage of theories. Unfortunately none of them is completely convincing.

One of the most intriguing (if controversial) comes from the little-known field of paleopsychology. According to this view, our civilized brains are built on a primitive, animalistic core known as the R-complex. Deep inside every one of us are the savage instincts of our apelike ancestors. For the vast majority of people, this basic, brute nature is kept in check by our more highly evolved faculties—reason, intelligence, and logic. But for various reasons, a small fraction of people are controlled by their primitive brains. In essence, advocates of this view see serial killers as throwbacks—bloodthirsty, Stone Age savages living in the modern world.

Freudian theorists take a similar view, though they talk about the id instead of the R-complex and see serial killers not as latter-day apemen but as profoundly stunted personalities, fixated at an infantile stage of psychosexual development. Because of their traumatic upbringings, compulsive killers never progress beyond the emotional development of a two-year-old. Put a porcelain vase in a toddler's hands and it will end up in little pieces. Serial killers act the same way. They love to destroy things. To them, a human being is just a breakable object—something to be taken apart for pleasure.

Other explanations run the gamut from the physiological (head injuries, hormonal imbalances, genetic deficiencies) to the sociological (class resentment, overpopulation, too much exposure to media violence). There are even environmental theories. One expert has proposed that serial murderers suffer from a disease caused, among other factors, by toxic pollutants.

Whatever other factors may or may not be involved, one common denominator seems to be that they all have an atrocious family background. The appalling **Upbringing** of most, if not all, serial killers clearly contributes to their pathology, turning them into people so full of hate and self-loathing that sadistic murder becomes their substitute for intimacy (see **Sadism**). Still, even a truly dreadful upbringing doesn't seem to be a sufficient explanation. After all, countless human beings suffer traumatic childhoods without growing up to be serial lust killers.

Ultimately, the root causes of serial murder are unknowable—as mysterious in their way as the sources of Mozart's musicianship or Einstein's mathematical genius. Perhaps the only possible answer is the one provided by the great American novelist Herman Melville in his masterpiece *Billy Budd*. Pondering the depravity of the villainous John Claggart, who sets out to destroy the innocent hero for no discernible reason, Melville concludes that Claggart's "evil nature" was "not engendered by vicious training or corrupting books or licentious living" but was "born with him and innate."

Sometimes, in short, "elemental evil" simply takes a human form.

> "Toward the accomplishment of an aim which in wantonness of atrocity would seem to partake of the insane, he will direct a cool judgment sagacious and sound. These men are madmen, and of the most dangerous sort."
>
> **HERMAN MELVILLE**
> *Billy Budd*

Cesare Lombroso and "Criminal Man"

A hundred years ago, an Italian physician named Cesare Lombroso invented the field of "criminal anthropology," a forerunner of the current theory of "paleopsychology." Lombroso believed that criminals were "atavisms"— savage, apelike beings born, by some unexplained evolutionary quirk, into the modern world. Because they were throwbacks to a prehistoric past, criminals could be identified by certain physical characteristics. They actually possessed the anatomical traits of apes—thick skulls, big jaws, high cheekbones, jutting brows, long arms, thick necks, etc.

A serial killer named Vincenz Verzeni helped convince Lombroso that his theory was valid. After strangling two women outside Rome, Verzeni disembowelled the corpses and, in one case, drank the victim's blood. Examining the vampire killer after his arrest, Lombroso discovered that the young man—with his large jaw, bull neck, malformed ears, and low forehead—was a perfect specimen of "primitive humanity." Before long, Lombroso was claiming that you could identify a "born criminal" purely by his physical features. Called to testify at the trial of one young suspect, Lombroso argued that the man must certainly be guilty because he had big ears, a crooked nose, a sinister look, and a tattoo.

Needless to say, Lombroso's theory of "criminal man" has been thoroughly discredited by now—especially his notion that you can identify a murderer just by looking at him.

At least thirty young women—who once met a handsome, clean-cut young fellow named Ted **Bundy,** who looked nothing in the world like an ape—could have told the famous criminologist just how wrong he was.

CHARACTERISTICS

Besides the obvious ones—sick minds, sociopathic personalities, unspeakable desires, etc.—serial killers tend to share a number of characteristics. In a paper presented to the International Association of Forensic Sciences in 1984, **FBI** Special Agents Robert Ressler, John Douglas, and several colleagues listed the following "general characteristics" of serial sex murderers:

1. The great majority are single white males.
2. They tend to be intelligent, with IQs in the "bright normal" range.
3. In spite of their high IQs, they do poorly in school, have a hard time holding down jobs, and often work as unskilled laborers.
4. They tend to come from markedly unstable families. Typically, they are abandoned as children by their fathers and raised by domineering mothers.
5. Their families often have criminal, psychiatric, and alcoholic histories.
6. They hate their fathers. They hate their mothers.

7. They are commonly abused as children—psychologically, physically, and sexually. Sometimes the abuser is a stranger. Sometimes it is a friend. Often it is a family member.
8. Many of them end up spending time in institutions as children and have records of early psychiatric problems.
9. They have a high rate of suicide attempts.
10. They are intensely interested from an early age in voyeurism, fetishism, and sadomasochistic pornography.

For other characteristics of serial killers, see the following entries: **Causes, Race and Racism, Triad, Upbringing,** and **Women.**

Andrei Chikatilo

According to the party line, serial killers didn't exist in the Soviet state. There was only one problem with this assertion. Even while Communist officials were declaring that serial murder was strictly "a decadent Western phenomenon," one of the most monstrous psychopaths in the annals of crime was at large in the Russian port city of Rostov.

He was Andrei Chikatilo—a mousy-looking forty-two-year-old factory clerk, married, with children. Possessed by a monstrous blood lust, he targeted easy prey—boys, girls, defenseless young women. Usually, he would lure them away from bus stops with the promise of a ride or a meal. Leading them into a lonely stretch of woods, he would pounce like a werewolf, committing unspeakable atrocities on his victims, often while they were still alive. (Cutting out their tongues, biting off their nipples, slicing off their noses, gouging out their eyes, devouring their genitals—these were just a few of the horrors he perpetrated.) So fierce was his appetite for human blood that during one four-week span in 1984, he butchered no fewer than six young victims.

Chikatilo's unwitting accomplice in these hideous crimes was the Soviet totalitarian system. According to Communist dogma, crime could not exist in a classless people's republic like the USSR. Rather than admit that they were wrong, Soviet authorities covered up Chikatilo's monstrous spree. As a result, during the "Mad Beast's" twelve-year reign of terror, Soviet citizens didn't even know that a serial killer was on the loose. Instead of being on their guard, they were left vulnerable to his advances.

The police finally nabbed Chikatilo in 1990. He was charged with a staggering fifty-three murders, though the true total may have been even higher. At his trial, he was kept locked inside a steel cage to protect him from his victims' relatives. He was executed in 1994.

For a compelling dramatization of the case, we highly recommend *Citizen X*, a 1995 made-for-cable movie (available on video) starring Stephen Rea, Donald Sutherland, Max von Sydow, and—in a thoroughly chilling portrayal—Jeffrey DeMunn as Chikatilo.

> "What I did was not for sexual pleasure. Rather it brought me some peace of mind."
>
> ANDREI CHIKATILO

CHILDHOOD

See **Upbringing**.

CIVIL SERVANTS

Government workers have never enjoyed the most glowing reputation among the general public. Just ask anyone who's ever had to deal with a surly clerk at the information desk of the local DMV, or been called in for an IRS audit.

The public's dim view of civil servants certainly wasn't helped any in 1986 when postal worker Patrick Sherrill strolled into his workplace in Edmond, Oklahoma, with a pair of Colt .45 semi-automatics and proceeded to relieve some of his work-related tension by killing fourteen people and himself. As it turned out, he was just the first of several USPS workers over the next ten years to teach the world the meaning of the phrase "going postal."

To be to fair to postal workers, theirs are not the only governmental ranks from which homicidal maniacs have sprung. In the late 1950s, a Scottish sociopath named Peter Manuel was holding down a civil service job with the

City of Glasgow Gas Board. During his off hours, however, Manuel was leading a sinister secret life. A lifetime criminal with a long record of convictions for offenses ranging from burglary to rape, Manuel murdered his first victim—a seventeen-year-old girl whose body he dumped on a golf course—in January 1956. Before long, he had slaughtered a total of eight people, including two entire families who were shot in their skulls as they slept in their beds at night.

Manuel's countryman, the notorious Dennis **Nilsen**—whose crimes bore a sickening resemblance to those of Jeffrey **Dahmer**—also worked as a civil servant. Employed by the British Manpower Services Commission, Nilsen was a dedicated professional who helped downtrodden young men find gainful work. By night, however, he was not assisting young men but preying on them. After having sex with one of his gay pickups, Nilsen would kill the young victim, then keep the rotting corpse around his flat for "companionship." When the decay became unbearable, Nilsen would finally dismember and dispose of the body.

Nilsen's monstrous career—which left fifteen victims dead—began in late 1978. Just one year earlier, the crimes of another notorious serial killer came to an end. In August 1977, the gun-crazy madman known as "Son of Sam" was apprehended after the biggest manhunt in New York City history. The public responded to his arrest with two equally intense emotions—relief at his capture and amazement at his identity. Instead of a slavering monster, the great boogeyman of the disco age turned out to be a pudgy-faced nonentity named David **Berkowitz,** regarded by his fellow employees as a quiet, courteous nebbish.

Berkowitz's job? He worked as a letter sorter for a post office branch in the Bronx.

Nearly thirty years later, the public had grown more accustomed to this sort of disparity between the mundane and the monstrous and was less taken aback to learn that the man charged with being the notorious **BTK** Strangler was a balding, bespectacled codes enforcer for the Wichita suburb of Park City. Unlike other serial-killer suspects who are often described as quiet and inoffensive, Dennis Rader could be a royal pain. In carrying out his not-so-civil duties, he would badger people over the most trivial infractions, going so far in some cases as to measure the height of the grass on neighbors' front lawns to make sure it complied with some obscure municipal ordinance.

Rader's job as code enforcer coincided with a period when the BTK murders had stopped. One criminologist thinks there may be a connection. Professor James Fox of Northeastern University theorizes that the sense of power Rader felt while harassing people might have been a substitute for the absolute power he felt while murdering his victims. In other words, as long as he was busting people's chops, he didn't feel the need to bind, torture, and kill them.

Just remember that, the next time you go to the DMV. If you happen to run up against an insufferable, bureaucratic jerk, his obnoxious behavior might just be a safety valve for even more hateful impulses—his way of not going postal.

Clans

In our age of splintered homes, broken marriages, and latchkey children, it's heartwarming to read about the large, close-knit families of yesteryear, bound together by common interests and shared activities. Unless, of course, those interests and activities included serial murder, gang rape, and even cannibalism—as was the case with two notorious killer clans of the past, the Beanes and the Benders.

According to legend, Sawney Beane was a fifteenth-century Scottish peasant who grew fed up with farming and turned to highway robbery. With his hard-bitten common-law wife, he holed up in a seaside cavern on the Galloway coast and sired a large brood of children. Eventually, through incestuous mating, the family swelled to forty-eight members, who subsisted by preying on unwary travelers, devouring their flesh, and pickling the leftover meat in seawater.

No one knows how many people fell victim to this feral clan—estimates run as high as one thousand. To the local inhabitants, the cause of these disappearances was a mystery. Was it a pack of man-eating wolves? Or some supernatural creature? The truth finally came to light when a husband and wife, returning from a village fair, were attacked by the barbarous Beanes, who fell upon the woman, slit her throat, and began feasting on her flesh. A second party, coming upon this appalling scene, informed the authorities. Before long, King James led a party of four hundred troops to the Galloway coast, where the Beanes' unspeakable hideout—its walls hung with human body parts—was uncovered. The entire family was captured and executed, the men put to slow torture, the women burned alive at the stake.

In our own country, a fiendish family known as the "Bloody Benders" perpetrated a string of atrocities during the 1870s. Headed by a brutish patriarch, John, and his equally savage wife (known only as "Ma"), the Benders were German immigrants who settled on the rugged Kansas frontier, where they ran a crude ramshackle "hotel." More than a dozen weary travelers who stopped there for a meal or a good night's rest never made it any farther. While daughter Kate served the stranger his dinner, Papa Bender and his son, John Jr., would sneak up from behind and smash the unwary victim on the skull with a sledgehammer. Then the body would be stripped, robbed, and buried. When a posse finally searched the place, they found the remains of a dozen victims, including a little girl who had been brutally raped before being buried alive beneath her father's corpse. By the time these atrocities were uncovered, however, the Benders had already fled. To this day no one knows what became of them.

The old-fashioned tradition represented by the Benders and the Beanes ("the family that slays together stays together") has been perpetuated in our own era by a family named the McCrarys. A nomadic band of small-time robbers, the McCrarys committed a string of holdups from coast to coast during a yearlong spree in the early 1970s. Along the way, the three McCrary males (father Sherman, son Danny, and son-in-law Raymond Carl Taylor) abducted twenty-two young women—waitresses, salesclerks, customers—from the crime scenes, then raped them, shot them in the head, and ditched the bodies. Through it all, the two McCrary women—mama Carolyn and daughter Ginger McCrary-Taylor—stood by their men. "I love my husband very much," declared Ginger after the vicious killer clan was apprehended. "And it never occurred to me to do anything other than to stay with him."

Sawney Beane on Film

Actually, there *are* no films about Sawney Beane. Two commendable horror movies, however, have been loosely inspired by the man-eating exploits of the legendary Scottish clan of cannibals.

The scarier of the pair is Wes Craven's low-budget shocker, *The Hills*

Have Eyes (1977), about a family of vacationing midwesterners whose station wagon breaks down in the California desert, where they are set upon by a clan of mutant cannibals whose members include a truly alarming character named Pluto (played by a truly alarming-looking actor, Michael Berryman). Craven's classic was given a stylish makeover in 2006 by French goremeister Alexandre Aja.

Less intense—though still well worth seeing—is the 1972 British horror movie *Raw Meat* (also known as *Death Line*). During the 1800s (according to the film) a gang of laborers, digging a tunnel for the London subway, were trapped underground by a cave-in. Since saving them was too expensive, they were simply abandoned down there. The movie concerns their modern-day descendants, a clan of inbred cannibals who still dwell in the subterranean reaches of the London subway system, preying on unlucky commuters. In spite of its lurid title and premise, the movie—starring Donald Pleasence, with a cameo by Christopher Lee—is surprisingly restrained and even (pardon the expression) tasteful.

COEDS

Though cinematic psychos like the brilliant and cultured Hannibal Lecter are often portrayed as criminal masterminds, few, if any, real-life serial killers possess genius-level **IQs**. Still, most are smart enough to know how to select vulnerable victims—what criminologists call "targets of opportunity." Often this means preying upon **Prostitutes.** It can also mean setting their sights on more respectable victims.

The winsome young females who abound on college campuses are a good example. Not only are these coeds alluring; they are often easy to manipulate. They're generally naïve about the darker dimensions of human nature; they are usually unsupervised for the first time in their lives; and they are sometimes tempted by new experiences that carry a whiff of the forbidden. In short, they make easy pickings for a certain breed of predatory killer.

By far the most infamous American coed killer was the silver-tongued Ted **Bundy.** While attending the University of Washington in 1974, he used his wholesome good looks and superficial charm to lure female students away from secure public places and lead them to isolated spots where he would unleash his inner Mr. Hyde. Toward the end of his appalling career,

Bundy dispensed with seduction. Breaking into a couple of sororities in Tallahassee, Florida, he set upon several of the sleeping residents and savaged their bodies in a frenzy of blood lust.

Predating Bundy by a few years was another notorious coed killer, John Norman Collins. Like Bundy, Collins cut a clean-cut all-American figure. His college English teacher, however, glimpsed another side of the seemingly normal young man when Collins handed in a paper on the right to commit murder. "If a person holds a gun on somebody—it's up to him to decide whether to take the other's life or not," Collins had written. "The point is: It's not society's judgment that's important, but the individual's own choice of will and intellect." Between 1967 and 1969, Collins—the star athlete and education major—put this theory into practice by raping, shooting, stabbing, strangling, and bludgeoning as many as nine young women.

Collins became known in the press as the "Coed Killer." But he wasn't the only murderer to earn that moniker. The same nickname was applied to one of the most appalling psychopaths of the era, Edmund **Kemper** III. At six-foot-nine and close to 300 pounds, Kemper didn't fit the Golden Boy mold of Bundy and Collins. Nor did he possess the slightest social skills when it came to the opposite sex. Rather than smooth-talking nubile young women into dropping their guard, he preferred simply to find them along the side of the road at a time when coeds were trusting enough to regard hitchhiking as a reasonable way to travel. Once he had them in the car, he would either shoot or stab his victims. Afterward, he would bring the corpses home and perform unspeakable atrocities on their bodies.

In effect, as Kemper calmly confessed to police, these abominations were his equivalent of taking an attractive young coed out on a date.

> "Alive, they were distant, not sharing with me. I was trying to establish a relationship [with them]."
>
> **EDMUND KEMPER,**
> *on his motive for butchering, dismembering, performing*
> *necrophiliac sex on, and cannibalizing his coed victims*

COOLING-OFF PERIOD

See **Definition**.

COPYCATS

There's nothing new about "copycat" killers—desperately disturbed individuals who feel impelled to imitate sensational, highly publicized crimes. Back in the late 1890s, for example, a San Francisco woman named Cordelia Botkin, after being dumped by her married lover, mailed a box of poisoned chocolates to the man's unwitting wife. The Botkin case, which received frenzied nationwide news coverage, inspired so many similar crimes that the country soon found itself in the midst of what the press (somewhat hysterically) called a "poison epidemic."

The situation tends to be different, however, when it comes to serial murder. True, the 1995 movie *Copycat* depicted a homicidal maniac who mimics the MO of such notorious psychos as David "Son of Sam" **Berkowitz,** the "**Hillside Stranglers,**" Ted **Bundy,** and Jeffrey **Dahmer.** But that is pure Hollywood fantasy. In real life, even the most infamous homicidal maniacs—the ones who receive the kind of saturation news coverage that turns them into media celebrities—rarely inspire imitators. Dahmer, for example, was page-one news from coast to coast and a *People* magazine cover boy. But no one has ever attempted to duplicate his atrocities. The reason is simple. The horrors perpetrated by such beings are the product of the deepest psychosexual compulsions. No one is going to disembowel, cannibalize, and perform necrophiliac sex on a bunch of teenage boys just because he read about it in the papers and it sounded like a cool thing to do.

There *have* been some acknowledged serial-killer copycats. Peter **Kürten,** the "Monster of Düsseldorf," was fascinated by **Jack the Ripper** and spent hours poring over accounts of Saucy Jack's atrocities. Kürten's monstrous compatriot, Fritz **Haarmann,** was an inspiration for the equally deranged Albert **Fish,** who collected all the newspaper clippings he could find about the "Vampire of Hanover."

A more recent example is Heriberto Seda. A deeply maladjusted young gun nut, Seda became obsessed with the infamous West Coast shooter known as **Zodiac.** Adopting the same nickname, he committed a string of murders in Brooklyn and Manhattan in the early 1990s, while sending bizarre communications to the press, complete with cryptic astrological messages. Unlike his psychopathic role model, however, Seda was finally captured in 1998 and sentenced to eighty-plus years behind bars.

While there have been relatively few serial-killer copycats in the strict sense of the term—people who try to replicate specific horrors they've read about in the news—there are a larger number who fall into a related category: psychopaths possessed of the sick ambition to win notoriety as serial murderers. For more on this phenomenon, see **Wannabes.**

COURTROOM THEATRICS

Given their bizarre psychological makeup, it's no wonder that when serial killers are brought to trial, they sometimes create outrageous scenes. After spending their lives in the shadows, like bugs under a rock, they suddenly find themselves thrust onto center stage, with an audience that (in the media age) can number in the millions. With the whole world watching, some of these psychos proceed to put on quite a show.

During his 1924 trial, Fritz **Haarmann**—the infamous "Vampire of Hanover," who murdered at least twenty-eight young boys by chewing through their throats—carried on like a talk-show host. Puffing on a fat cigar, he heckled the witnesses and made frequent quips about his appalling crimes.

Haarmann's countryman, the German sex murderer Rudolph Pleil, used his trial as a platform for establishing his lethal preeminence. Pleil was charged with the rape-murder of nine women. Possessed of a perverse vanity, Pleil was indignant at these accusations, insisting that he was actually responsible for twenty-eight homicides. At his trial, he demanded that the official transcript refer to him as *"der beste Totmacher"*—"the best death-maker."

At roughly the same time in America, the "Lonely Hearts Killers," Martha Beck and Raymond Fernandez, were on trial for a trio of killings, including the murder of a two-year-old child (see **Killer Couples**). At one point, the mountainous Beck—determined to demonstrate her undying love— detoured on her way to the witness stand to hurl herself into the arms of her skinny Latin lover (a scene not unlike the one in Walt Disney's *Fantasia* when the hippo ballerina dives into the arms of her reptilian dance partner).

Few trials, however, have been as outrageous as that of Charles **Manson** and his "family" of drug-crazed hippie assassins. Manson began the proceedings by marching into the courtroom with a big *X* carved into his forehead. "I have X-ed myself out of your world," was his lucid explanation for this bizarre self-mutilation. At the height of the trial's madness, Manson lunged at the judge and tried to assault him.

Since the psychology of serial killers is such an unholy blend of derangement and cunning, it's hard to know when their weird courtroom behavior is genuine and when they are just putting on an act. The latter may well have been the case in the trial of Andrei **Chikatilo,** the Russian "Mad Beast" who murdered, raped, and cannibalized more than fifty young women and children. Chained inside an iron-barred cage—which was installed in the courtroom to protect him from the vengeful relatives of his victims—Chikatilo spent his time swaying autistically, spewing obscenities, baying at the judge, and shouting out insane remarks (at one point, he began yelling about his one-man battle against the Assyrian Mafia; at another, he claimed he was pregnant and lactating). If Chikatilo's behavior was a calculated act, designed to persuade observers of his legal insanity, it did not meet with success. He received the ultimate pan for his performance—a bullet to the back of the skull from a Russian executioner.

CSI

Since its premiere in the fall of 2000, the CBS TV series *CSI: Crime Scene Investigation* has become a bona fide cultural phenomenon. It has not only spawned two hit spin-offs—*CSI: Miami* and *CSI: New York*—but has also produced powerful reverberations in the real world of academics and law. Enrollment in Baylor University's forensic science program, for example, has increased tenfold since the show went on the air. Dozens of other colleges have created forensic science majors to meet the growing demands of young CSI-wannabes.

The impact of the show has also become evident in the courtroom—so much so that prosecutors, defense lawyers, and judges now speak of the *"CSI* effect." Jurors who used to fall asleep when lawyers began talking about scientific evidence now look forward to the testimony of DNA technicians and other forensic specialists. While some legal experts applaud the program for creating a more scientifically informed jury pool, others criticize it for raising unrealistic expectations. After all, not every crime can be proved with hard scientific evidence. And in the real world, even DNA findings can be unreliable, particularly since—unlike Gil Grissom and his glamorous crew—actual human technicians have been known to make errors.

Grissom, the lead character in the original entry in the *CSI* franchise, is played by William Petersen. This seems particularly apt, since Petersen started his film career matching wits with Hannibal Lecter in Michael Mann's 1986 *Manhunter,* the first cinematic version of Thomas Harris's *Red Dragon.* In *CSI,* too, Petersen comes up against an assortment of highly creative serial killers: a sex murderer known as the "Blue Paint Killer," whose coed victims are all found with paint stains on their hands; a sadist called the "Strip Strangler," who deliberately plants misleading evidence; a madman who compulsively re-creates his father's murder (which he witnessed as a boy) by shooting victims in the bathtub; a maniac who snares married couples looking for sexual kicks, then kills the husband after forcing him to slit the wife's throat; and others.

Of course, for all its veneer of scientific hypersophistication, *CSI* is, at heart, a very traditional show. Strip away Gil Grissom's state-of-the-art gadgetry—the gas spectrometers and fiber-optic fluorometers, the electromagnetic dusting kits and ultraviolet flashlights—and you're left with a Las Vegas version of Sherlock Holmes: a solitary eccentric, his head stuffed with esoteric information, who solves crimes through close observation and a remarkable ability to draw clever deductions from the smallest scraps of physical evidence. In the end, the real message of the show seems to be that while technology is providing police with ever more useful tools, what ultimately counts when it comes to tracking down serial killers and other criminals is good old-fashioned detective work.

CULTS

In essence, a cult is a surrogate family, headed by a strong, charismatic leader who functions as a father substitute. Cult members are required to behave like obedient children and do whatever Daddy says—whether that involves committing mass suicide by swallowing poison-spiked Kool-Aid or committing serial murder.

Undoubtedly the most notorious crimes of the Aquarian Age were the Tate-LaBianca murders, carried out by Charles **Manson**'s renegade "family" of psycho-hippies. The crimes became a worldwide sensation, partly because of their appalling savagery—seven people butchered over two nights, including the pregnant actress Sharon Tate. But equally unsettling were the killers themselves. Beginning as more or less typical "flower children"— part of the mass migration of drugged-out adolescents who drifted to California during the Summer of Love—they had been transformed into the pawns of a malevolent spellbinder willing to commit random slaughter at his whim.

According to some reports, Manson and his tribe dabbled in satanism. Ever since the 1960s, America has been terrified (and titillated) by reports of rampant devil worship, involving everything from ritual animal mutilation to the use of human "breeders"—fertile young women who are impregnated for the express purpose of producing sacrificial infants. If TV tabloid shows like *Geraldo* are to be believed, our country is full of satanic cults, generally made up of diabolical suburbanites or wild-eyed teens who receive

Charles Manson; from
52 Famous Murderers
trading cards
(Courtesy of Roger Worsham)

their instructions from Lucifer by playing Black Sabbath records in reverse. Fortunately, most of these reports are nothing more than the quasi-pornographic fantasies of religious nuts or people who have watched one too many viewings of *Rosemary's Baby.* Devil cults that perform human sacrifice are blessedly rare. But they do exist—as a young man named Mark Kilroy was unlucky enough to discover in March 1987.

Kilroy, a twenty-one-year-old student at the University of Texas, was on spring vacation with some friends in Matamoros, Mexico, when he disappeared during an evening of bar hopping. His whereabouts remained a mystery until investigators were led to a remote ranch that served as the headquarters for a local drug-smuggling gang. The leader of this blood-thirsty crew was a self-styled sorcerer named Adolfo de Jesus Constanzo—aka *El Padrino* ("The Godfather")—who preached a hodgepodge of Cuban Santeria, Haitian Voodoo, Aztec Santismo, and an obscure African-derived religion called Palo Mayombe. Whenever a big drug deal was about to go down, Constanzo's cult would seek supernatural protection by sacrificing a human victim, whose heart and brain would be cooked in a cauldron and devoured in a cannibal feast. When the *federales* finally rounded up the gang, they found the mutilated remains of fifteen victims (including Kilroy) who had been sacrificed to the cult's crazy-quilt religion.

====== **Cult of Doom** ======

Your average modern-day thug tends to be a relatively scary character, particularly when he's armed with a 9mm handgun. Still, compared to the original Thugs—a notorious cult of killers that existed in India for at least six centuries—even a Mafia hitman seems like a wimp.

A secret society of robbers and murderers, the Thugs were devotees of the cannibal goddess Kali, in whose name they committed their innumerable crimes. The word *thug* itself is a bastardization of the Hindu word *thag,* meaning a rogue or deceiver. Deception was crucial to their murderous technique. Posing as innocent travelers, a group of Thugs would join up with a party of pilgrims or traders (their favorite targets). Then—after luring the party to a suitable spot—the Thugs would sneak up on their victims and strangle all of them at once while chanting prayers to the goddess. After mutilating and gutting the corpses, the killers would bury the bodies and hold a ritual feast on the graves.

Generation after generation of Thugs strangled countless victims throughout India. (Children of cult members were inducted into the society and taught the prescribed method of murder on clay dummies.) Finally, beginning in 1830, the British launched a virtual war on the Thugs, wiping out the death cult by 1860.

For sheer exotic evil, the Thugs are hard to beat; it's no surprise that two of the most colorful adventure films of all time have used these Kali-worshipping cultists as villains—George Stevens's *Gunga Din* and Steven Spielberg's *Indiana Jones and the Temple of Doom*.

Other films that deal with the Thugs include the gleefully gruesome 1959 Hammer horror film, *The Stranglers of Bombay*, and—at the opposite end of the cinematic spectrum—the artsy 1988 thriller *The Deceivers*, in which a young British officer (played by a pre-007 Pierce Brosnan) infiltrates the Kali-worshipping cult.

D

Jeffrey Dahmer

JEFFREY DAHMER

Jeffrey Dahmer; from
*True Crime Trading Cards
Series Two: Serial Killers and
Mass Murderers;*
art by Jon Bright
*(Courtesy of Jon Bright and
Valarie Jones)*

Folklorists sometimes refer to "Forbidden Chamber" stories—tales about young men or women who, while exploring an ogre's castle, open a secret door and discover a roomful of butchered bodies. In 1991, this nightmare really happened—not in a decaying castle somewhere deep in the Black Forest but in a rundown apartment house in a seedy neighborhood of Milwaukee.

On the night of July 22, a dazed and terrified young man, with a pair of handcuffs dangling from one wrist, flagged down an MPD squad car. A "weird dude" had just tried to kill him, he told the police. His story led the officers to apartment no. 213 of a nearby building. Inside, they discovered a virtual warehouse of human remains. The sickening inventory included a human head sitting on a refrigerator shelf, skulls stashed in a closet, body parts packed in a blue plastic barrel, decomposed hands lying in a lobster pot, an assortment of bones stored in cardboard boxes, and a freezer full of viscera—lungs, livers, intestines, kidneys. There was also a collection of sickening Polaroids, including one of a male torso eaten away by acid from the nipples down. The occupant of this charnel house, a meek, soft-spoken young man named Jeffrey Dahmer, made no effort to conceal the stomach-churning evidence of his unspeakable crimes.

Dahmer had killed seventeen men in all, most of them young African Americans he had picked up in gay bars. He drugged them, strangled them, and dismembered their bodies with an electric saw. He ultimately confessed to the most unimaginable depravities, including cannibalism and necrophiliac rape (disembowelling a corpse and having sex with the viscera was one of his particular pleasures). On several occasions, he also performed makeshift lobotomies on his still-living victims, drilling holes in their skulls and injecting their brains with muriatic acid in an effort to turn them into **Zombies.**

Dahmer's deranged appetites went all the way back to his childhood. As a boy, he loved to collect and dissect roadkill and to butcher small creatures. Former acquaintances would recall finding cats and frogs nailed to trees in the woods behind the Dahmer home. On one occasion, some neighborhood boys came upon a dog's head impaled on a stick.

Dahmer progressed from **Animal Torture** to homicide at the age of eighteen, when—after picking up a young male hitchhiker and bringing him home for sex—he bludgeoned the young man to death, then dismembered the body and buried the parts in the woods. Two years later, Dahmer exhumed the decomposed remains, pulverized the bones with a sledgehammer, and scattered the pieces around the woods.

The "Milwaukee Monster" was ultimately sentenced to fifteen consecutive life sentences, amounting to a total of 936 years. But his prison term—and his life—came to an abrupt end in 1994, when he was beaten to death by a fellow inmate.

> **"I really screwed up this time."**
>
> **JEFFREY DAHMER,**
> *to his father*

DEATH WISH

It's obvious that, in one sense, *all* serial killers have a death wish—they wish to inflict death on as many people as possible. But many of them also have a death wish in the strict Freudian sense of the term: a desire to bring about their own destruction. The long list of serial killers who have either committed or attempted suicide includes such notorious figures as Karl Denke, Georg Grossmann, Gary **Heidnik**, Joseph Kallinger, and Henry Lee **Lucas**.

Some of these psychopaths have killed themselves as a way of escaping the law. Joe Ball, the Florida hardcase who disposed of his unwanted lovers by feeding them to his pet alligators, put a bullet through his heart rather than submit to arrest (see **Alligators**). Leonard Lake—who built a torture bunker on his California ranch where he and his partner, Charles Ng, murdered an indeterminate number of victims—swallowed a cyanide capsule immediately after his arrest (see **Partners**).

By contrast, other serial killers fulfill their death wish by engineering their own capture and eventual execution. Six years after murdering and then cannibalizing a twelve-year-old girl, Albert **Fish** sent a note to her mother describing the crime. Though Fish scratched out the return address embossed on the envelope, he did such a halfhearted job that police had no trouble deciphering the address and tracking him down. The criminal career of serial sex killer Bobby Joe Long came to an abrupt end when he simply let one of his kidnapped victims go. The young woman instantly went to the police and provided them with a detailed description of her abductor, his apartment, and his car. That some serial killers desperately want to be captured was made clear by the famous lipstick-scrawled plea that sex killer William Heirens left on a bedroom wall—"For heaven's sake catch me before I kill more. I cannot control myself."

It's not very surprising that serial killers are often suicidal. Brought up by dreadfully abusive parents who fill them with the sense that all human beings—beginning with themselves—are just so much worthless garbage, serial killers are consumed with despair and self-loathing. After his conviction for first-degree murder, Harvey Murray Glatman—a sadistic creep who shot photos of his bound-and-gagged victims before strangling them to death—suggested that execution would be the most appropriate punishment. When the judge obliged by sentencing him to the gas chamber, Glatman remarked, "It's better this way. I knew this is the way it would be." Other serial killers—like Mormon-missionary-turned-child-killer Arthur Gary Bishop—have expedited their own deaths by refusing to appeal their death sentences. For killers like these, life becomes a growing nightmare. Eventually they yearn for escape.

It is possible that the most famous of all serial killers, **Jack the Ripper,** fell into this category. Though his identity remains a mystery, the fact that his crimes ceased abruptly after his fifth and final atrocity suggests that—overwhelmed by revulsion at the growing horror of his deeds—the "Whitechapel Monster" took his own life.

Indeed, some serial killers seem to look forward to their impending deaths with positive excitement. Michael Ross, who raped and murdered eight teenage girls in the 1980s, put a stop to any further appeals to his death sentence in 1992 and finally had his death wish come true when prison guards strapped him to a lethal-injection gurney in May 2005. According to one observer, when Ross learned that the execution was finally going to happen, he "became upbeat and started joking around."

Weird as that may seem, it's nothing compared to the way Peter **Kürten**—the "Monster of Düsseldorf"—anticipated his own, much harsher execution. His mood, according to certain accounts, can only be described as positively giddy. Aroused since childhood by the sight and sound of spurting blood, Kürten claimed he would die a happy man if he could hear the blood gushing from his own neck stump at the moment of beheading.

DEFINITION

Like certain other terms—*obscenity,* for example—*serial killing* is surprisingly tricky to define. Part of the problem is that police definitions tend to differ from popular conceptions. According to some experts, a serial killer is any murderer who commits more than one random slaying with a break between the crimes. There is certainly some validity to this viewpoint. If (for example) Ted **Bundy** had been caught after committing only a couple of atrocities, he wouldn't have gained worldwide notoriety—but he still would have been what he was: a demented personality capable of the most depraved acts of violence. Still, it's hard to think of someone as a serial killer unless he's killed a whole string of victims.

How many victims constitute a "string"? Again, it's hard to be precise. The most infamous serial killers—Bundy, **Gacy, Dahmer,** etc.—are the ones responsible for double-digit murders. Most experts seem to agree, however, that to qualify as a serial killer, an individual has to slay a minimum of three unrelated victims.

The notion of a string implies something else besides sheer number. A serial killer must perpetrate a number of random killings with an emotional "cooling-off" period between each crime. This hiatus—which can last anywhere from hours to years—is what distinguishes the serial killer from the **Mass Murderer,** the homicidal nut who erupts in an explosion of insane violence, killing a whole group of people all at once. Thus, the official **FBI** definition of serial homicide is "three or more separate events with an emotional cooling-off period between homicides, each murder taking place at a different location."

There are several problems with this definition, however. For one thing, not all serial killers commit their murders in different locations. The nearly three dozen victims of John Wayne Gacy, for example, all met their horrible deaths in the basement of his suburban ranch house. And there are murderers who commit three or more separate homicides over extended periods of time who aren't serial killers: mob hitmen, for example.

What distinguishes a professional hitman from a serial murderer, however, is that one kills for money—it's his job—while the other kills purely for depraved pleasure. A hitman may enjoy his work, but murder isn't his primary source of sexual gratification. The situation is different with psychos like Gacy, who reach the heights of ecstasy while perpetrating their atrocities. According to many experts, in other words, true serial homicide always involves an element of unspeakable sexual **Sadism.**

Taking these issues into account, the National Institute of Justice offers a definition we find more useful than the FBI's: "A series of two or more murders, committed as separate events, usually but not always committed by one offender acting alone. The crimes may occur over a period of time ranging from hours to years. Quite often the motive is psychological, and the offender's behavior and the physical evidence observed at the crime scenes will reflect sadistic, sexual overtones."

(For more on the element of sexual sadism in serial murder, see **Women.**)

Coining a Phrase

In earlier times, psychopathic killers who butchered a succession of random victims were generally described in supernatural terms—demons, fiends, monsters. In the late 1800s, one ingenious journalist, searching for a way to describe the infamous Dr. H. H. **Holmes,** invented the term "multi-murderer"—a snappily alliterative coinage that never caught on. Other common terms used to describe these creatures include "lust-murderers," "recreational killers," "homicidal maniacs," and "stranger-killers." During most of the mid-twentieth century, all criminals who slaughtered a number of victims were lumped together as "mass murderers."

By the late 1960s, however, it became clear that a distinction had to be drawn between the kind of killer who blows away a whole bunch of people at once and the compulsive killer who commits a string of atrocities over an extended period of time. Ultimately, the term "mass murderer" was reserved for the former—the rampage killer who "goes postal"—while the term "serial killer" was applied to the kind of predatory sex slayer exemplified by **Bundy, Gacy,** et al.

Credit for the phrase "serial killer" has generally been given to (and claimed by) former Special Agent Robert K. Ressler, one of the pioneers of the **FBI**'s Behavioral Science Unit. According to Ressler's account (published in his 1992 book, *Whoever Fights Monsters*), he was lecturing at the British Police Academy when one of the participants referred to "crimes in series." Impressed with the phrase, Ressler began using a variation— "serial killers"—in his classes at Quantico.

In point of fact, however, the phrase "serial murderer" can be traced at least as far back as 1961, when it was used by the German film critic Siegfried Kracauer to describe the psychopathic child killer played by Peter Lorre in Fritz Lang's classic thriller, *M*. Five years later, British crime writer John Brophy used the same phrase repeatedly in his 1966 book, *The Meaning of Murder*.

It's possible that, while in England, Ressler picked up the phrase (perhaps subliminally) from Brophy or someone familiar with Brophy's book. Still, Ressler deserves credit for altering the term from "serial murderer" to the slightly more snappy "serial killer." And it was certainly Ressler and his colleagues at Quantico who popularized the term, which quickly became a part of everyday American speech.

Albert DeSalvo

In his short, deranged life, Albert DeSalvo acquired several nicknames. In his late twenties, he became known as the "Measuring Man," a serial sex molester who went from door to door, posing as a scout for a modeling agency. If a woman fell for this line and invited him in, he would produce a tape measure and proceed to check out her assets—a ploy that allowed him to indulge his taste for crude sexual fondling.

A few years later, after serving a brief prison sentence, he progressed from molestation to rape, assaulting hundreds of women throughout New England during a two-year span in the early 1960s. During this period, he was known as the "Green Man," so called because of the green work clothes he favored while committing his crimes.

It was his third nickname, however, that ensured him enduring infamy. In 1962, DeSalvo became known as the "Boston Strangler," a smooth-talking sadist who savagely murdered thirteen women during an eighteen-month reign of terror.

Or, at least, that has been the official version for the last forty years. Recent developments have raised some questions about DeSalvo's guilt.

The generally accepted story begins with DeSalvo's insanely brutal **Up-bringing,** when he acquired an early taste for **Sadism.** One of his favorite childhood pastimes was placing a starving cat in an orange crate with a puppy and watching the cat scratch the dog's eyes out. He got married while in the army and maintained a more or less normal facade as a husband and father, even while committing some of the most shocking crimes in American history. (Of course there were strains in the marriage. Among other things, DeSalvo was possessed of a demonic libido and demanded sex as often as six times a day.)

The earliest victims of the Boston Strangler were elderly women. Each had willingly let the killer into her apartment. Posing as a building repairman, the glib, smooth-talking sex slayer had no trouble gaining entrance. Besides raping and strangling the women, he enjoyed desecrating their corpses, sometimes by shoving bottles or broomsticks into their vaginas. After finishing with his victim, he would leave a grotesque signature, knotting his makeshift garrote (often a nylon stocking) into a big, ornamental bow beneath the dead woman's chin.

Toward the end of 1962, the Strangler's MO suddenly changed. He began preying on much younger women. And his murders became even more vicious—and bizarre. In one instance, he stabbed his victim nearly two dozen times. He left another corpse propped against the headboard of her bed, a pink bow tied around her neck, a broomstick handle jutting from her vagina, and a Happy New Year's card resting against her left foot.

Eventually, DeSalvo was arrested not for the Boston Strangler murders but for one of the Green Man rapes. During a stint at a state mental hospital, however, he began boasting of his strangling career to a fellow inmate. Only then did authorities discover that they had unwittingly nabbed the infamous killer.

In the end, DeSalvo was never punished for the Boston Strangler crimes. Through a deal struck by his lawyer—F. Lee Bailey—DeSalvo was spared the chair and given a life sentence for the Green Man rapes instead. Not that Bailey's efforts did DeSalvo much good in the end. He was stabbed to death by a fellow inmate in November 1973.

DeSalvo's death, however, was not the end of the story. For years, questions about his guilt swirled around the case. Some skeptics believed that DeSalvo confessed for mercenary motives—i.e., because he believed he'd profit from book and movie rights. Others remained convinced there was more than one Strangler.

In 2001, forensic experts lent support to the doubters when DNA taken from the exhumed corpse of the Strangler's last victim did not provide a match with DeSalvo. The controversy over his involvement in the other ten cases, however, rages unabated. Whether science will ever be able to resolve the issue of his guilt remains to be seen.

"Me? I wouldn't hurt no broads. I love broads."

ALBERT "BOSTON STRANGLER" DESALVO

DISPOSAL

To get away with gruesome murder again and again, a serial killer has to possess a fairly high degree of fiendish cunning. Snaring a victim is the first challenge he has to meet. Once he has perpetrated his atrocities, he is faced with another, even more pressing problem—what to do with the remains. The solutions to this grisly dilemma range from the straightforward to the diabolically elaborate.

Some serial killers simply leave their victims where they lie, occasionally taking the time to wreak some grotesque indignity on the remains. For example, Albert **DeSalvo,** the "Boston Strangler," liked to tie big ornamental bows around the throats of his female victims, as though he were leaving a gift-wrapped present for the police.

DeSalvo's bizarre bow-tying practice made for an unmistakable "signature." Understandably enough, many other homicidal maniacs prefer to leave no trace of their identities at all. For some sociopaths, the simplest approach to corpse disposal is the best. Ted **Bundy,** the "**Hillside Stranglers,**" and the Green River Killer, for example, simply dumped the bodies of their victims out in the open—in forests, along riverbanks, on the slopes bordering freeways. Others made perfunctory attempts at concealment, burying the bodies in shallow graves or shovelling dead leaves over the remains. John Wayne **Gacy** didn't even bother to leave home. He simply stuck the dead bodies of his young male victims under the crawl space of his house—at least until he ran out of room, at which point he began tossing them into a nearby river.

By contrast, there are some serial killers who go to great lengths to obliterate every trace of their victims, often by immersing the bodies in acid, covering them with **Quicklime,** or incinerating them in **Ovens.**

Then there are those serial killers whose disposal methods can best be described as wildly (if not insanely) unorthodox. Joe Ball, for example, got rid of his murdered mistresses by feeding their flesh to his pet **Alligators,** while the monstrous Fritz **Haarmann** chopped up his victims and sold their flesh to his neighbors, passing it off as black-market beef.

The longer a serial killer remains on the loose, of course, the more proficient he tends to become. With corpse disposal, as with most human skills, practice makes perfect. Special agents of the **FBI**'s Behavioral Science Unit describe one serial killer who was thrown into a state of almost panicky confusion when faced with the ravaged remains of his first victim. By the time he committed his second homicide, he had already worked out a sophisticated disposal method, taking four painstaking hours to dismember the body in his bathroom before bagging up the parts and depositing them in supermarket Dumpsters.

Of course, there are some serial killers who prefer not to dispose of their victims at all. Both Dennis **Nilsen** and his American counterpart, Jeffrey **Dahmer,** were so desperate for companionship that they went to great, highly deranged lengths to keep the corpses close by. Of course, since both men occupied cramped apartments, even they had to face up to the fetid reality after a while and get rid of their rotting house guests. Nilsen's solution was sublime in its simplicity, if not entirely practical—he chopped up the bodies and flushed the chunks down the toilet, a method that eventually led to his arrest when the plumbing in his apartment building became clogged with gobs of decomposing human flesh.

DOCTORS

From Dr. Jekyll to Dr. Lecter, the fiendish physician has long been a staple of horror fantasy. Unfortunately, this nightmarish figure is not just a figment of the pop imagination. The annals of crime contain notable examples of psy-

"I got a dead body on my hands. People saw me come in here. How am I going to pack this one out? Am I gonna put it in a double bag or a sheet and carry it out of here? I figured the smaller the better. I chopped the body up, stuffed some in the refrigerator, dumped the guts in a vacant lot, throwing pieces here and there, whatever came out of the bag first. I was scared."

Anonymous serial killer,
describing his first experience with body disposal

chopathic M.D.'s who stand the Hippocratic Oath on its head by using their skills to do harm.

Given his dexterity at dissection, there has always been speculation that **Jack the Ripper**—the first and most famous of modern serial killers—was someone with surgical training. "Ripperologists" have come up with several candidates: a Russian doctor and homicidal maniac named Michael Ostrog, who ended up in a mental asylum; another Russian, Dr. Alexander Pedachenko, described as a "criminal lunatic" exiled to London by the tsar's secret police; and an English surgeon named Stanley who allegedly confessed to the Whitechapel murders on his deathbed.

Jack's contemporary, H. H. **Holmes**, was America's original M.D.—i.e., Medical Deviate. After receiving his degree from the University of Michigan at Ann Arbor, Holmes made his way to Chicago, where he constructed his notorious "Murder Castle," complete with a basement dissection lab. Though Holmes worked as a pharmacist, not a physician, he was able to put his surgical training to profitable use by selling the stripped and mounted skeletons of his victims to local anatomy schools.

At roughly the same time, a British psychopath named Thomas Neill Cream—who received his medical degree from Montreal's McGill University and did postgraduate work at the prestigious Royal College of Physicians and Surgeons at Edinburgh—was busily dispatching victims on both sides of the Atlantic. After killing several women through botched, illegal

Herman Mudgett,
aka Dr. H. H. Holmes; from
*True Crime Trading Cards
Series Two: Serial Killers and
Mass Murderers;*
art by Jon Bright
*(Courtesy of Jon Bright and
Valarie Jones)*

HERMAN MUDGETT

abortions, Dr. Cream—who was residing in Chicago at the time—poisoned his mistress's husband by lacing the man's epilepsy medicine with strychnine. Released after a ten-year stint in Joliet, he sailed for England, where he embarked on a career as a serial killer of prostitutes—poisoning five London streetwalkers before he was caught, tried, and hanged in 1892. Dr. Cream is regarded as another Ripper candidate, since he is reputed to have cried, "I am Jack the—" just as he plunged through the trapdoor of the gallows.

Fifty years later and across the English Channel, residents of the Rue Le Sueur in Paris were assaulted by an overpowering stench issuing from a neighborhood building. When firemen broke in, they were horrified to discover a stack of dismembered bodies decomposing in the basement. The building, it turned out, belonged to Dr. Marcel **Petiot,** who claimed that the corpses were those of Nazi collaborators killed by the Resistance. It wasn't until the war ended that the appalling truth emerged: the victims were actually wealthy French Jews, desperate to flee Nazi-occupied France. Posing as a Resistance member who would smuggle them to freedom—for a fee— Petiot arranged to have the unsuspecting victims arrive at his house with all their valuables. Then he would administer an "immunization shot"— actually a lethal injection of strychnine—lock them in a chamber (where, through a peephole, he could watch them die in agony), appropriate their belongings, and dispose of their remains in his furnace. Unrepentant to the end, Dr. Petiot went to the guillotine with a smile in 1946.

Some of the most notorious serial killers of recent years have been physicians. Though convicted of only three murders, Dr. Michael Swango—a classic psychopath who confessed to feeling turned on by the "sweet, husky, close smell of indoor homicide"—is believed to have dispatched as many as sixty victims, all of them recuperating hospital patients who suffered sudden mysterious heart seizures while under his "care." (The story of Swango—and the American medical establishment that willfully ignored his nefarious doings—is brilliantly told in James Stewart's 2000 bestseller, *Blind Eye*.) Even more appalling was Dr. Harold Shipman, who took more innocent lives than any other killer in the annals of British crime.

Dr. Death

No one will ever know exactly how many lives were taken by Dr. Harold Frederick Shipman during the years he treated patients in northern England. A total of 459 people died under his care, but some of those surely perished of natural causes. The most reliable estimate is that, between 1971 and 1998, the genial general practitioner committed no fewer than 250 murders, making him the most prolific serial killer in British—and possibly world—history. (See **Records**.)

The vast majority of his victims were elderly women, who warmed to his charming bedside manner. Shipman's MO was always the same. He would pay an unexpected afternoon house call on a fairly healthy patient, kill her with an injection of the painkiller diamorphine (medical-grade heroin, legal in the U.K.), then hurry away. Later—often summoned by a frantic call from a relative who had discovered the corpse—he would return and sign the death certificate, attributing the unexpected death to natural causes.

It was not until 1997 that someone—a woman named Debbie Brambroffe, the daughter of the local undertaker—realized that something sinister was going on. Struck by the unusually high death rate among Dr. Shipman's elderly female patients—and by the bizarre fact that their bodies were invariably found fully dressed and seated in their favorite easy chairs or resting on the settee—Ms. Brambroffe shared her suspicions with another local physician, Dr. Susan Booth. Before long, an investigation was under way.

Though Shipman became aware that authorities had begun to examine the death certificates of his patients, he could not stop killing. He was finally caught after murdering an unusually fit octogenarian, Mrs. Kathleen Grundy, then crudely forging a will in her name that left him her entire fortune of nearly $400,000. As soon as Mrs. Grundy's daughter set eyes on the document, she saw it was a fake and contacted the police, who already had Shipman in their sights. Before long, Mrs. Grundy's body was exhumed and autopsied. When lethal amounts of diamorphine were discovered, Shipman was arrested.

What drove him to kill? Some psychiatrists claim that Shipman was unusually attached to his mother and deeply traumatized by witnessing her slow death from cancer when he was in his teens. According to this theory, the sight of the family physician administering morphine injections to ease her final agonies left an indelible mark on his psyche, one that drove him, in later life, to re-create that traumatic scene again and again. At Shipman's trial in January 2000, the prosecuting attorney, Richard Henriques, offered a simpler explanation: Shipman killed for pleasure. "He was exercising the ultimate power of controlling life and death," argued Henriques, "and repeated the act so often he must have found the drama of taking life to his taste."

Shipman, who consistently denied his guilt, was convicted of killing fifteen patients and sentenced to life in prison. On January 13, 2004— one day before his fifty-eighth birthday—he took one final life: his own. He hanged himself with his bedsheets from the bars of his cell—an act applauded by the British tabloids, which urged other incarcerated serial killers to follow Shipman's example.

Escape

With their diabolical cunning, serial killers are often able to elude the law for long periods of time—months, years, sometimes forever (see **Whereabouts Unknown**). There have also been a number of notorious serial killers who have been captured after massive manhunts, only to pull off successful escapes.

Back in the 1920s, when Harry Houdini was wowing audiences by miraculously extricating himself from submerged steamer trunks, buried coffins, and other apparently escape-proof receptacles, Earle Leonard **Nelson** contrived some impressive feats of his own. Sentenced to a state mental asylum, he managed to break out so often that the authorities finally gave up trying to recapture him. In 1926, Nelson embarked on his lethal career as a serial rapist and strangler, a terrifying figure who came to be known as the "Gorilla Murderer." After committing a score of murders across the United States, he made his way up into Canada, where the police finally apprehended him. Nelson was taken to Killarney jail, stripped of his boots, and tossed into a double-locked cell. Left unguarded for fifteen minutes, he somehow managed to escape, setting off a citywide panic and the largest manhunt in Manitoba history, which ended when he was recaptured less than twelve hours later.

Perhaps the most fear-provoking escape ever engineered by a serial killer occurred in 1967 when Albert **DeSalvo,** the "Boston Strangler," slipped out of custody. Countless women barricaded themselves in their homes as terror gripped New England. As it turned out, however, DeSalvo's escape was a symbolic act, not a serious attempt to break free and resume his career of crime. DeSalvo was unhappy with his lack of psychiatric treatment, and the escape was his way of protesting. When police finally caught up with him, he made no effort to resist.

Just one year earlier, a psychopathic runt named Charles Schmid, who came to be known as the "**Pied Piper** of Tucson," was sentenced to fifty-five years in prison for the rape-murder of a fifteen-year-old girl, one of his three teenaged victims. Five years after his conviction, Schmid managed to break out of prison. Before he was recaptured a few days later, there were some very nervous people in Arizona. At his trial, Schmid had vowed to "get the people" who had testified against him.

One of the most cunning of all modern serial killers was Ted **Bundy.** In January 1977, Bundy was extradited to Colorado to stand trial for murder. Since Bundy (who had been a law student in Utah) insisted on overseeing his own defense, he was allowed access to the law library at the Pitkin County courthouse in Aspen. On the morning of June 7, 1977, after being left alone in the library for a few minutes, Bundy leapt to freedom through an open second-story window. He was back in custody a few days later, but in late December of that year, he managed to saw a hole in the ceiling of his jail cell and escape. This time, he eluded the authorities for more than a month. Before he was captured again, in mid-February 1978, he had made his way to Florida and brutally murdered three more young women.

EVIL

The atrocities committed by some serial killers are so extreme—torturing children while tape-recording their agonized pleas for help, drilling holes in the skulls of living victims and injecting their brains with acid to turn them into "sex **Zombies**," castrating boys and forcing them to eat their own genitals—that, in attempting to account for such behavior, some forensic psychiatrists have thrown up their hands and resorted to an age-old explanation: pure, elemental evil.

One of these experts is Dr. Michael Stone of Columbia University, who, after studying the biographies of several hundred British and American serial killers, concluded that while some were clearly suffering from severe mental illness, many others were technically sane; their ghastly crimes were committed for sheer pleasure. According to Stone, these beings—Ted **Bundy,** John Wayne **Gacy,** and **Moors Murderer** Ian Brady, among others—cannot be diagnosed according to the usual psychiatric categories: malignant narcissism, criminal psychopathology, antisocial personality disorder, etc. "Such people make a rational choice to commit terrible crimes over and over again," says Stone. "They are evil, and we should be able to say that formally."

Not everyone agrees. Some of Stone's peers believe that talking of evil smacks of medieval superstition. The well-known forensic psychiatrist Dr. Park Dietz, for example, says of serial killers that "As far as we can tell, the causes of their behavior are biological, psychological, and social, and so far do not demonstrably include the work of Lucifer."

Others, however, side with Stone in what has been called the "mad or bad" debate. These forensic specialists believe that only one concept can adequately describe creatures like Fred and Rose West, the British **Killer Couple** who raped, tortured, and murdered a string of young victims, including several of their own children.

Evil, plain and simple.

EXCREMENT

It's hard to say which of the many **Paraphilias** practiced by serial killers is the most disgusting, though coprophagy—i.e., deriving sexual pleasure from eating feces—clearly ranks high on the list. Needless to say, this was a favorite pastime of the monstrously perverted Albert **Fish.** During Fish's 1935 trial for the cannibal murder of little Gracie Budd, his attorney cited the old man's fondness for eating human excrement as evidence of his extreme abnormality. The prosecution countered by calling a psychiatrist who insisted many "very successful people, successful artists, successful teachers, successful financiers" regularly engaged in the same activity. Such people, he declared, were "socially perfectly all right"—a bit of testimony that left many spectators wondering who was crazier, Fish or the supposed expert witness.

EXECUTIONS

Back in the old days—when public executions were a major form of popular entertainment—putting a serial killer to death was quite a production. When the fifteenth-century cutthroat Sawney Beane was finally brought to justice, he and all the other male members of his cannibal clan had their hands and legs chopped off. Then the women were tossed into three blazing bonfires after being forced to watch their men bleed to death. All this, of course, took place before a large crowd of eager spectators. (For more details on the bestial Beanes, see **Clans**.)

A century or so later, in the late sixteenth century, a German serial killer named Peter Stubbe committed such unspeakable deeds that he was regarded as a literal werewolf. (Among his other atrocities, Stubbe murdered his own son, then cracked open the boy's skull and devoured his brain.) When Stubbe was finally arrested, authorities meted out a punishment commensurate with his crimes. After being tortured on the rack, he was broken on the wheel. Then red-hot pincers were used to tear out chunks of his flesh, his arms and legs were crushed with an axe head, and his head was cut off and his body incinerated.

As everyone knows, of course, we live in a much less barbarous age. Nowadays, even a creature like John Wayne **Gacy** ends up being treated like a beloved, ailing pet—put to sleep by lethal injection. Still, there have been exceptions. Unsurprisingly, one particularly nasty exception occurred under the most barbarous regime of modern times. Between 1928 and 1943, a German laundry deliveryman named Bruno Ludke murdered as many as eighty women. Nazi officials repeatedly bungled the investigation, but when they finally caught up with Ludke, they reacted with characteristic brutality. Bypassing the usual channels, they shipped him off to a "research hospital" in Vienna, where he was used as a human guinea pig. Only when the Nazi torture doctors were done with him was Ludke executed by lethal injection.

Of course, when you're dealing with serial killers, it's not always clear that putting them to death is a form of punishment. Some of these maniacs actually look forward to the experience. Ludke's countryman Peter

Kürten—the "Monster of Düsseldorf"—couldn't wait to be beheaded; the sound of his own gushing blood, he claimed, would be a source of ultimate pleasure. The American child killer Albert **Fish** seemed to feel the same way. Fish was not only a sadistic killer but also a world-class masochist, who enjoyed shoving sewing needles into his groin (among other extravagant forms of self-abuse). When Fish was given the death sentence for the savage murder of a twelve-year-old girl, the newspapers quoted him as saying, "What a thrill it will be to die in the electric chair! It will be the supreme thrill—the only one I haven't tried!"

FAIRY TALES

Fairy tales may be set in the enchanted neverland of "Once upon a time," but they also reflect the real-world conditions of the European peasants who originally told them. And from the evidence of these supposedly charming little kiddie stories, that world was full of violence, brutality, and the kind of remorseless cutthroats we now call serial killers.

Take "The Robber Bridegroom." The heroine of this well-known Grimm Brothers tale finds herself betrothed to the leader of a gang of cannibal killers who abduct young women, cut them into pieces, boil the parts in a big kettle, then consume the flesh with generous portions of salt.

Another Grimm tale, "Fitcher's Bird," is an example of a folklore tradition that scholars call "bloody chamber" narratives: stories about innocent young women who discover that they are married to monsters when they enter forbidden rooms filled with the reeking remains of their hubbies' previous victims. The villain of "Fitcher's Bird" is a serial axe murderer who keeps the dismembered corpses of his female victims in a "great bloody basin" stored in a locked room. When his latest wife sneaks into the room and discovers his terrible secret, he chops off her head, cuts her into pieces, then "tosses her into the basin with the rest."

One of the most famous of all fairy tales, "Little Red Riding Hood," is generally interpreted as a cautionary tale about the very real dangers that unprotected young girls face from sexual predators. Some scholars believe that the big, bad wolf is meant to represent real-life "lycanthropes"—serial mutilation murderers who killed with such savage ferocity that they were thought to be actual wolfmen. The most famous example was Peter Stübbe, a sixteenth-century German lust killer who slaughtered, dismembered, and cannibalized more than a dozen children, often tearing out their hearts and eating them "panting hot and raw."

In one of his bestselling records, Frank Sinatra croons, "Fairy tales can come true, it can happen to you." If you're familiar with Grimm Brothers stories like "The Robber Bridegroom" and "Fitcher's Bird," all you can say is, "I hope not."

FAN CLUBS

Though it's common for serial killers—even the most repugnant—to attract **Groupies,** few possess enough broad-range appeal to generate fan clubs. One exception is Ed **Gein,** Wisconsin's most notorious native son. Undoubtedly because of his unique status as the most influential psychokiller since **Jack the Ripper,** Gein—whose ghoulish crimes inspired *Psycho, The Texas Chainsaw Massacre,* and *The Silence of the Lambs*—has attracted a sizable worldwide cult following.

Evidence of Gein's appeal is the existence of the Official Ed Gein Fan Club, information about which can be found on the aptly named Web site www.evilnow.com. For a modest fee, new members receive a card, a badge, and a shot glass adorned with Ed's mug, as well as specially discounted offers on such must-have collectibles as a purported chunk of Gein's gravestone, a sample of dirt from his grave, and a gravestone rubbing.

Another celebrity psycho who has always exerted widespread fascination is the scarily charismatic Charles **Manson.** The Web page www.charles mansonfanclub.com proudly offers "the best in Charlie Manson Memorabilia," from "Charlie Fan Club" T-shirts to Zippo lighters emblazoned with a portrait of the hippie-era Manson surrounded by the slogan: "Remember Kids, Charlie Loves You."

Needless to say, these psycho-worshipping fan clubs—and the cheerfully tasteless souvenirs they traffic in—inspire profound indignation among many people. For more on the phenomenon of what one outraged critic has labeled "murderabilia," see **Cards, Comics, and Collectibles.**

Official Ed Gein Fan Club membership certificate and lapel pin
(Courtesy of Damon Fox)

FANTASY

Though we're sometimes loath to admit it (even to ourselves), everyone harbors socially unacceptable thoughts—forbidden dreams of sex and violence. There's a big difference, though, between the fantasies of serial killers and those of ordinary people. For one thing, the former are a whole lot sicker. An average guy might imagine himself making love to a super-model. The serial killer, on the other hand, will think obsessively about shackling her to a wall, then slicing up her body with a hunting knife.

There's a second, even scarier difference: unlike a normal person (who might indulge in an occasional daydream about, say, hiring a hit-man to bump off his boss), serial killers aren't satisfied with *thinking* about taboo behavior. They are compelled to act out their fantasies—to turn their darkest imaginings into real-life horrors.

People who grow up to be serial killers begin indulging in fantasies of sadistic activity at a disturbingly young age—sometimes as early as seven or eight. While their peers are pretending to be sports stars or superheroes, these incipient psychopaths are already daydreaming about murder and mayhem. Interviewed in prison after his arrest, one serial killer explained that as a child he spent so much time daydreaming in class that his teachers always noted it on his report cards. "And what did you daydream about?" asked the interviewer. His answer: "Wiping out the whole school."

Another serial killer recalled that his favorite make-believe game as a little boy was "gas chamber," in which he pretended to be a condemned prisoner undergoing an agonizing execution. Fantasizing about a slow, painful death was a source of intense boyhood pleasure to this budding psycho.

Unlike other people, the serial killer never outgrows his childhood fantasies. On the contrary. Cut off from normal human relationships, he sinks deeper and deeper into his private world of grotesque imaginings. From the outside, he might appear perfectly well adjusted—a hard worker, good neighbor, and all-around solid citizen. But all the while, bizarre, blood-drenched dreams are running rampant inside his head.

Since psychopaths lack the inner restraints that prevent normal people from acting out their hidden desires, there is nothing to keep a serial killer from trying to make his darkest dreams come true. Eventually, this is exactly what happens. His perverted fantasies of dominance, degradation, and torture become the fuel that sets his crimes in motion. For this reason, former **FBI** agent Robert K. Ressler—the man who popularized the term "serial killer"—insists that it is not child abuse or early trauma that turns people into serial killers. It is their dreams.

As Ressler puts it, creatures like Ted **Bundy**, John Wayne **Gacy**, and their ilk are "motivated to murder by their fantasies."

FBI

J. Edgar Hoover's G-men earned their reputation by battling such Depression-era outlaws as John Dillinger and Pretty Boy Floyd. But compared to today's serial killers, those tommy-gun-toting badmen of yore seem almost quaint. To combat the growing threat of random violence in America, the Bureau has had to come up with sophisticated new crime-fighting techniques.

Beginning in the late 1970s, agents of the FBI's Behavioral Science Unit (BSU), headquartered at the Bureau's Training Academy on the Quantico marine base in eastern Virginia, embarked on the Criminal Personality Research Project—an ambitious effort to probe into the minds of serial murderers. Traveling to prisons throughout the United States, these agents (whose forensic feats have been immortalized in the megahit movie *The Silence of the Lambs*) interviewed nearly forty of America's most notorious figures, including Ed **Gein**, Charles **Manson**, Richard **Speck**, David **Berkowitz**, John Wayne **Gacy**, and Ted **Bundy**. Flattered by the Bureau's attention, most of these killers were happy to chat about themselves. The insights gained from this survey enabled the BSU to devise a revolutionary "criminal personality profiling" method that has proven to be a major new weapon in the fight against violent crime (see **Profiling**).

With serial killings multiplying at an alarming rate, the FBI perceived the need for a national clearinghouse that would provide assistance to police officers throughout the country in their efforts to solve the most monstrous and baffling of murders. The result was the creation of the National Center for the Analysis of Violent Crimes (NCAVC), designed for the express purpose (as Ronald Reagan put it when he announced its establishment in June 1984) of "identifying and tracking repeat killers." Administered by the Behavioral Science Unit, NCAVC not only offers its criminal profiling service to stymied police agencies throughout the country but also serves as the world's leading resource center for the pursuit and capture of serial killers.

Besides profiling, the most powerful weapon in NCAVC's arsenal is the Violent Criminal Apprehension Program (VICAP), the brainchild of a former Los Angeles homicide detective named Pierce Brooks. Back in the late 1950s, Brooks was investigating a brutal murder that seemed to be the work of a veteran killer who kept on the move. Having hit a dead end in his investigation, Brooks decided to see if there were other unsolved homicides in the country with similar characteristics. Unfortunately, there was only one way to check—by going to the public library during his off-hours and plowing through newspapers from around the United States. It took him a solid year to find what he was looking for—a case in Ohio that bore all the earmarks of the LA crime.

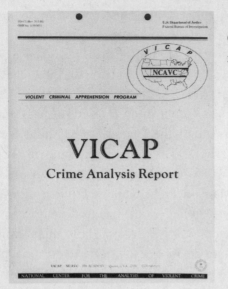

Cover of VICAP crime analysis report form

Perceiving the need for a more efficient way of tracking America's growing population of elusive, highly mobile killers, Brooks came up with the concept of a nationwide, computerized network designed to collate and provide leads on thousands of unsolved crimes. As a result of Brooks's efforts, VICAP finally became operational in 1985.

VICAP has had some problems: serious underfunding and the reluctance of local police to fill out the hellishly complex forms on their unsolved crimes. But the forms have been simplified, and the program received a major infusion of money from Congress in 1994. If VICAP lives up to its potential, creatures like Ted Bundy might soon go the way of other obsolete scourges, like leprosy and the black plague.

Tales of the "Psyche Squad"

Two founding members of NCAVC—Robert K. Ressler and John Douglas—have published gripping accounts of their experiences. Readers interested in learning more about the Bureau's crack team of criminal personality profilers (aka the "Psyche Squad") shouldn't fail to check out *Whoever Fights Monsters* by Robert K. Ressler and Tom Schachtman (New York:

Simon & Schuster, 1992) and *Mindhunter: Inside the FBI's Elite Serial Crime Unit* by John Douglas and Mark Olshaker (New York: A Lisa Drew Book/ Scribner, 1995). Also recommended: H. Paul Jeffers's *Who Killed Precious?* (New York: St. Martin's, 1992), a lively, behind-the-scenes look at the history and operations of the FBI's Behavioral Science Unit, and Stephen G. Michaud's *The Evil That Men Do* (New York: St. Martin's, 1999), which details the career of Roy Hazelwood, another pioneering profiler and cofounder of VICAP.

FETISH OBJECTS

See **Trophies.**

Albert Fish

Albert Fish has been called "America's boogeyman"—and for good reason. A cannibal ogre in the guise of a kindly old man, he was every parent's worst nightmare: a fiend who lured children to destruction with the promise of a treat.

The crime that brought Fish to public attention was the 1928 kidnapping-murder of a pretty twelve-year-old girl named Grace Budd. After befriending her parents, Fish made up a diabolical lie. He said that his niece was having a birthday party and asked if Grace would like to go. Mr. and Mrs. Budd—who had no way of knowing that the grandfatherly old man was a monster—agreed.

Dressed in her Sunday finest, the trusting little girl went off with Fish, who led her to an isolated house in a northern suburb of New York City. There, he strangled her, butchered her body, and carried off several pounds of her flesh. Back in his lodgings, he turned her "meat" (as he called it) into a cannibal stew, complete with carrots, onions, and bacon strips. He spent the next nine days locked in his room, savoring this unholy meal and compulsively masturbating.

For the next six years, Fish remained at large, but throughout this time he was doggedly pursued by a New York City detective named William King, who had made the Grace Budd case his personal crusade. Even so, Fish

Albert Fish; from
*True Crime Trading Cards
Series Two: Serial Killers and
Mass Murderers;*
art by **Jon Bright**
*(Courtesy of Jon Bright and
Valarie Jones)*

ALBERT FISH

probably would have gotten away with the crime if it hadn't been for his own inner demons. In 1934, he felt compelled to send Mrs. Budd one of the sickest **Letters** ever written. In the end, King was able to track down his quarry through the letterhead stationery Fish had used.

Once Fish was in custody, authorities quickly realized that they had their hands on a killer of unimaginable depravity, one who had spent his whole lifetime inflicting pain—on himself as well as on others. Like a number of serial killers, Fish was a religious maniac, and he subjected himself to grotesque forms of torture as penance for his sins—flagellating himself with leather straps and nail-studded paddles, eating his own excrement, shoving sewing needles up into his groin. The children he mutilated and murdered were, in his demented eyes, sacrificial offerings to the Lord. Noted New York City psychiatrist Dr. Frederic Wertham—who was called in by the defense to examine Fish—declared that the old man had practiced "every sexual perversion known," as well as a few that no one had ever heard of (among his grotesque pleasures, Fish liked to insert rose stems into his urethra). X rays of his pelvic region taken in prison revealed that there were twenty-nine needles lodged around his bladder.

Though the jury at his 1935 trial acknowledged that he was insane, they believed he should be electrocuted anyway. After receiving the death sentence, the bizarre old man reportedly exclaimed, "What a thrill it will be to die in the electric chair! It will be the supreme thrill—the only one I haven't tried!"

On January 16, 1936, the sixty-five-year-old Fish went to the chair—the oldest man ever put to death in Sing Sing.

FOLIE À DEUX

Would the Columbine massacre have taken place if Eric Harris had never met Dylan Klebold? Would Nathan Leopold have tried his hand at "thrill killing" without the encouragement of Richard Loeb? In both these instances, the answer is: it's possible but highly unlikely. Cases like these—in which two individuals egg each other on to insane acts of violence that neither one, individually, would have dared to commit on his own—are examples of a phenomenon that psychiatrists call *folie à deux:* a madness shared by two people (otherwise known as "double insanity," "reciprocal insanity," or "insanity in pairs").

Not all criminals caught up in a *folie à deux* are serial killers. Some, like Klebold and Harris, are mass murderers. Others, like Leopold and Loeb, perpetrate a single spectacular act of gratuitous violence.

Conversely, not all serial killers who operate in pairs are in the grip of a *folie à deux.* Henry Lee **Lucas** and the unspeakable Ottis Toole, for example, teamed up for a while, but each was already a confirmed serial killer. A true *folie à deux* involves two people who, separately, might daydream about murder but would never have the nerve to commit it. Only when they form a bond with another, equally toxic personality do they take the plunge into full-blown homicidal behavior.

Among the most notorious of these pernicious partnerships are Leonard Lake and Charles Ng, two wildly vicious sadists who raped, tortured, and murdered a string of victims in a specially designed concrete bunker in northern California during the early 1980s; Lawrence Bittaker and Roy Norris, another deadly California duo who abducted and killed a half-dozen teenage girls in a customized van they dubbed "Murder Mack"; and the **"Hillside Stranglers."**

A significant number of *folies à deux* involve male-female couples. In cases like these it is usually the man who instigates the crimes and the woman who serves as his willing, even eager, accomplice. For more on this phenomenon see **Killer Couples.**

FOREIGNERS

America may no longer be the world's leading manufacturer of cars, cameras, and color TVs, but we're still way ahead of the pack when it comes to serial killers. Not only do we turn them out in far greater quantity than any other civilized nation, we've also produced most of the really big-name psychos of the late twentieth century: **Manson, Bundy, Gacy,** et al. Still, it would be the height of chauvinism to believe that the United States of America is the only country capable of creating homicidal sex maniacs.

From the days of **Jack the Ripper,** Great Britain has been home to lots of serial killers (see **Rippers**). In the past few decades alone, Shakespeare's "blessed isle" has produced a number of world-class psychos, including the unspeakably heinous Fred and Rosemary West (see **Killer Couples**) and Dr. Harold Shipman, one of the most prolific serial killers in history (see **Records**). France, too, has produced its fair share—from Joseph **Vacher** to Dr. Marcel **Petiot** to Thierry Paulin (the "Monster of Montmartre," who murdered at least twenty old ladies in the mid-1980s). Some of the most monstrous lust murderers in history, including Peter **Kürten** and Fritz **Haarmann,** were born and bred in Germany. Among Italian homicidal maniacs, special mention must be made of the "Monster of Florence," a sexually sadistic **Lovers' Lane** killer who preyed mostly on young couples in the 1970s and 1980s. Even Belgium, the last place on earth you'd expect to find serial killers, has turned out some scary specimens. In the 1930s, for example, a serial poisoner named Marie Becker knocked off a dozen people (Becker had a knack for picturesque descriptions. During her trial, she told the judge that one of her female victims resembled "an angel choked on sauerkraut.") More recently, a Belgian pedophile, Marc Dutroux, was at the center of a scandal involving child abduction and serial murder.

With all of these killers in Western Europe (to say nothing of the U.S.), can serial murder be seen as a symptom of capitalist decadence? That's certainly what Soviet officials used to claim. Their position was somewhat undermined, however, when the victims of Andrei **Chikatilo,** the "Beast of

Rostov," began piling up. Nor did a Communist social system prevent China from producing at least one notorious sex slayer, Lu Wenxian, aka the "Guangzhou Ripper," responsible for thirteen mutilation murders in the early 1990s. There is reason to suspect that there have been other serial killers in China, though it's unlikely that the world will ever hear about their crimes, since that's not the sort of news a state-controlled media tends to play up.

For such a sparsely populated country, Australia has turned out a surprising number of serial murderers, including "Granny Killer" John Wayne Glover, Edward Leonski (aka the "Singing Strangler"), and William McDonald, the "Sydney Mutilator." South America can lay claim to having produced the terrifyingly prolific Pedro Lopez, the "Monster of the Andes," responsible for the deaths of as many as three hundred young girls in Ecuador, Colombia, and Peru.

In South Africa, a soft-spoken ex-convict named Morris Sithole slaughtered thirty-eight young women between January and October 1995, a case that received international attention, particularly after **FBI** "mindhunter" Robert Ressler was brought in as a consultant. The Japanese take justifiable pride in the safety of their society, but during the 1940s, a former naval officer named Yoshio Kodaira confessed to the rape-murder of seven women. More recently, the country was rocked by the case of the "Kobe School Killer," an underage psycho who placed the severed head of an eleven-year-old boy by the entrance of a junior high school, along with a taunting note stuffed in the victim's mouth.

From Norway to New Zealand, Portugal to Pakistan, serial murder is clearly an international phenomenon. To paraphrase the song, it's an appalling world after all.

The Iranian Spider

Here's a philosophical conundrum: Is serial murder a crime if the perpetrator lives in a society where people condone—even applaud—his behavior? That was the issue surrounding the case of Iranian sex killer Saeed Hanaei.

For more than a year, the thirty-five-year-old construction worker trolled the streets of the holy city of Mashhad, luring sixteen prostitutes to his home, where they were strangled with their scarves, then wrapped in their black chadors and dumped by the roadside or in open sewers. Arrested in July 2001, Hanaei—known as the "Spider" for his skill at snaring victims—displayed not a trace of remorse. On the contrary, he took positive pride in his crimes, describing himself as a holy crusader against sin and corruption. "I realized God looked favorably upon me, that he had taken notice of my work," proclaimed Hanaei, who described himself as an "anti-streetwalker activist."

To be sure, other "harlot killers" have felt they were doing God's work. The "Yorkshire **Ripper,**" Peter Sutcliffe, for example, believed that he was "just cleaning the streets" by slaughtering prostitutes. And the German lust murderer, Heinrich Pommerencke was inspired to go out and butcher "sinful" women after watching the Golden Calf sequence in Cecil B. DeMille's *The Ten Commandments.*

In Western nations, however, such psychopaths tend not to receive widespread, enthusiastic support for their malevolent acts of misogyny. The case was different in Iran, where Hanaei became a folk hero to religious hardliners, who rallied to his defense, arguing that his victims were a "waste of blood" and that, in disposing of them, Hanaei was only obeying Islamic law.

Their support waned only after Hanaei revealed that he had had sex with the women before killing them. He went to the gallows in April 2002, convinced to the bitter end that his ideological allies would step in at the last minute and save him.

Hanaei's case is the subject of Maziar Bahari's fascinating 2002 documentary, *And Along Came a Spider,* which explores his crimes in the context of a society bitterly torn between fundamentalism and reform.

Was Jack the Ripper Really a Yank?

Forget Shakespeare, Churchill, and the Beatles. As far as crime buffs are concerned, the most significant Englishman of all time was **Jack the Ripper.** There's only one problem with this belief. According to a pair of writers named Stewart Evans and Paul Gainey, Saucy Jack was really an American!

In their 1995 book, *The Lodger: The Arrest and Escape of Jack the Ripper,* Evans and Gainey argue that the legendary "Whitechapel Monster" was actually an Irish-American quack, Dr. Francis Tumberty. A bizarre personality who had once been arrested for the assassination of Abraham Lincoln, Tumberty was a self-confessed woman hater. He had developed a grudge against the opposite sex after discovering that his wife was moonlighting as a prostitute. Among his other eccentricities, he kept a personal collection of preserved female organs, which he liked to display to his guests during dinner parties.

While residing in London in the late 1880s, Tumberty became a prime suspect in the Ripper crimes. Arrested in mid-November 1888—just days after what turned out to be the last of the Whitechapel murders—he was held for a week before being bailed out by loyal employees. Hopping a steamer back to the States, he holed up in his Manhattan apartment, then disappeared again with Scotland Yard inspectors still hot on his trail. Not long afterward, a series of grisly prostitute murders—identical in method to the Whitechapel slayings—occurred in Jamaica and later in Managua, Nicaragua. Evans and Gainey believe that Tumberty was responsible, making him "the world's first traveling serial killer."

G

John Wayne Gacy

13. JOHN WAYNE GACY

John Wayne Gacy;
from *Murderers!*
trading card set
(Courtesy of Roger Worsham)

John Wayne Gacy was a man of many masks. There was the mask of masculinity. To live up to the two-fisted name bestowed by his tyrannical father, Gacy cultivated a gruff, swaggering air. There was the mask of middle-class respectability, symbolized by his tidy ranch-style house in a Chicago suburb.

He even wore a literal mask, making himself up as a grinning clown called Pogo to entertain hospitalized children.

But Gacy was one of the most monstrously divided sociopaths in the annals of crime, and his masks concealed a hideous reality. Beneath his "man's man" persona, he was a tormented, self-loathing homosexual who preyed on young males. Beneath the smiling face, he was a leering, implacable sadist. Beneath the crawl space of his suburban house, more than two dozen corpses moldered in the slime.

Raised by an abusive, alcoholic father—who spent much of his time deriding his son as a sissy—Gacy grew up to be a pudgy hypochondriac whose homosexual drives were a source of profound self-hatred. He also possessed a terrifyingly antisocial personality.

For a long time, however, he managed to conceal his real character beneath the veneer of an ambitious Middle American businessman. By the time he was twenty-two, he was a married man and father, a highly respected member of the Junior Chamber of Commerce, and the successful manager of a Kentucky Fried Chicken outlet in Waterloo, Iowa. But he was also leading a secret life as a seducer and molester of young males. In 1968, after being arrested on a sodomy charge, he was hit with a ten-year sentence, though he proved to be such a model prisoner that he was paroled after only eighteen months.

Gacy—whose first wife had divorced him on the day of his sentencing—relocated to Chicago, where he soon reestablished himself as an apparent pillar of the community, remarrying, starting a thriving contracting business, becoming active in local politics (on one occasion, he was photographed shaking hands with First Lady Rosalynn Carter). Before long, however, his darkest impulses reasserted themselves—this time in an even ghastlier form. He became a human predator who tortured and murdered his young male pickups for his own depraved pleasure.

Cruising the streets for hustlers, drifters, and runaways, Gacy (who sometimes coerced them into his car by posing as a plainclothes cop) would bring them back to his house. There he would handcuff them and then subject them to hours of rape and torture before strangling them slowly. Their bodies would end up in the crawl space of his house.

In 1978, police finally set their sights on the civic-minded contractor when a teenage boy dropped out of sight after telling friends that he was on his way to see Gacy about a job. Digging into Gacy's past, police uncovered records of his previous sex offenses. In the fetid muck of his crawl space, they exhumed the decomposing remains of twenty-seven victims.

Gacy had buried two more elsewhere on his property and dumped another four corpses in a nearby river, bringing the number of his victims to thirty-three.

At first, Gacy maintained that he was the victim of multiple personality disorder, and that his atrocities were actually the work of an evil alter ego named Jack. But the ploy didn't work. He was given the death sentence in 1980. After fourteen years on death row, the "Killer Clown" was finally executed by lethal injection.

Edward Gein

Ed Gein
(AP/Wide World Photos)

If a serial killer is defined as someone who murders at least three victims over an extended period of time, then—strictly speaking—Edward Gein was not a serial killer, since he appears to have murdered no more than two women. And yet his crimes were so grotesque and appalling that they have haunted America for almost forty years.

Gein was raised by a fanatical, domineering mother who ranted inces-

santly about the sinful nature of her own sex. When she died in 1945, her
son was a thirty-nine-year-old bachelor, still emotionally enslaved to the
woman who had tyrannized his life. Boarding up her room, he preserved it
as though it were a shrine. The rest of the house, however, soon degener-
ated into a madman's shambles.

When Gein wasn't earning his meager living doing odd jobs for neighbors, he passed his lonely hours poring over lurid magazine pieces about
sex-change operations, South Seas headhunters, and Nazi atrocities. His
own atrocities began a few years after his mother's death. Driven by his
desperate loneliness—and burgeoning psychosis—he started making noc-
turnal raids on local graveyards, digging up the bodies of middle-aged
women and bringing them back to his remote farmhouse. In 1954, he aug-
mented his necrophiliac activities with murder, shooting a local tavern
keeper named Mary Hogan and absconding with her two-hundred-pound
corpse. Three years later—on the first day of hunting season, 1957—he
killed another local woman, a fifty-eight-year-old grandmother who owned
the village hardware store.

Ed Gein exhuming a corpse;
art by Chris Pelletiere

Suspicion immediately lighted on Gein, who had been hanging around
the store in recent days. Breaking into his summer kitchen, police discovered the victim's headless and gutted corpse suspended upside-down
from a rafter like a dressed-out game animal. Inside the house itself, the

stunned searchers uncovered a large assortment of unspeakable artifacts—chairs upholstered with human skin, soup bowls fashioned from skulls, a shoebox full of female genitalia, faces stuffed with newspapers and mounted like hunting trophies on the walls, and a "mammary vest" flayed from the torso of a woman. Gein later confessed that he enjoyed dressing himself in this and other human-skin garments and pretending he was his own mother.

The discovery of these Gothic horrors sent shock waves throughout Eisenhower-era America. In Wisconsin itself, Gein quickly entered local folklore. Within weeks of his arrest, macabre **Jokes** called "Geiners" became a statewide craze. The country as a whole learned about Gein in December 1957, when both *Life* and *Time* magazines ran features on his "house of horrors."

After ten years in a mental hospital, Gein was judged competent to stand trial. He was found guilty but insane and institutionalized for the rest of his life, dying of cancer in 1984.

By then, however, Gein had already achieved pop immortality, thanks to horror writer Robert **Bloch,** who had the inspired idea of creating a fictional character based on Gein—a deranged mama's boy named Norman Bates. In 1960, Alfred Hitchcock transformed Bloch's pulp chiller, *Psycho,* into a cinematic masterpiece. Insofar as *Psycho* initiated the craze for "slasher" movies, Gein is revered by horror buffs as the "Grandfather of Gore," the prototype of every knife-, axe-, and cleaver-wielding maniac who has stalked America's movie screens for the past thirty years.

Ed Gein, Superstar

Ed Gein's ghoulish crimes have served as the inspiration for the three most terrifying films of the past thirty years: *Psycho, The Texas Chainsaw Massacre,* and *The Silence of the Lambs.*

Though Robert **Bloch,** the original author of *Psycho,* insisted that his book was not simply a fictionalized version of Gein's crimes, his immortal character, Norman Bates, was clearly inspired by Gein. (Indeed, in Bloch's original novel, Norman himself points out the parallels between his own crimes and Gein's.)

Ed Gein; from *True Crime Trading Cards Series Two: Serial Killers and Mass Murderers;* art by Jon Bright

(Courtesy of Jon Bright and Valarie Jones)

Tobe Hooper, the director of *The Texas Chainsaw Massacre,* reportedly heard stories about Gein from Midwestern relatives and grew up haunted by these tales. In his splatter-movie classic, the Gein-inspired character is not a mild-mannered motel keeper with a split personality but a bestial hulk named Leatherface, who sports a mask made of dried human flesh.

Thomas Harris researched the **FBI**'s files on Gein before creating his fictional serial killer Jame Gumb (aka "Buffalo Bill"), a transsexual wannabe who attempts to fashion a suit from the flayed torsos of his victims. Jonathan Demme's Oscar-winning movie version relied on Harold Schechter's book *Deviant: The Shocking True Story of the Original "Psycho"* to create the squalid look of Gumb's Gein-inspired house.

Psycho, Chainsaw, and *Silence* all take considerable liberties with the Gein story. The film that sticks closest to the facts is a 1974 low-budget shocker called *Deranged,* which has developed a major cult following among horror buffs. Some video versions of *Deranged* are prefaced by a brief documentary on Gein called *A Nice Quiet Man,* which includes the only known footage of some of his hideous human-flesh artifacts.

GRAVE ROBBING

See **Necrophilia.**

> **"Every man to his own tastes. Mine is for corpses."**
> **HENRI BLOT**

GROUPIES

Fame can be a powerful aphrodisiac—even when a person is famous for committing serial murder. Celebrity killers have attracted groupies for at least a century. During a ten-day span in 1895, a handsome San Francisco medical student and Sunday school teacher named Theo Durrant—the Ted **Bundy** of his day—lured two young women into an empty church, then murdered them and raped their corpses, leaving one body inside the church library, the other in the belfry. Durrant's trial was a nationwide sensation, exerting a morbid fascination on people from coast to coast. A young woman named Rosalind Bowers, however, carried her fascination to what most observers felt was an unseemly extreme. Virtually every day of the trial, the dainty Miss Bowers appeared in court with a bouquet of sweet pea flowers, which she presented to the "Demon of the Belfry" as a gesture of support. Before long, Miss Bowers had gained a measure of celebrity herself, being dubbed by the papers the "Sweet Pea Girl."

In the century since the Durrant case, high-profile serial killers have continued to attract almost as many groupies as rock stars. While some of these murderers have possessed a certain superficial charm (like Bundy) others have been seriously repellent (John Wayne **Gacy**, for example) or just plain over-the-top bizarre (like Richard the "Night Stalker" **Ramirez**). But no matter how loathsome or grotesque the killer, there have always been women who considered him a dreamboat. Even Ed **Gein**—a dim-witted, middle-aged necrophiliac with the approximate sexual magnetism of Gomer Pyle—received frequent letters from women begging for locks of his hair.

One of the most startling examples of this strange erotic phenomenon came to light only recently with the publication of the book *Love Letters to Adolf Hitler,* culled from the collection of a man named William Emker. Shortly after the end of World War II, Emker—then a U.S. Army officer—was searching through Hitler's bombed-out headquarters when he came upon a trove of letters written to the Führer by female admirers. "Sweetest love," one typical letter begins, "favorite of my heart, my dearest, my truest and hottest beloved. I could kiss you a thousand times and still not be satisfied. My love for you is endless, so tender, so hot and so complete." Emker found thousands of missives like this one, addressed to "My darling, sugar-sweet Adolf," "My beloved Führer," or sometimes simply "Dear Adi." The fact that the greatest **Mass Murderer** of the twentieth century could stimulate such overheated fantasies only confirms the disquieting point: there is something about monsters that just turns certain women on.

Fritz Haarmann

One of the most infamous lust slayers of the twentieth century, Haarmann was born to a working-class couple in Hanover, Germany, in 1879. He was a sullen and slow-witted child whose favorite pastime was dressing up like a girl. At seventeen, he was committed to an asylum after being arrested for child molesting. Six months later, he escaped to Switzerland and made his way back to Hanover.

For a while, he attempted to lead a respectable life, taking a job in a cigar factory, getting engaged to a young woman. But this period of relative normalcy didn't last. Deserting his fiancée, he ran off and joined the army. When he returned to Hanover in 1903, he launched into a life of petty crime. Throughout his twenties, he was in and out of jail for offenses ranging from being a pickpocket to burglary. He spent World War I behind bars.

Released in 1918, he returned to his native city and joined a postwar smuggling ring that trafficked, among other things, in black-market beef. He also served as a police stool pigeon, a sideline that afforded him protection for his illicit activities. In 1919, however, after being caught in bed with a young boy, Haarmann was shipped back to prison.

It was after his release nine months later that Haarmann began his career of unparalleled depravity. Living in Hanover's seamy Old Quarter, he fell under the thrall of a homosexual prostitute named Hans Grans. Together, the two set about preying on the young male refugees who were flooding into the war-ravaged city. Though Haarmann was ultimately charged with twenty-seven murders, it seems likely he was responsible for as many as fifty. The method he employed to kill his victims was always the same.

After luring the hungry boy to his room, Haarmann would feed him a meal, then overpower him (often with Grans's assistance) and fall upon the boy's throat, chewing through the flesh until he had nearly separated the head from the body. Generally, he would experience a sexual climax while battening on the boy.

Afterward, Haarmann and Grans would butcher the body and dispose of the flesh by peddling it as black-market beef. The victim's clothes would also be sold, and the inedible portions of the body dumped in a canal.

As the number of missing boys mounted, police suspicion began to fall on Haarmann. A woman who had purchased one of his black-market "steaks" became convinced it was human flesh and turned it over to the police. In the summer of 1924, several skulls and a sackful of bones were found on the banks of the canal. Searching Haarmann's rooms,

Fritz Haarmann; from
Bloody Visions trading cards
(© & ™ 1995 M. H. Price and Shel-Tone Publications. All rights reserved.)

18: FRITZ HAARMANN:
"The Ogre
of Hanover"

detectives discovered bundles of boys' clothing. The landlady's son was wearing a coat—given to him by Haarmann—that belonged to one of the missing boys.

In the end, Haarmann confessed. He was tried in 1924, found guilty, and sentenced to death. While awaiting execution, the "Vampire of Hanover" (as he'd been dubbed by the press) produced a written confession in which he described, with undisguised relish, the pleasure he had derived from his atrocities. At his own request, he was beheaded with a sword in the city marketplace. Afterward, his brain was removed from his skull and shipped to Goettingen University for study. Unfortunately, nothing came of this effort. Seventy years later, science is still no closer to comprehending the evil of monsters like Fritz Haarmann.

Actor Götz George turns in a chillingly persuasive performance as Haarmann in the 1995 German art film *Der Totmacher (The Deathmaker)*. With a screenplay based on the actual transcripts of Haarmann's psychiatric interviews, the movie (available on DVD) is confined entirely to a stark interrogation room where, shortly before his execution, the wild-eyed lust killer is being examined by an impassive shrink. As Haarmann leers, rants, blubbers, and boasts, a terrifying portrait of homicidal madness emerges. Don't look for fast-paced action or hardcore gore. The movie is all talk—though of a thoroughly compelling kind. Think *My Dinner with Andre* meets *The Silence of the Lambs*.

HEAD INJURIES

When faced with a phenomenon as incomprehensibly evil as serial murder, it's natural for people to search for some kind of rational explanation. After all, if researchers could only identify the sources of serial murder, then it might be possible to come up with a cure—or at least identify potential psychos before they have a chance to hurt anybody. In their urgent efforts to solve this problem, criminologists have come up with all sorts of theories, from "negative parenting" to screwed-up hormones (see **Causes**). Some specialists put the blame on "juvenile cerebral trauma"—or, in plain English, getting whacked on the head as a kid. The brain damage done by such an injury can, according to these experts, turn people into serial killers.

It's certainly true that a high percentage of serial killers have suffered head injuries during their childhoods. Earle Leonard **Nelson,** for example—the notorious "Gorilla Man" who murdered almost two dozen women in the mid-1920s—was thrown off his bike by a trolley when he was ten and lay comatose for nearly a week. He finally recuperated, but his behavior (which wasn't entirely normal to begin with) became even more bizarre from then on. The serial rapist and killer Bobby Joe Long—convicted in 1984 on nine counts of first-degree murder—must have set some kind of record for head injuries. At five he was knocked unconscious in a fall from a swing. At six he had a bike accident that sent him flying headfirst into a parked car. At seven he fell off a pony and onto his skull. From that point on, he managed to avoid any more head traumas—until he reached his early twenties, when he got into a motorcycle accident, slamming headfirst into the asphalt with such force that his helmet was crushed. These are only two of many examples. The list of head-battered psychos includes some of the most infamous names in the annals of serial murder—John Wayne **Gacy**, Richard **Speck**, Charles **Manson**, and Henry **Lucas**.

Unfortunately, the cerebral trauma theory of serial murder has the same limitations as other reductive explanations. Head injuries are an everyday fact of childhood life. Millions of kids fall off bikes and swings and see-saws and land on their heads. But only a tiny fraction turn out to be psycho-pathic killers. On the other hand, combined with other predisposing factors, a serious head trauma may well contribute to incipient psychopathology.

So—can serial murder be caused by something as simple as a knock on the head? Probably not.

But it sure doesn't help.

Gary Heidnik

The average tabloid headline is the printed equivalent of a sideshow barker's pitch—a shrill, attention-grabbing come-on that tends to promise much more than it can possibly deliver by way of lurid thrills. On rare occasions, however, even the most sensational headlines fall short of the terrible truth. Such was the case on March 26, 1987, when papers from coast to coast trumpeted front-page phrases like "Madman's Sex Orgy" and "Torture Dungeon." Titillating as these headlines were,

they couldn't begin to convey the shocking reality of Gary Heidnik's house
of horrors.

Alerted by a frantic 911 call from a woman named Josefina Rivera—who
claimed that she had been held captive for months in Heidnik's cellar—the
cops entered the suspect's rundown home in North Philadelphia and found
a scene that might have been dreamed up by the Marquis de Sade. In the
dank and squalid basement, two naked women were shackled to pipes. Another sat quaking in a fetid pit that had been dug in the earthen floor. All
three had been beaten, starved, tortured, raped.

Eventually, authorities would learn that Heidnik had abducted and imprisoned a total of six young women. Josefina Rivera had been lucky
enough to escape. Two others had died. Heidnik had killed one by forcing
her into the pit, filling it with water, then electrocuting her with a live wire.
The other victim had perished after Heidnik left her dangling by the wrists
for a week. He had dismembered her body, ground up some of her flesh in a
food processor, and mixed it with dog food. Then he had forced the other
captives to devour this unspeakable mush. Searching Heidnik's house, police discovered a charred human rib in the oven and a forearm in the
freezer. Not surprisingly, Heidnik turned out to be a former mental patient
and convicted sex offender with a history of preying on mentally retarded
black women. In spite of his flagrant psychopathology, he was something of
a financial whiz, who had parlayed a modest investment into a half-million-
dollar fortune. As one pundit put it, Heidnik was an expert in "stocks and
bondage." He owned several expensive cars, including a Rolls-Royce. He
had managed to avoid paying taxes on his income by founding his own
church and appointing himself bishop.

Aspiring to the role of Old Testament patriarch, he had begun
kidnapping women in late 1986, intending to assemble a personal
harem of ten women who would provide him with a whole tribe of offspring.
"We'll be just one big happy family," Heidnik told his captives, even as
he was busily shoving screwdrivers into their ears, raping each one in
turn while the others were forced to watch, and making them into
unwitting cannibals.

At his arraignment, Heidnik offered a novel defense, claiming that the
women were already there when he moved into the house. For some reason, the judges failed to believe him. He was convicted of two counts of
murder and sentenced to death. While in prison, he seemed to share the
opinion of many people that his life was not worth saving. During the eleven

years he languished on death row, he made several attempts to kill himself. On July 6, 1999, prison personnel finished the job via lethal injection.

> "Any person who puts dog food and human remains in a food processor and calls it a gourmet meal and feeds it to others is out to lunch."
>
> **ATTORNEY CHUCK PERUTO JR.,**
> *referring to his client Gary Heidnik*

The Hillside Stranglers

When the corpses started piling up—young women who had been tortured, raped, and strangled—the papers blared the news: a serial killer was on the loose. They dubbed him the "Hillside Strangler" because the bulk of the bodies were deposited on hillsides around the Los Angeles area. But the newspapers were wrong. The grisly crimes weren't the work of a serial killer.

They were the demented teamwork of *two* serial killers.

The first to die was a black prostitute, whose naked corpse was dumped near Forest Lawn Cemetery in mid-October 1977. Two weeks later, the body of a fifteen-year-old female runaway turned up in the Los Angeles suburb of Glendale. Over the next few months, eight more bodies would be found. The victims ranged in age from twelve to twenty-eight. All had been sexually violated (sometimes with objects like soda bottles), strangled, and tortured in a variety of ways. One had been burned with an electric cord. Another had been injected with cleaning solution. Yet another had been killed with voluptuous cruelty—strangled to the point of unconsciousness, then revived, then strangled again, and so on until her tormentor finally put her to death.

From early on in their investigation, police suspected that two killers were involved, since semen found inside the victims indicated that the women had been raped (often both vaginally and anally) by different men. That suspicion was confirmed when an eyewitness caught sight of two men forcing a young woman into their car.

As a rule, serial killers keep murdering until they are caught. In February 1978, however—four months after they started—the Hillside Stranglings abruptly ceased. The killers might well have gotten away with their atrocities—if it hadn't been for the twisted compulsions of one member of the unspeakable duo.

One year after the last of the Los Angeles murders, two young women were raped and strangled in Bellingham, Washington. Suspicion immediately lighted on a twenty-six-year-old security guard named Kenneth Bianchi, who had recently moved to Bellingham from Los Angeles. Before long, police had ferreted out the truth—Bianchi and his forty-four-year-old cousin, a brutish sociopath named Angelo Buono, were the Hillside Stranglers.

Though Buono led an outwardly respectable life as the owner of a successful auto upholstery business, he was also a sadistic pimp with a long history of violence against women. (He allegedly once sodomized his wife in front of their children after she refused to have sex with him.) Bianchi was a small-time con artist who had moved in with his cousin after relocating from Rochester, New York, in 1976. Separately, neither one had ever been known to commit murder—but together, they brought out the most monstrous impulses in each other. (See **Folie à Deux.**)

For a while, Bianchi had authorities believing that he suffered from a split personality. Ostensibly, it was his evil alter ego, "Steve," who had participated in the murders. But a psychiatric expert finally established that "Steve"—a sadistic sex killer who emerged under hypnosis—was a ruse.

In the end—in order to avoid a death sentence—Bianchi agreed to plead guilty to the murders and to testify against his cousin, who was convicted after a highly protracted trial. Both Hillside Stranglers are currently serving life sentences.

HISTORY

Reviewing the history of serial murder is a tricky proposition, since it's hard to know exactly where to begin. On the one hand, serial killing seems like a uniquely modern phenomenon, a symptom of the various ills afflicting late-twentieth-century America—alienation, social decay, sexual violence, rampant crime, etc. On the other hand, the savage, sadistic impulses that underlie serial murder are undoubtedly as old as humankind.

Any historical survey of serial murder would have to begin at least as far back as ancient Rome, when the emperor Caligula was busily indulging his taste for torture and perversion. During the Middle Ages, depraved **Aristocrats** like Gilles de Rais (the original "**Bluebeard**") and Elizabeth Bathory (the "Blood Countess") fed their unholy lusts on the blood of hundreds of victims, while psychopathic peasants like Gilles Garnier and Peter Stubbe butchered their victims with such bestial ferocity that they were believed to be literal werewolves (see **Lycanthropy**). Other homicidal monsters of the premodern era include the Scottish cannibal Sawney Beane (see **Clans**) and Vlad the Impaler, the real-life Dracula (see **Vampires**).

Most crime buffs agree that the first serial sex killer of the modern era was **Jack the Ripper,** whose crimes—the ghastly slaughter of five London streetwalkers—sent shock waves throughout Victorian England. One hundred years later, the serial slaying of prostitutes has become such a commonplace activity that (to cite just one of many examples) when, in July 1995, a former warehouse clerk named William Lester Suff was convicted of killing thirteen hookers in Southern California, the media barely noted the event. That shift sums up the history of serial murder in the twentieth century: its appalling transformation from a monstrous anomaly into an everyday horror.

Jack the Ripper's American contemporary, H. H. **Holmes,** who confessed to twenty-seven murders in the late 1890s, is regarded as America's first documented serial killer. Two full decades would pass before another one appeared on the scene: the unknown maniac dubbed the "Axeman of New Orleans," who terrorized that city between 1918 and 1919 (see **Axe Murderers**).

Though it was a violent and lawless decade, the Roaring Twenties produced only two authentic serial killers: Earle Leonard **Nelson**—the serial strangler nicknamed the "Gorilla Murderer"—and the viciously depraved Carl **Panzram**. Serial killers were equally few and far between in the 1930s and 1940s. The cannibalistic pedophile Albert **Fish** and the anonymous psycho known as the "Mad Butcher of Kingsbury Run" (aka the "Cleveland Torso Killer") are the only known serial killers of Depression-era America. The roster of 1940s serial killers is also limited to a pair of names: Jake Bird, a homicidal burglar who confessed to a dozen axe murders, and William Heirens, famous for his desperate, **Lipstick**-scrawled plea: "For heaven's sake catch me before I kill more. I cannot control myself."

It wasn't until the post–World War II period that serial murder became rampant in this country. Its shadow was already beginning to spread during the sunny days of the Eisenhower era. The 1950s witnessed the depredations of Wisconsin ghoul Ed **Gein**; the voyeuristic horrors of Californian Harvey Murray Glatman (who photographed his bound, terrorized victims before murdering them); the crimes of homicidal scam artists Martha Beck and Raymond Fernandez (the "Lonely Hearts Killers"); and the bloody rampage of Charles Starkweather, who slaughtered a string of victims as he hot-rodded across the Nebraska badlands.

The situation became even grimmer during the 1960s, a period that produced such infamous figures as Melvin "Sex Beast" Rees, Albert "Boston Strangler" **DeSalvo,** Richard **Speck,** Charles **Manson,** and the still-unknown **Zodiac.** By the time the 1970s rolled around, the problem had become so dire that, for the first time, law enforcement officials felt the need to define this burgeoning phenomenon as a major category of crime (see **Definition/ Coining a Phrase**). The 1970s was the decade of **Berkowitz** and **Bundy, Kemper** and **Gacy,** Bianchi and Buono (the "**Hillside Stranglers**"), and more.

By the 1980s, some criminologists were bandying words like *plague* and *epidemic* to characterize the problem. Though these terms smack of hysteria, it is nevertheless true that serial homicide has become so common in our country that most of its perpetrators stir up only local interest. Only the most ghastly of these killers, the ones who seem more like mythic monsters than criminals—Jeffrey **Dahmer,** for example—capture the attention of the entire nation and end up as creepy household names.

In view of this grim chronicle, it's hard not to agree with Voltaire's famous definition. "History," he wrote, "is little else than a picture of human crime and misfortune."

H. H. Holmes

At the same time that **Jack the Ripper** was terrorizing London, America was home to its own psychopathic monster. Calling himself Dr. H. H. Holmes, he was at least as notorious in his own day as "Saucy Jack." But while the latter's fame has grown through the years, Dr. Holmes—for unexplained reasons—has largely been forgotten. In the chronicle of American crime, however, he occupies a special place: he was our country's first documented serial killer.

Dr. H. H. Holmes, the
nineteenth-century
"multi-murderer"
*(Courtesy of the Illinois State
Historical Society)*

Much about his life and crimes remains shrouded in mystery. We know
that his real name was Herman Mudgett, that he was born in the tiny New
Hampshire village of Gilmanton Academy, and that—like other budding sociopaths—he enjoyed conducting "medical experiments" on small, living
creatures during his childhood.

In his early twenties, he wed a young female acquaintance—the first of
several wives he would acquire without ever bothering with the formality of
a divorce. He abandoned her within a few years of the marriage. After a year
of college in Vermont, he transferred to the University of Michigan at Ann
Arbor, graduating with a medical degree in 1884. By then, he was already
an accomplished swindler who had learned to bilk insurance companies of
thousands of dollars. His method was simple. He would take out a life insurance policy for a fictitious person, obtain a corpse, claim that the corpse
was the insured individual, and cash in on the policy. Of course, the scheme
depended on Mudgett's ability to acquire dead bodies. But at this activity,
too, he grew proficient.

In 1886, he showed up in Chicago under a new name—Henry Howard
Holmes. Within a few months, he had taken a job as a druggist in the fashionable suburb of Englewood. The pharmacy was owned by an elderly

widow, who mysteriously disappeared a few months later, leaving Holmes as the new proprietor. A consummate con artist, he had no trouble finagling large sums of cash from gullible investors. Combined with the proceeds from assorted scams, this money allowed him to construct a magnificient residence on a vacant lot across from his store. He called it "The Castle." It contained dozens of rooms, linked by secret passageways, hidden staircases, fake walls, concealed shafts, and trapdoors. Some of the rooms were soundproofed, lined with asbestos, and equipped with gas pipes connected to a large tank in the cellar. From a control panel in his office, Holmes could fill these chambers with asphyxiating gas. A pair of chutes ran from the second and third floors to the basement, where Holmes kept a fully equipped dissection lab.

Inside the walls of this Gothic horror house, an indeterminate number of people disappeared—including a string of susceptible young women who had fallen under the spell of Holmes's insidious charm. During the 1893 Chicago World's Fair, Holmes also rented rooms to tourists, many of whom were never seen again. Throughout this period, local medical schools—in desperate need of high-grade anatomical specimens—purchased a regular supply of human skeletons from Dr. Holmes, no questions asked.

He was finally arrested for the murder of a confederate, Ben Pitezel. Holmes used Pitezel's corpse to try to pull off his favorite insurance scam, but he was caught by clever investigators. Following his trial—the most sensational of its day—he confessed to twenty-seven murders. The enormity of his deeds made him the most infamous criminal of his age, known throughout the land as "Holmes, the Arch Fiend." He was hanged in Philadelphia on May 7, 1896.

"I was born with the devil in me. I could not help the fact that I was a murderer, no more than the poet can help the inspiration to sing. . . . I was born with the Evil One standing as my sponsor beside the bed where I was ushered into the world, and he has been with me since."

From the confession of Dr. H. H. Holmes

HOMEBODIES

Some serial killers range far and wide in search of their prey. Others, however, have a more domestic bent. Luring their victims to their houses or apartments, these psychos commit their gruesome murders in the comfort of their own homes—and sometimes even conceal the dead bodies right on the premises.

Shortly after a mousy little man named John Reginald Christie vacated his London flat in 1953, the new tenants began noticing an unpleasant smell that seemed to be emanating from a hollow place in the kitchen wall. Tearing down the wallpaper, they discovered a concealed cupboard containing three female corpses. When police made a search of the premises, they found a fourth decomposed body—that of Christie's own wife—under the dining room floorboards, and the skeletal remains of two other victims buried in the backyard. (See **The Wrong Man.**)

In the 1970s, both Dean Corll and John Wayne **Gacy** turned their homes into suburban torture chambers, committing dozens of atrocities on bound and helpless young men. Each of these sociopaths perpetrated more than thirty at-home murders without ever arousing the suspicions of his next-door neighbors. Corll buried the corpses along the shore of a nearby lake (see **Partners**). Gacy likewise dumped some of his victims in a river—but not until he had run out of room on his property, where police eventually dug up twenty-nine bodies.

Jeffrey **Dahmer** was another homebody homosexual killer, who not only turned his cramped Milwaukee apartment into a death chamber but filled it with an appalling assortment of human remains. His British counterpart, Dennis **Nilsen,** played out twisted little scenes of domesticity with the dead bodies of his male victims—bathing them, snuggling with them in bed, propping them up in front of the TV, or seating them at the dinner table.

One of the most gruesome of all domestic serial killers was a deranged German innkeeper named Karl Denke. Denke was so reluctant to leave home that he didn't even bother to go out shopping for food. During the post-World War I era, he murdered almost three dozen lodgers, then butchered their carcasses, pickled the meat in brine, and stored it in his basement. When Denke was finally arrested in 1924, he told the police that he had been eating nothing but human flesh for the past three years (see **Cannibalism**).

HOMOSEXUALITY

In a tome called *A Casebook of Murder,* British crime maven Colin Wilson makes the rather remarkable statement that Ed **Gein,** the infamous Wisconsin ghoul, was "a sexually normal man." Since, among other things, Gein was guilty of digging up the bodies of elderly women, dismembering the corpses, and performing unspeakable atrocities upon them, it takes a moment to figure out that what Wilson really means is that, whatever other kind of creature Gein was, at least he wasn't a *homosexual.* While the implications of Wilson's remark are truly staggering (i.e., that grave robbing, necrophilia, dismemberment, etc., are more "normal" than homosexuality), he does manage to put his finger on a salient fact of serial murder. The great bulk of its practitioners are, indeed, heterosexuals.

More specifically, criminologists estimate that at least 86 percent of male serial killers are heterosexual—meaning that they derive their deepest gratification from raping, mutilating, and murdering women. Still, though numerically inferior, gay serial killers include some of the foremost monsters of our time.

Throughout his two marriages, for example, John Wayne **Gacy** was busily having sex with teenage boys—twenty-seven of whom ended up buried in the crawl space beneath his suburban house. Likewise, Jeffrey **Dahmer** preyed exclusively on young males. So did the infamous British serial killer Dennis **Nilsen,** whose murders—like Dahmer's—seemed at least partly motivated by a desperate desire to prevent his male pickups from leaving in the morning. Less well known—though every bit as heinous—was California's "Freeway Killer," William George Bonin, a Vietnam vet and truck driver responsible for torturing and then murdering twenty-one young men during the 1970s.

Serial sex murder, as practiced by men, is virtually unknown among **Women,** homosexual or otherwise. A recent exception is the lesbian hooker Aileen **Wuornos,** who killed a string of male motorists along a Florida highway in 1989 and 1990.

Certain lust murderers are possessed of such ravening appetites that they are, in effect, bisexual, preying indiscriminately on both male and female victims. During a three-year span in the late 1890s, for example, a hideously disfigured maniac named Joseph **Vacher,** armed with knives, scissors, and a butcher's cleaver, roamed the French countryside, savaging nearly a dozen victims before his capture in August 1897. Vacher's victims—who suffered unspeakable sexual mutilations at his hands—ranged from a fifty-eight-year-old widow to a fourteen-year-old boy. Andrei **Chikatilo,** the Russian "Beast of Rostov," likewise tortured, mauled, raped, and cannibalized members of both sexes, many of them adolescents. And while the desperately deranged American pedophile Albert **Fish** preferred to commit his atrocities on boys, he was happy to settle for a pretty little girl when a male victim wasn't available.

Homosexual Serial Killers in the Cinema

Gay serial killers—psychopathic homosexuals who prey on members of their own gender—are a rarity in movies. Aileen Wuornos, for example—whose sordid story is told in the Oscar-winning biopic *Monster*—was a lesbian, but her homicidal rage was directed strictly at men. Conversely, "Buffalo Bill"—the flagrantly effeminate psychokiller of *The Silence of the Lambs*—targets only female victims.

The only mainstream Hollywood movie (so far as we know) to deal with homosexual serial murder is William Friedkin's 1980 *Cruising*. Friedkin's shocker was widely—and, to a large extent, deservedly—reviled by critics (in his *Movie and Video Guide,* Leonard Maltin tosses around words like "distasteful," "sick," and "degrading"). Still, it's a deeply unsettling film, starring Al Pacino as a New York City cop on the hunt for a gay homicidal maniac in pre-AIDS Greenwich Village.

HOUSEKEEPERS

Contrary to what some people claim, not all serial killers are men. **Women** commit serial murder, too—they just do it in a more, well, *womanly* way. Male serial killing is essentially old-fashioned phallic aggression carried to a monstrous extreme—the violent penetration of a victim's body with a sharp, pointed implement. Female serial killers, on the other hand, are like grotesque parodies of female stereotypes: **Black Widow** brides instead of adoring wives. Lethal **Nurses** instead of loving nurturers. And instead of happy homemakers, Housekeepers from Hell.

In the early years of the nineteenth century, an embittered German widow named Anna Zwanziger, who bore a striking resemblance to an over-sized toad, hired herself out as a housekeeper and cook to a succession of middle-aged judges. Apparently, Zwanziger hoped that one of these wor-thies would become so dependent on her domestic skills that he would end up proposing. Of course, there was one small problem with Anna's plan—namely, the inconvenient fact that each of the men was already married or engaged to another woman. Anna hit on an ingenious solution: she poi-soned two of the women with arsenic. For good measure, she also poisoned one of the judges, several servants, and a baby (who died after eating a bis-cuit soaked in arsenic-spiked milk). Just before her execution in July 1811, Anna told her jailers, "It is perhaps better for the community that I should die, as it would be impossible for me to stop poisoning people."

While Zwanziger appears to have been motivated by some lethal combi-nation of desperation and crushed hope, other homicidal housekeepers have killed for more obscure reasons. Roughly ten years after Zwanziger's beheading, another German cook named Gessina Gottfried poisoned an en-tire family named Rumf—papa, mama, and five children—by sprinkling ar-senic over every meal she prepared for them. Her admitted motive was sheer malevolent pleasure—at her trial in 1828, she confessed that the sight of her victims' death agonies threw her into a transport of ecstasy. Equally ap-palling was the French domestic Helene Jegado. Between 1833 and 1851, she fatally poisoned at least twenty-three and perhaps as many as thirty men, women, and children. Her victims included several nuns and her own sister.

"Wherever I go," she was once heard to remark, "people die."

IMPOTENCE

Sigmund Freud argued that when normal sexual drives are warped, they tend to vent themselves as violence. The impulse to love turns into an urge to destroy. His theory is confirmed with brutal clarity in the behavior of serial killers, who commonly substitute murder for sex. This is especially evident in the cases of those psychopathic killers who suffer from sexual impotence.

John Reginald Christie, the "Monster of Rillington Place," was so plagued by impotence that he couldn't consummate his marriage for more than two years. Murder was his sick way of compensating for this deficiency. Gassing and strangling women served as a sexual turn-on for Christie. Once his victims were dead he had no trouble raping them (see **The Wrong Man**).

Christie's potency problem probably wouldn't have surprised his acquaintances. Bald, bespectacled, and a known hypochondriac, he wasn't exactly a picture of self-confident virility. Paul John Knowles, on the other hand, cut an impressively masculine figure. Charming and ruggedly handsome, he became known in the mid-1970s as the "Casanova Killer." At least eighteen people who crossed his path—and perhaps as many as thirty-five—ended up shot, stabbed, or strangled. In the course of his deadly wanderings, Knowles met a British journalist named Sandy Fawkes who, like so many other young women, took an immediate fancy to him. The two ended up in bed, but Knowles was unable to perform sexually with a willing partner. When Fawkes abruptly broke off their short-lived relationship, Knowles reverted to the only kind of sex he was capable of, seeking out one of Fawkes's close friends and attempting to rape her at gunpoint.

Some serial killers, on the other hand, suffer from the opposite problem—not impotence but a sex drive of almost demonic intensity. When Bobby Joe Long, for example, was in his twenties, even the combination of twice-daily intercourse with his wife and compulsive masturbation couldn't slake his sexual hunger. Soon he began pursuing an additional outlet, raping at least fifty Florida women and murdering as many as ten.

INSANITY

When it comes to a killer who flays the skin from corpses, tans it like animal hide, and tailors it into a suit, the question of sanity would seem to be cut and dried (so to speak). And, in fact, Ed "Psycho" **Gein**—who actually did fashion garments out of human skin—was deemed officially insane and committed for life to a state mental institution.

Gein, however, represents the exception rather than the rule. Though at least one psychiatric expert has flatly declared that serial killers are "almost always insane," persuading a jury is another matter. Statistics tell the story. Of all the multiple murderers brought to trial in the past century, fewer than 4 percent have resorted to an insanity plea. And of those, only one in three has been found NGRI (not guilty by reason of insanity).

Still, the poor odds haven't stopped some notorious serial killers from trying. David "Son of Sam" **Berkowitz,** for example, did his best to persuade psychiatrists that his mind was controlled by his neighbor's dog, a black Labrador retriever that was ostensibly possessed by the spirit of a six-thousand-year-old demon named Sam. The "Voices from Beyond" gambit was also employed (unsuccessfully) by the "Yorkshire **Ripper,**" who slaughtered thirteen women in the late 1970s. The "Yorkshire Ripper" turned out to be a happily married truck driver named Peter Sutcliffe, who insisted that he was simply acting on orders from God, whose voice he heard issuing from a grave in a local cemetery. Sutcliffe's countryman John George Haigh—the

> **"As a result of our psychiatric examination,
> we are of the opinion that this man at the present time
> is not insane."**
>
> *From a 1930 Bellevue Hospital report on Albert Fish, who
> two years earlier had abducted, dismembered, and
> cannibalized a twelve-year-old girl*

notorious "Acid Bath Murderer" of the 1940s—tried a different tack to impress jurors with his lunacy: he drank his own urine.

Other serial killers have tried their hands at the popular multiple-personality ploy. William Heirens (famous for the **Lipstick**-scrawled plea he left in a victim's apartment, "For heaven's sake catch me before I kill more") blamed his crimes on an alternate personality named "George Murman." Similarly, both John Wayne **Gacy** and Kenneth "**Hillside Strangler**" Bianchi claimed that their crimes were the handiwork of evil alter egos, named "Jack" and "Steve," respectively. None of these ruses worked.

The problem for defense lawyers with serial-killer clients is that even the most horrific acts—crimes no normal person could even imagine, let alone commit—are not necessarily proof of legal insanity. A killer like Jeffrey **Dahmer** can dismember his still-living victims, eat their flesh, store their heads in his refrigerator, etc., and still be deemed sane according to the law. Though legal definitions vary, most states rely on the McNaughton rule, which says, in essence, that the criterion for sanity is the ability to distinguish right from wrong. Since most serial killers go to great pains to cover up their crimes, it's hard to prove that they don't know they're engaged in wrongdoing.

The difficulty of winning an NGRI verdict is vividly illustrated by the case of Albert **Fish,** certainly one of the most bizarre minds in the annals of American crime. A frighteningly sadistic child killer and cannibal, Fish was a true psychiatric phenomenon, who indulged (according to expert testimony) "in every known sexual perversion and some perversions never heard of before." Though the jury agreed that Fish was suffering from severe mental derangement, they found him guilty and sentenced him to the chair. As one juror explained after the trial (expressing a sentiment that many people would endorse), "we believed he was insane, but we thought he deserved to die anyway."

INTERNET

In just a few years the Internet has evolved from an online grab bag of highly dubious information to a legitimate, even indispensable, research tool (though there's still a lot of highly dubious information floating around).

The single best Web site for serial killer biographies—as well as for highly informative articles on subjects like "Team Killers" and "Necrophilia"—is Court TV's Crime Library (www.crimelibrary.com). Serial Killer Central (www.skcentral.com) offers up-to-the-minute news, along with a host of psycho-related material, including serial-killer art, poetry, and short stores. The Internet Crime Archives (www.mayhem.net) is another rich, if slightly headache-inducing, source of information, some of it relating to obscure murderers ignored by other media outlets.

Google the name of any notorious serial killer and you are sure to come up with a sizable number of hits. Psychos who tend to generate the most obsessive interest in the public often have entire Web sites built around them. One of the best of these is Tom Voigt's **Zodiac** page (www.zodiackiller.com). There is also—as one would expect—a very impressive site devoted exclusively to the most legendary serial killer of all, **Jack the Ripper** *(www.case book.org).*

If the Internet has become a very useful tool for people interested in serial killers, there's some indication that it may also prove to be a resource for serial killers themselves. There have already been two known cases of psychos who trolled for victims in cyberspace: the German cannibal Armin Meiwes, who found a sacrificial volunteer by posting an ad on the Web, and online predator John E. Robinson, responsible for at least seven homicides.

An Eagle Scout at thirteen and an aspiring priest, Robinson dropped out of seminary prep school and embarked on a career as a con artist, forger, and embezzler. His scams took a murderous turn in 1985, when he killed a young unwed mother and sold her four-month-old baby to his own brother and sister-in-law, who believed they were receiving a legally adopted child.

In the meantime, Robinson was also running a prostitution ring specializing in sadomasochistic sex, an activity that brought him to the attention of the **FBI** and eventually landed him in jail. Released in 1993, he quickly discovered the Internet and—under the name "Slavemaster"—began participating in sexually explicit chatrooms. With his con-man wiles, it didn't take him long to snare a series of submissive women who traveled to meet him and ended up rotting in sealed barrels.

Robinson's increasingly reckless behavior brought him under police surveillance, and he was finally arrested in 2000 at the age of fifty-six. A search of some desolate property he owned in Kansas, as well as of a rented storage facility across the state line in Missouri, turned up five large chemical drums, each containing the decomposed corpse of a woman.

In January 2003, "the first Internet serial killer," as he was dubbed in the press, was sentenced to death.

IQ

Though no real-life psychopath comes close to matching the evil genius of Dr. Hannibal Lecter, serial killers tend to be smart. When special agents of the **FBI**'s Behavioral Science Unit began their criminal **Profiling** program, they discovered that the mean IQ for serial killers was bright normal.

The above-average intelligence of these psychopaths is one of the scariest things about them, making it possible for them not only to snare victims with relative ease but also to elude the police, sometimes forever (see **Whereabouts Unknown**). It also accounts for the striking number of serial killers who have done well in terms of worldly success. Ted **Bundy** was a law student, John Wayne **Gacy** ran a thriving business, Gary **Heidnik** made a fortune playing the stock market, and a considerable number of serial killers have been **Doctors.**

On the other hand, it's also true that because of their severe personality problems, many serial killers end up working at menial jobs that are far beneath their intellectual capacities.

Jack the Ripper

The horrors began in the early morning hours of August 31, 1888. At roughly 3:45 A.M., while walking down a deserted, dimly lit street in London's East End, a market porter named George Cross stumbled upon what he took to be a tarpaulin-wrapped bundle. Peering closer, he saw that the sprawling heap was the butchered body of a woman, later identified as a forty-two-year-old prostitute named Mary Anne Nicholls. Her throat had been slashed, her belly slit, her vagina mutilated with stab wounds.

Though no one could have suspected it at the time, the savaging of Mary Anne Nicholls was a grisly landmark in the history of crime. Not only was it the first in a string of killings that would send shock waves throughout London and, eventually, the world, but it also signified something even more momentous—the dawn of the modern age of serial sex murder.

A week after the Nicholls atrocity, the mutilated remains of Annie Chapman, a wasted forty-seven-year-old prostitute suffering from malnutrition and consumption, were discovered in the rear of a lodging house a half mile from the site of the first murder. Chapman's head was barely attached to her body—the killer had severed her neck muscles and nearly succeeded in sawing through her spinal column. She had also been disembowelled.

The true identity of the killer would never be known. But several weeks later, the Metropolitan Police received a taunting **Letter** by a writer who claimed to be the culprit and signed his note with a sinister nom de plume. The name caught on with the public. From that point on, the mad butcher of Whitechapel would be known by this grisly nickname—Jack the Ripper.

Two days after police received the Ripper's letter, the killer cut the throat of a Swedish prostitute named Elizabeth Stride. Before he could commit any further atrocities on the victim, he was interrupted by the sounds of an approaching wagon. Hurrying away, the Ripper encountered Catherine Eddowes, a forty-three-year-old prostitute who had just been released from a police station, where she had spent several hours sobering up after having been found lying drunk on the pavement. The Ripper lured her into a deserted square, where he slit her throat. Then, in the grip of a demoniacal frenzy, he disfigured her face, split her body from rectum to breastbone, removed her entrails, and carried off her left kidney.

The final crime committed by the Ripper was also the most hideous. On

---

"The throat had been cut right across with a knife, nearly severing the head from the body. The abdomen had been partially ripped open, and both of the breasts had been cut from the body. . . . The nose had been cut off, the forehead skinned, and the thighs, down to the feet, stripped of the flesh. . . . The entrails and other portions of the frame were missing, but the liver, etc., were found placed between the feet of this poor victim. The flesh from the thighs and legs, together with the breasts and nose, had been placed by the murderer on the table, and one of the hands of the dead woman had been pushed into her stomach."

From an 1888 newspaper description of Jack the Ripper's final victim, Mary Kelly

the evening of November 9, he picked up a twenty-five-year-old Irish prostitute named Mary Kelly, three months pregnant, who took him back to her
rooms. Sometime in the middle of the night, he killed her in bed, then spent
several leisurely hours butchering her corpse—disembowelling her, slicing
off her nose and breasts, carving the flesh from her legs.

Following this outrage, the Whitechapel horrors came to an abrupt end.
The Ripper vanished forever, stepping out of history into the realm of myth.

Since then, armchair detectives have proposed a host of suspects,
from a kosher butcher to an heir apparent to the English throne (see **Ripper
Theories**). Most of these "solutions" make for colorful reading, but the
Ripper's true identity remains what it has been for a hundred years—
a tantalizing, probably insoluble mystery.

Ripper Theories

There is a basic (and disheartening) law of police work: if a case isn't
cracked right away, then the odds of ever solving it rapidly shrink to zero. So
the chances of coming up with the solution to a hundred-year-old crime are
essentially less than nil. Still, that hasn't stopped a host of armchair detectives from offering up theories on the most tantalizing murder mystery of
all: Who was the knife-wielding serial prostitute killer known as **Jack the
Ripper**? For the most part, these theorists are harmless cranks, like the
people who spend their time trying to prove that there was a second gunman on the grassy knoll, or that Amelia Earhart ended up in a Japanese
nunnery. The most likely truth is that—like virtually every other serial killer
in history—the Ripper was a complete nonentity whose only remarkable
trait was a staggering capacity for violence. But—as is so often the case
with reality—that simple explanation is infinitely less satisfying than more
colorful alternatives. Following are some of the more entertaining hypothe-
ses put forth by various "Ripperologists":

1. *The Mad Russian.* Supposedly Rasputin himself wrote a book called
Great Russian Criminals in which he claimed that Jack the Ripper was actually a deranged Russian doctor named Pedachenko, who was dispatched to
London by the tsarist police in an effort to create consternation in England
and embarrass the British authorities.

2. *The Black Magician.* The Ripper was actually Dr. Roslyn D'Onston

Stephenson, a self-styled conjurer obsessed with the occult, who supposedly committed the East End murders as part of a satanic ritual.

3. *The Jewish Slaughterman.* A *shochet,* or kosher butcher, decided to use his carving skills on women of the night.

4. *Jill the Ripper.* The homicidal maniac was not a man at all but a demented London midwife.

5. *The Lodger.* An unnamed boarder in a London roominghouse acted suspiciously at the time of the Ripper murders and might have been the East End fiend. Although the vaguest of the Ripper solutions, this theory has distinguished itself as the basis for four entertaining movies, including an early Hitchcock thriller (see **Le Cinéma de Jack**).

6. *The Deadly Doctor.* A man named Dr. Stanley committed the murders as an act of revenge, after his son contracted syphilis from a prostitute.

7. *The Lethal Lawyer.* A failed attorney named Montague John Druitt committed the Ripper crimes, then drowned himself in the Thames.

8. *The Polish Poisoner.* A multiple murderer named Severin Klosowski (aka George Chapman), who poisoned three of his wives, presumably committed the Whitechapel slayings out of his pathological hatred of womankind in general.

9. *The Evil Aristocrat.* HRH Prince Albert Victor, Duke of Clarence—Queen Victoria's grandson and heir to the British throne—went on a killing spree after he was maddened by syphilis.

10. *The Crazed Cotton Merchant.* A diary that surfaced in the early 1990s "revealed" that the Ripper was a drug-addicted businessman named James Maybrick. Unfortunately, the diary was declared a hoax by renowned document experts.

11. *The Psycho Painter.* Patricia Cornwell, the popular crime novelist with a flair for forensic science, spent six million dollars of her own money to prove that Victorian painter Walter Sickert was the real Ripper. Cornwell's theory—set forth in her 2002 book *Portrait of a Killer: Jack the Ripper, Case Closed*—rests partly on Sickert's penchant for dark, sexually disturbing subject matter and partly on some highly dubious DNA testing that indicated that Sickert could have been one of thousands of people who wrote a Ripper letter that might very well have been a hoax.

Despite the crowing subtitle of Cornwell's book, most serious Ripperologists scoff at her theory. One reviewer (Caleb Carr, author of the bestselling historical thriller *The Alienist*) went so far as to demand that Cornwell issue a public apology for slandering Sickert's reputation.

Le Cinéma de Jack

It's not surprising that **Jack the Ripper**—the most famous of all serial killers—has been a longtime favorite of filmmakers. Following is a list of his most memorable big-screen appearances:

1. *Pandora's Box* (1928). Classic silent film by G. W. Pabst, starring screen legend Louise Brooks as the femme fatale Lulu, who ends up as a streetwalker in London. And guess who her very first (and last) customer is?

2. *The Lodger* (1944). Based on a 1913 novel by Marie Belloc Lowndes, this suspense thriller—about a family named Bunting who suspect that their new boarder is Jack the Ripper—had already been filmed by Alfred Hitchcock in 1926. But Hitchcock's version is like *Hamlet* without the prince, since it turns out that the Buntings are wrong. The 1944 version, directed by German émigré John Brahm, is more faithful to the original— Saucy Jack really is living in the Bunting house and taking a lively (or deadly) interest in their young daughter, Daisy.

3. *Room to Let* (1950). Adapted from a BBC radio play of the same title, this modest little thriller (in which Jack turns out to be a sinister physician named Dr. Fell) was an early production of the fledgling Hammer Film Company, beloved by horror buffs for the lurid fright films it began turning out in the late 1950s.

4. *Man in the Attic* (1954). Still another version of *The Lodger,* this one starring the inimitable Jack Palance as the Ripper. Talk about type-casting.

5. *Jack the Ripper* (1960). A low-budget British shocker with a memorable gimmick. Though the entire film is in black and white, the climactic sequence—in which Jack is crushed to death by a falling elevator—was shot in color so the audience could enjoy the vivid red of his gushing blood.

6. *A Study in Terror* (1965). What a concept! Sherlock Holmes battles Jack the Ripper in this brisk, entertaining thriller, produced with the cooperation of Adrian Conan Doyle, son of Holmes's creator.

7. *Hands of the Ripper* (1971). Suffering from the traumatic aftereffects of watching Daddy stab Mommy, Jack the Ripper's angelic daughter turns into a homicidal maniac whenever a guy kisses her. She ends up in treatment with an early disciple of Freud. A Hammer movie classic!

8. *Murder by Decree* (1979). Another Holmes vs. Ripper movie, this

one with a stellar cast: Christopher Plummer, James Mason, Donald Sutherland, Genevieve Bujold, David Hemmings, John Gielgud, and Anthony Quayle.

9. *Time After Time* (1979). Nifty little fantasy written and directed by Nicholas Meyer in which Jack the Ripper travels from Victorian England to modern-day America via H. G. Wells's time machine.

10. *Jack the Ripper* (1988). Originally a two-part TV movie, this is a solid, lavish telling of the Ripper case, starring Michael Caine as a Scotland Yard inspector hot on the trail of Saucy Jack. It sticks to the facts except for its conclusion, when the hero succeeds in unmasking the killer.

11. *From Hell* (2001). Though it could have benefited from a bit more terror and suspense—not to mention the sort of grisly violence one hopes for in a Jack the Ripper movie—this handsome adaptation of Alan Moore and Eddie Campbell's acclaimed graphic novel does an impressive job of conjuring up the sordid underbelly of Victorian London. Johnny Depp gives a typically compelling performance as the opium-using Scotland Yard sleuth who uncovers a high-level conspiracy in his pursuit of Saucy Jack.

JEKYLL/HYDE

Plenty of people lead double lives: suburban matrons with lovers on the side; happily married hubbies who sneak off at night to cruise the gay bars; successful corporate executives supporting costly heroin habits. But cases like these pale beside the lives of certain serial killers. Ted **Bundy** was so bright and personable that he could have run for elected office if he hadn't also been a sadistic sex killer who murdered dozens of young women. John Wayne **Gacy** liked to dress up as a clown and entertain hospitalized children when he wasn't torturing teenage boys in his suburban home. And the Swedish physician Dr. Teet Haerm, who mutilated and killed at least nine young women, was a respected forensic pathologist who actually ended up performing the autopsies on some of his victims.

Killers like these possess such monstrously split personalities that they seem slightly unreal, as if they stepped from the pages of a horror story. More specifically, they seem like the flesh-and-blood incarnations of a figure first dreamed up by British writer Robert Louis Stevenson in the 1880s:

Dr. Henry Jekyll, who spends half his life as an idealistic scientist and the other half as a hideous creature named Edward Hyde.

"Dreamed up" is not just a figure of speech, since the idea for the story reportedly came to Stevenson in a nightmare. He dashed off a first draft in just three days, but his wife was so shocked by this version that Stevenson burned it, then rewrote it in a slightly less sensational form. Like *Dracula* and *Frankenstein, Dr. Jekyll and Mr. Hyde* is one of those stories that everyone knows, even if they've never read the original. This is largely because it's been made into so many movies, beginning with a 1920 silent version starring John Barrymore. It comes as a surprise, therefore, to discover that Stevenson's novelette is not so much a horror story as a mystery, revolving around the question of Edward Hyde's identity—who is this evil being and what is his relationship to the distinguished Dr. Jekyll? The answer to these questions isn't revealed until the very end, when readers discover that Hyde is really Jekyll's alter ego, the living embodiment of the good doctor's bestial, hidden self.

For people who only know *Dr. Jekyll and Mr. Hyde* from the movies there are other surprising aspects of the original story. On film, Hyde is typically portrayed as a fanged, hairy creature—a kind of werewolf in Victorian clothing. In the book, however, he is less overtly monstrous. There is something deeply repellent about him, but exactly where this quality comes from is hard to say. "He is not easy to describe," one character remarks. "There is something wrong with his appearance; something displeasing, something downright detestable. I never saw a man I so disliked, and yet I scarce know why. He must be deformed somewhere; he gives a strong feeling of deformity, although I couldn't specify the point. He's an extraordinary looking man, and yet I really can name nothing out of the way."

Furthermore, though Stevenson tells us that Hyde has a history of vile and violent deeds, he doesn't appear to be a homicidal maniac. Rather, he is the personification of the nasty, lawless impulses that lurk beneath our civilized veneers: what Sigmund Freud called the Id. Indeed, in Stevenson's story, Edward Hyde commits only a single murder—the clubbing of a distinguished old gentleman named Sir Danvers Carew.

In short, though serial killers like Bundy and Gacy are often described as Jekyll-and-Hydes, they are really far worse. Compared to them, Stevenson's bestial creation was a pussycat.

JOKES

Serial murder is no laughing matter. But that hasn't stopped people from making fun of it—any more than it's kept them from swapping sick jokes about other lurid and sensational subjects, from O. J. Simpson to Lorena Bobbitt, the Virginia housewife who, in 1993, sliced off her husband's penis while he slept because she was unhappy with their sex life. The latter, in fact, costarred in this widely circulated rib tickler with one of America's premier serial killers, the late Jeff "The Chef" **Dahmer:**

What did Jeffrey Dahmer say to Lorena Bobbitt?
  "You going to eat that?"

Dahmer's cannibalistic crimes inspired a host of sick jokes. One day, for example, his mother came over for dinner. "Jeffrey," she complained, halfway through the meal, "I really don't like your friends." "Then just eat the vegetables, Ma," Dahmer replied.

The phenomenon of serial-killer humor appears to have originated in relation to another celebrity psycho who (like Dahmer) resided in Wisconsin: Edward **Gein.** Not long after Gein's atrocities came to light, jokes about the "Plainfield Ghoul" began circulating throughout the Midwest. These crude riddles—known as "Geiners"—drew the attention of a psychologist named George Arndt, who published an article about them in a psychiatric journal. Among Arndt's examples were the following:

Why did Ed Gein's girlfriend stop going out with him?
  Because he was such a cut-up.

What did Ed Gein say to the sheriff who arrested him?
  "Have a heart."

Why won't anyone play poker with Ed Gein?
  He might come up with a good hand.

Why do serial-killer jokes exist? Are they an expression of pure callousness and cruelty? Probably not. Like other gross and nasty jokes, serial-killer humor offers an outlet for our fears—in the same way that a child walking past a graveyard will whistle a lively tune to calm his nerves. It's a way of warding off terror with levity. As the saying goes, we laugh to keep from crying.

"A Visit from Old Ed"

Woodcut portrait of Ed Gein
by Chris Pelletiere

Sick jokes about Ed **Gein** weren't the only kind of black humor circulating in the months following the discovery of his crimes. Researching local reaction to Gein's atrocities, psychologist George Arndt recorded this ghoulish parody of Clement Moore's "A Visit from St. Nicholas":

'Twas the night before Christmas, when all through the shed,
All creatures were stirring, even old Ed.

The bodies were hung from the rafters above,
While Eddie was searching for another new love.

He went to Wautoma for a Plainfield deal,
Looking for love and also a meal.

When what to his hungry eyes should appear,
But old Mary Hogan in her new red brassiere.

Her cheeks were like roses when kissed by the sun.
And she let out a scream at the sight of Ed's gun.

Old Ed pulled the trigger and Mary fell dead,
He took his old axe and cut off her head.

He then took his hacksaw and cut her in two,
One half for hamburger, the other for stew.

And laying a hand aside of her heel,
Up to the rafters went his next meal.

He sprang to his truck, to the graveyard he flew,
The hours were short and much work must he do.

He looked for the grave where the fattest one laid,
And started in digging with shovel and spade.

He shoveled and shoveled and shoveled some more,
Till finally he reached the old coffin door.

He took out a crowbar and pried open the box,
He was not only clever but sly as a fox.

As he picked up the body and cut off her head,
He could tell by the smell that the old girl was dead.

He filled in the grave by the moonlight above,
And once more old Ed had found a new love.

"He had a bizarre sense of humor."

One of Jeffrey Dahmer's former schoolmates

JUVENILES

Little boys who grow up to be serial killers tend to be extremely sadistic, but the targets of their cruelty are almost always small animals, not other children (see **Animal Torture**). An exception to this rule was the juvenile psychopath Jesse Pomeroy, one of the most unsettling criminals of nineteenth-century America.

Pomeroy suffered a difficult boyhood. He was raised in hardship by a widowed mother, who scraped together a meager living as a seamstress in South Boston. And he was cursed with a grotesque appearance—his mouth was disfigured by a harelip, and one eye was covered with a ghastly white film. Still, his contemporaries weren't inclined to attribute his atrocities to childhood trauma. To them, he was simply a natural-born fiend.

Little is known about Pomeroy's early life until he reached the age of eleven—at which point, he began preying on other children. Between the winter of 1871 and the following fall, he attacked seven little boys, luring them to a secluded spot, then stripping, binding, and torturing them. His first victims were subjected to savage beatings. Later, Pomeroy took to slashing his victims with a pocketknife or stabbing them with needles.

Arrested at the end of 1872, Pomeroy was sentenced to ten years in a reformatory but managed to win probation after only eighteen months by putting on a convincing show of rehabilitation. No sooner had he been released, however, than he reverted to his former ways. But by this time, the teenage psychopath wasn't content merely to inflict injury. At this point, he was homicidal.

In March 1874 he kidnapped ten-year-old Mary Curran, then mutilated and killed her. A month later, he abducted four-year-old Horace Mullen, took him to a remote stretch of marshland, and slashed him so savagely with a pocketknife that the boy was nearly decapitated.

When Mullen's body was found, suspicion immediately lighted on Pomeroy, who was picked up with the bloody weapon in his pocket and mud on his boots that matched the soggy ground of the murder site. When police showed Pomeroy the victim's horribly mutilated body and asked if he had killed the little boy, Pomeroy simply said, "I suppose I did." It wasn't until July that Mary Curran's corpse was found, when laborers uncovered her decomposed remains while excavating the earthen cellar of the Pomeroys' house.

Pomeroy's 1874 trial was a nationwide sensation. Moral reformers blamed his crimes on the lurid "dime novels" of the day (very much like those modern-day bluenoses who attribute the current crime rate to gangsta rap and violent videogames). Unfortunately, their position was undermined by Pomeroy's insistence that he had never read a book in his life.

In spite of his age, Pomeroy was condemned to death, but his sentence was commuted to life imprisonment with a harsh proviso: the so-called boy-fiend would serve out his sentence in solitary. And indeed, it wasn't until forty-one years later that he was finally allowed limited contact with other inmates. He died in confinement in 1932, at the age of seventy-two.

Pomeroy makes a brief but memorable appearance in Caleb Carr's best-selling 1994 novel, *The Alienist*, when the titular hero—seeking insight into the mind of an unknown serial killer—travels to Sing Sing to interview the former boy-fiend and finds him locked in a punishment cell, his head encased in a cagelike "collar cap."

During the late 1990s—a century after Pomeroy's crimes—America was shocked by a rash of horrendous killings committed by juvenile sociopaths. In Pearl, Mississippi, sixteen-year-old Luke Woodham killed three schoolmates and wounded seven others after knifing his own mother to death. In West Paducah, Kentucky, fourteen-year-old Michael Carneal gunned down three fellow students and wounded five others at an early-morning prayer meeting. In Springfield, Oregon, fifteen-year-old Kip Kinkel murdered his parents, then shot twenty-seven students, killing two. In Jonesboro, Arkansas, Andrew Golden and Mitchell Johnson—ages eleven and thirteen—set off a fire alarm to draw their classmates outside, then opened fire, killing four students and a teacher.

The most notorious of these incidents occurred in April 1999, when seventeen-year-old Dylan Klebold and eighteen-year-old Eric Harris massacred their schoolmates and teachers at Columbine High School in Littleton, Colorado, leaving thirteen dead and twenty-five wounded. Like others of their ilk, however, Klebold and Harris were not serial killers but **Mass Murderers:** suicidal rampage killers so full of rage and despair that they chose to end their own lives after inflicting a terrible vengeance on the world they had come to find unbearable.

"Despite both the shackles on the collar cap, Jesse had a book in his hand and was quietly reading. . . . 'Pretty hard to get an education in this place,' Jesse said, after the door had closed. 'But I'm trying. I figure maybe that's where I went wrong—no education. . . .' "

"Laszlo nodded. 'Admirable. I see you're wearing a collar cap.'

"Jesse laughed. 'Ahh—they *claim* I burned a guy's face with a cigarette while he was sleeping. . . . But I ask you—' He turned my way, the milky eye floating aimlessly in his head. 'Does that sound like me?' "

From Caleb Carr's The Alienist

K

Edmund Kemper

In August 1963, when Edmund Kemper was fifteen years old, he stepped up behind his grandmother and casually shot her in the back of the head. After stabbing her a few times for good measure, he calmly waited for his grandfather to return from work, then gunned him down, too. His motive? "I just wondered how it would feel to shoot Grandma," he explained to the police.

In retrospect, this homicidal outburst wasn't really very surprising. From his earliest years, Kemper had been what his mother euphemistically described as a "real weirdo." One of his favorite childhood games was to pretend that he was being asphyxiated in the gas chamber. He also enjoyed decapitating his sisters' dolls.

By the time he was ten, he had graduated to **Animal Torture,** chopping up a cat with a machete and stashing the dismembered parts in his closet. He buried another cat alive, then—after exhuming the corpse—cut off its head, which he proudly displayed in his bedroom.

Deemed mentally unsound after the double murder of his grandparents, Kemper was committed to a maximum-security mental hospital in 1963.

Just six years later, he was released. Physically, he had undergone a striking change, having grown into a hulking, six-foot-nine, three-hundred-pounder. Psychologically, however, he was the same as ever—a sadistic psychopath obsessed with necrophiliac fantasies.

Two years after his discharge from the mental hospital, Kemper picked up a pair of hitchhiking coeds, drove them to an isolated spot, and stabbed them to death. After smuggling their bodies back home, he amused himself for several hours with his "trophies"—photographing them, dissecting them, having sex with their viscera. Eventually, he bagged and buried the body parts and tossed the heads into a ravine.

Four months later, he abducted another teenage hitchhiker, strangled her, raped her corpse, then took it home for more fun and games. The same pattern would repeat itself with three more female victims, all of them hitchhiking students. Though Kemper clearly enjoyed the killing, it was the postmortem perversions that gave him the most satisfaction. He decapitated all of the women and enjoyed having sex with their headless bodies. He also liked to dissect the corpses and save various "keepsakes." On at least two occasions, he cannibalized his victims, slicing the flesh from their legs and cooking it in a macaroni casserole.

By January 1973, Santa Cruz authorities were aware that a serial murderer—dubbed the "Coed Killer"—was on the loose, though they never suspected Kemper, who, in fact, had befriended a number of local police officers. Several months later, on Easter weekend, Kemper committed matricide, hammering in the skull of his sleeping mother, then cutting off her head. After raping the decapitated body, he ripped out her larynx and jammed it down the garbage disposal. ("That seemed appropriate," he would later tell the police, "as much as she'd bitched and screamed and yelled at me over so many years.") Afterward, he telephoned his mother's best friend and invited her over for dinner. When she arrived, he crushed her skull with a brick and subjected her corpse to the usual postmortem outrages.

On Easter Sunday, Kemper got in a car and headed east. When he reached Colorado, he telephoned his pals on the Santa Cruz police force and confessed. Convicted of eight counts of murder, he was asked what he thought a fitting punishment would be. "Death by torture," was his reasonable reply. Instead, he was sentenced to life in prison.

> Q. "What do you think when you see a pretty girl
> walking down the street?"
> A. "One side of me says, 'I'd like to talk to her,
> date her.' The other side of me says, 'I wonder how
> her head would look on a stick?' "
>
> EDMUND KEMPER,
> *during a magazine interview*

KIDNEY

This vital organ has a special significance for crime buffs, since it figures prominently in the case of the most famous serial killer of all time.

On the evening of September 30, 1888, the anonymous madman who would become known as **Jack the Ripper** committed two atrocities in quick succession. First, he slit the throat of a Swedish prostitute named Elizabeth Stride. Then—after being interrupted by an approaching wagon—he accosted a forty-three-year-old prostitute named Catherine Eddowes and lured her into a deserted square, where he slashed her windpipe and savaged her body, removing her left kidney.

Two weeks later—on October 16—a parcel arrived at the home of George Lusk, head of the Whitechapel Vigilance Committee, a group of local tradesmen who had organized to assist in the search for the killer. The parcel contained a ghastly surprise—a chunk of kidney (with an inch of renal artery still attached), accompanied by an equally appalling letter addressed to Lusk: "Sir I send you half the kidne I took from one woman prasarved it for you tother piece I fried and ate it was very nise I may send you the bloody knif I took it out if you only wate a whil longer." It was signed "Catch me when you can Mister Lusk."

The sender's address on the upper-right-hand corner of the letter said simply: "From Hell."

In the weeks since the Ripper first struck, the police had been inundated with letters from cranks claiming to be the killer, and at first, there were many who declared that this latest communication was nothing but a depraved hoax. The kidney, they proclaimed, had either been taken from a dog or removed from a dissecting room. Examination by a specialist from the London Hospital Museum, however, revealed not only that the kidney was human but that it had come from a middle-aged alcoholic woman who suffered (as did Catherine Eddowes) from Bright's disease. Moreover, the inch of renal artery still attached to the preserved piece of kidney precisely matched the severed arterial remains in Eddowes's eviscerated body.

There seemed little doubt that the ghastly human artifact sent to George Lusk was the real thing—or that the note that accompanied it was an authentic communication from the Whitechapel Butcher. To this day, the "From Hell" letter is regarded as the only apparently genuine message ever sent by the legendary killer.

KILLER COUPLES

Can a woman live with a man for many years without knowing he is a homicidal sex maniac? Apparently so. Some of the most infamous serial killers in history—among them Albert "Boston Strangler" **DeSalvo,** Peter **Kürten**, and Andrei **Chikatilo**—were married to women who had no inkling of their husbands' sinister secret lives. It's possible to feel sorry for such women, who eventually discover, to their uttermost dismay, that they've been mated to monsters.

There is, however, another type of woman who—far from inspiring sympathy—elicits only loathing and disbelief. This is the wife or lover of a serial killer who is not only aware of the horrors her man commits but also actively participates in them.

Perhaps the most infamous of this breed is Myra Hindley. A shy, twenty-three-year-old typist from Manchester, England, Hindley led an unremarkable life until she hooked up with Ian Brady, a psychopathic creep with a taste for sadomasochistic porn and Nazi paraphernalia. Before long, Hindley was dressing up in S.S. regalia and posing for Brady's obscene photos—a kinky but relatively harmless pastime compared to the horrors that followed. Beginning in July 1963, the perverted pair murdered a series of children, then buried the corpses in the desolate moors outside Manchester. In the case of one of their victims—a pretty ten-year-old girl named Leslie

Ann Downey—the couple forced the child to pose for pornographic pictures, then tape-recorded her tormented pleas before killing her. When the tape was played at the 1966 trial of the **Moors Murderers,** spectators and jurors alike wept uncontrollably.

Ian Brady and Myra Hindley;
from *Bloody Visions*
trading cards

(© & ™ 1995 M. H. Price and Shel-Tone Publications. All rights reserved.)

Like Brady and Hindley, some deadly duos are unmarried lovers who enjoy serial murder the way other couples savor candle-lit dinners and romantic weekends at a country inn. The "Lonely Hearts Killers," Martha Beck and Raymond Fernandez, committed an indeterminate number of homicides in the late 1940s (they confessed to three but were suspected of twenty), including the murder of a two-year-old girl. Right to the bitter end, Beck persisted in seeing their vile affair as a storybook romance, vowing undying love for her sleazeball companion even as she was being led to the chair.

Carol Bundy took romantic devotion to even more hideous lengths. In the early 1980s, Bundy was the live-in lover of Douglas Clark, a psychopathic killer of prostitutes and necrophiliac dubbed the "Sunset Strip Slayer." Among his various pleasures, Clark liked to lure young women into his car, shoot them in the temple while they were fellating him, then carry their decapitated heads home for further fun and games. On at least one occasion, Bundy helped out by playing beautician—applying lipstick and makeup to one of the heads and giving it a pretty hairdo. As soon as she was done, her boyfriend took the head into the bathroom and used it for oral sex. "We had a lot of fun with her," Bundy later confessed. "I made her up like a Barbie."

In the early 1990s, Barbie was invoked again in the case of a killer couple. Only this time, the doll's name was connected not to a victim but to one of the perpetrators.

Known as the "Ken and Barbie" killers because of their golden good looks, Paul Bernardo and Karla Homolka were a Canadian husband-wife team, perfectly matched in their mutual depravity. Their first victim was Homolka's own fifteen-year-old sister, Tammy. In December 1990, after a Christmas Eve dinner in the Homolka home, Paul plied the teenager with tranquilizer-laced drinks. Once she was out cold, he videotaped Karla as she performed oral sex on her little sister. Bernardo then raped the young girl while Karla held a drug-soaked cloth over Tammy's mouth to keep her unconscious. Unfortunately, the drug—an animal sedative called halothane stolen from the veterinary clinic where Karla worked—caused the girl to throw up and choke to death on her own vomit.

In the following two years, the monstrously depraved pair kidnapped and videotaped the rape, sexual torture, and murder of two more Ontario teenagers: fifteen-year-old Kirsten French and fourteen-year-old Leslie Mahaffy, who was strangled by Bernardo with an electrical cord while she clutched a teddy bear Homolka had given her for comfort.

Eventually, the pair was arrested. Bernardo was sent to prison for life. In exchange for her full cooperation, Homolka received a lenient sentence. To the outrage of many of her countrymen, she was released in July 2005, after serving twelve years for her role in the atrocities.

There are other cases of husbands and wives who share a taste for serial murder—couples who add spice to their marriage by indulging in unspeakable crime. Between 1978 and 1980, Charlene Gallego helped procure teenage victims for her sadistic husband, Gerald, by luring them into his car with the promise of marijuana. She would then sit in the front seat and watch while he raped, sodomized, and beat them to death with a hammer. In 1992, the British couple Fred and Rosemary West were charged with the grisly torture-murder of ten young women—including their own seventeen-year-old daughter.

The monstrous Mrs. West, however, is no longer part of a killer couple. She became a widow on New Year's Day when her abominable mate hanged himself in his jail cell.

━━━━━━ **The "Honeymoon Killers"** ━━━━━━

Martha Beck; from *Bloody Visions* trading cards

(© & ™ 1995 M. H. Price and Shel-Tone Publications. All rights reserved.)

The loathsome love story of Martha Beck and Raymond Fernandez made it to the screen in the 1970 sleeper *The Honeymoon Killers,* starring Shirley Stoler and Tony LoBianco. Writer-director Leonard Kastle does an outstanding job of capturing the creepy essence of this repugnant romance. In spite (or perhaps because) of its cheapness, this black-and-white low-budget chiller is extremely effective—just watching it makes you feel vaguely unclean.

A Couple of Crazy Kids

Portrait of Charles
Starkweather
by Chris Pelletiere

Charlie "Little Red" Starkweather—a nineteen-year-old garbage collector from Lincoln, Nebraska—saw himself as a romantic young rebel like his teen idol, James Dean. In reality, he was a sociopathic punk with a grudge against everyone in the world except his fourteen-year-old sweetheart, Caril Ann Fugate. On December 1, 1957, Starkweather knocked over a gas station in Lincoln, abducted the twenty-one-year-old attendant, drove him out to the countryside, and gunned him down in cold blood.

That was just a warm-up for the most notorious murder spree of the 1950s.

Seven weeks later, Charlie went to visit Caril, who hadn't come home yet from school. Her mother—who had a justifiably low opinion of Stark-weather—let him know what she thought of him. Charlie shot her and her husband to death with his trusty .22-caliber rifle. Caril arrived home just as her psycho boyfriend was choking her baby sister to death by ramming the rifle barrel down her throat. After Caril tacked a note to the front door— "Stay a Way. Every Body is Sick With the Flu"—the loathsome lovebirds settled in to watch TV, pig out on junk food, and screw.

When the food ran low and suspicious relatives began coming round, the pair made off in Charlie's jalopy. Stopping at a local farmhouse, they shot both the seventy-year-old owner and his dog, then hitched a ride with two high school sweethearts, Robert Jensen and Carol King. After abducting them at gunpoint, Charlie killed the boy, then raped the girl and shot her. In an apparent fit of jealousy, Caril reportedly mutilated the dead girl's genitals with a hunting knife.

Heading back to Lincoln, they invaded the home of a wealthy businessman, C. Lauer Ward, where Charlie tortured, raped, and killed Mrs. Ward and the fifty-one-year-old housemaid. After breaking the neck of the family dog, Charlie settled down to wait for Mr. Ward to return from work, blasting him as he stepped over the threshold.

Escaping in Ward's limousine, the pair headed for Washington state. By then, a 1,200-man posse was hunting for the killer couple. Deciding to switch vehicles, they stopped outside Douglas, Wyoming, where Charlie shot a salesman named Merle Collison as he dozed in his car. Charlie was wrestling the corpse from behind the steering wheel when a passing motorist stopped and began to grapple with the little killer. Starkweather managed to leap into the limo and roar away just as the sheriffs arrived. Leading them on a high-speed chase, he surrendered after being grazed by a police bullet. The twenty-six-day murder spree, which left ten people dead, was over. Charlie was electrocuted on June 24, 1959. Caril was sentenced to life but was paroled in 1977.

Sordid as it was in reality, their story contained enough seductive ingredients—doomed young outlaw lovers on the lam—to give it romantic appeal. It has been told and retold in various forms, from Bruce Springsteen's song "Nebraska" to Terrence Malick's 1973 cult film, *Badlands,* to the 2004 novel *Outside Valentine* by Liza Ward (whose own grandparents were among the victims of the sociopathic young pair).

KRAFFT-EBING

Anyone who thinks that serial murder is strictly a modern-day phenomenon will be quickly disabused of that notion by a glance at *Psychopathia Sexualis,* the classic nineteenth-century text on sexual deviation. Its author was

Dr. Richard von Krafft-Ebing (1840–1902), a distinguished German physician who was regarded as the most important neuropsychiatrist of his day.

Krafft-Ebing's massive compendium covers every known perversion, from foot fetishism to **Necrophilia.** For the student of serial murder, the most interesting portions are the case histories of notorious lust murderers. Krafft-Ebing covers all the big-name sex killers of the nineteenth century, including **Jack the Ripper** and Joseph **Vacher.** He also discusses a number of lesser-known, but seriously alarming, psychopaths, such as the English clerk "Alton" who—after dismembering a child—made the following entry in his personal diary: "Killed to-day a young girl; it was fine and hot."

Another obscure but horrifying case recorded by Krafft-Ebing is that of "a certain Gruyo, aged forty-one, with a blameless past life, [who] strangled six women in the course of ten years. They were almost all public prostitutes and quite old. After the strangling, he tore out their intestines and kidneys through the vagina. Some of the victims he violated before killing, others, on account of the occurrence of impotence, he did not. He set about his horrible deeds with such care that he remained undetected for ten years."

Krafft-Ebing's pioneering work makes it shockingly clear that though serial slaughter is unquestionably on the rise, the crime itself has always been with us.

> **"I opened her breast and with a knife cut through the fleshy parts of the body. Then I arranged the body as a butcher does beef, and hacked it with an axe into pieces. . . . I may say that while opening the body, I was so greedy that I trembled and could have cut out a piece and eaten it."**
>
> *Lust murderer Andreas Bichel,*
> *as quoted by Professor Richard von Krafft-Ebing*

Peter Kürten

In his own words, Peter Kürten aspired to become "the most celebrated criminal of all time." He didn't quite make it—other criminals are more famous, including his role model, **Jack the Ripper.** Still, though Kürten fell short of that goal, he can lay claim to another distinction. In a century that has produced a slew of sadistic lust killers, Kürten, in the view of many experts, may have been the most appalling of all.

The household Kürten grew up in—a single room occupied by ten family members—was a hotbed of depraved sex. His father was a vicious drunk who habitually forced himself on his wife in front of the children and was jailed for the rape of his thirteen-year-old daughter. Kürten, too, engaged in sex with his sisters.

Young Kürten's favorite form of sexual activity, however, wasn't incest but bestiality. A neighbor who worked as a dog catcher taught the boy how to torture and masturbate animals, forging an early link in Kürten's already twisted psyche between sadistic cruelty and sexual release. Between the ages of thirteen and fifteen, he committed countless acts of bestiality with pigs, sheep, and goats, deriving particularly intense pleasure from stabbing the animal to death while having intercourse with it.

At fifteen, Kürten—already a habitual thief—was arrested and jailed, the first of a long string of prison sentences. Altogether, he would spend more than half of his forty-seven years behind bars. Between 1899 and 1928, during those periods when he managed to remain at large, he may have committed as many as three murders, though none was ever pinned on him. A raging pyromaniac, he also derived sexual satisfaction from torching barns, another of his favorite pastimes.

Kürten took a wife in 1921, winning the consent of his bride-to-be in an unconventional (if characteristic) way: he threatened to kill her if she refused to marry him. Until Kürten himself confessed to the unspeakable truth, his loyal, long-suffering wife remained completely unaware that she was wed to the infamous "Monster of Düsseldorf."

Kürten earned that nickname in 1929. During that year, he unleashed an unprecedented torrent of violence, attacking twenty-nine people between February and November. This blood spree came to an end with the strangling and frenzied stabbing of a five-year-old girl, Gertrude Alberman. A few days later—in emulation of his idol, Jack the Ripper—Kürten sent the police a letter. In it, he directed them to the savaged remains of the Alberman girl, as well as to the body of another of his victims, a housemaid he had stabbed twenty times and sodomized after death.

For more than a year, the citizens of Düsseldorf lived in terror. The police did everything possible to track down the killer, questioning nearly a thousand suspects and following hundreds of leads. But Kürten was hellishly difficult to track. Most lust killers prefer a single kind of weapon and a certain type of victim. But Kürten used axes, scissors, hammers, knives, and his bare hands to kill the young and old, male and female alike.

In May 1930, Kürten mysteriously let a young woman go after attempting to rape her. Seventy-two hours later, he was under arrest. In custody, he spilled out his unspeakable story in amazing detail. Among other facts, authorities learned that—besides his other perversions—Kürten was a **Vampire,** who drank the blood of various victims, and he had once experienced an ejaculation after cutting the head off a sleeping swan and guzzling the blood from the neck stump. Convicted of nine murders, he was guillotined in July 1931.

> "In the case of Ohliger, I also sucked blood from the wound on her temple, and from Scheer from the stab in the neck. From the girl Schulte I only licked the blood from her hands. It was the same with the swan in the Hofgarten. I used to stroll at night through the Hofgarten very often, and in the spring of 1930 I noticed a swan sleeping at the edge of the lake. I cut its throat. The blood spurted up and I drank from the stump and ejaculated."
>
> *From the confessions of Peter Kürten*

LADY-KILLERS

The conventional image of a serial killer is someone like Norman Bates—a guy so nice and harmless-looking that you'd never suspect he was a homicidal maniac. Clearly, this is a popular misconception. There have been plenty of scary-looking serial killers: hard-bitten losers like Henry Lee **Lucas,** wild-eyed madmen like Charles **Manson,** Mephistophelian creeps like Richard "Night Stalker" **Ramirez.** Still, stereotypes often possess a kernel of truth—and there have, in fact, been a number of serial killers who look not just normal but downright presentable. Unlike such psychotic dweebs as David **Berkowitz** and Edward **Gein**—who couldn't get the time of day from a woman—these debonair sociopaths are highly attracted to the opposite sex. They are genuine lady-killers—in more ways than one.

Though Ted **Bundy** is undoubtedly the best known of this breed, he certainly wasn't the first. A hundred years ago, another attractive young fellow who shared Bundy's first name—Theodore Durrant—earned nationwide notoriety as one of the most heinous killers of the century. A bright and personable twenty-three-year-old who still lived at home with his parents, Durrant appeared to be a paragon of young American manhood: a medical student, Sunday school teacher, and a member of the California militia signal corps. He was good-looking, too: tall, trim, and athletic, with fine, almost feminine features. Women found him hard to resist. On April 3, 1895, Durrant lured one of his lady friends into an empty church, then strangled her, raped her corpse, and hid it in the belfry. Nine days later, he dispatched another young woman in a similar way. It wasn't long before Durrant—who quickly became known as the "Demon of the Belfry"—was arrested, tried, and condemned to death. Public detestation of Durrant was so intense that, after he was hanged, no cemetery in San Francisco would agree to bury him. His parents had to take his body to Los Angeles for cremation.

Durrant's contemporary Dr. H. H. **Holmes** was also catnip to the ladies. A dapper, smooth-talking sociopath, Holmes had no trouble working his seductive charm on scores of young women, an indeterminate number of whom met their ends in the depths of his infamous "Murder Castle." A model of Gilded Age enterprise, Holmes found a way to make a profit from his crimes by peddling the mounted bones of his victims to local medical schools.

Ted Bundy; from *True Crime Trading Cards, Series Two: Serial Killers and Mass Murderers;* art by Jon Bright

(*Courtesy of Jon Bright and Valarie Jones*)

TED BUNDY

Theo Durrant hauls a victim to the belfry in this nineteenth-century engraving

The twentieth century produced more than its share of lethal ladies' men. One of the most notorious was the English psychokiller Neville Heath. Tall, handsome, and charming, Heath looked like a Hollywood version of a British war hero. He was, in fact, a military officer who saw action as an RAF bomber pilot in World War II. Unfortunately, he was also a sadistic sociopath whose taste for bondage and flogging blossomed into full-blown blood lust. In June 1946, a part-time actress named Margery Gardner accompanied Heath to his hotel room for a night of kinky sex. When Gardner's body was found the next day, the condition of her corpse shocked even hardened policemen. Tied up and suffocated with a gag, she had been savagely whipped with a riding crop. Her nipples had nearly been bitten off, and a poker had been thrust between her legs. Not long afterward, Heath murdered and mutilated another young woman he had met at a Bournemouth hotel. Arrested shortly afterward, he pled not guilty by reason of insanity at his trial, but the jury took less than an hour to convict him. He remained suave to the end. On the day of his hanging, he requested a double whiskey from the warden like a gentleman ordering a drink at a hotel bar.

> "You *feel* the last bit of breath leaving their body.
> You're looking into their eyes.
> A person in that situation is God!"
>
> **TED BUNDY,**
> *on the joy of murder*

LETTERS

There is some dispute as to whether Ted "Unabomber" Kaczynski—the antitechnological terrorist responsible for a string of letter bomb attacks between 1978 and his arrest in 1996—can be considered a serial murderer. Some people say he most certainly was: after all, he killed three people and seriously injured almost two dozen more. Others, however, regard him as a revolutionary zealot who resorted to violence as a way of promoting his beliefs. This question remains a matter of debate, but one thing's for sure—the guy could write. In August 1995, he sent a letter to the *New York Times,* offering to refrain from violence if the paper agreed to publish his tract, "Industrial Society and Its Fate"—a 35,000-word manifesto that (however crackpot in some of its views) is a model of literacy, clarity, and coherence.

Unfortunately, Kaczynski also put his writing skills to less impressive uses. At the same time that he sent his letter to the *Times,* he also wrote to one of his victims, Dr. David Gelernter of Yale University, taunting the professor as a "techno-nerd." In this regard, the Unabomber was, in fact, typical of serial killers, a number of whom have taken delight in communicating through taunting missives.

During the height of the "Whitechapel Horrors," the London police were inundated with letters purporting to be from the shadowy killer. Almost all of these were hoaxes, but one was signed with a sinister pseudonym that would quickly become the most infamous name in criminal history:

Dear Boss,

I keep on hearing the police have caught me but they won't fix me just yet. I have laughed when they look so clever and talk about being on the right track. . . . I am down on whores and I shan't quit ripping them till I do get buckled. Grand work the last job was. I gave the lady no time to squeal. How can they catch me now. I love my work and want to start again. You will soon hear of me with my funny little games. . . . My knife is nice and sharp I want to get to work right away if I get a chance. Good luck.

Yours truly
Jack the Ripper

Ninety years later, the New York City psycho who, until that time, had been known as the ".44-Caliber Killer" received a new and permanent nickname when he left a ranting letter at a crime scene. Addressed to a Queens police captain, the letter began:

I am deeply hurt by your calling me a wemon hater. I am not. But i am a monster. I am the "son of Sam." I am a little brat.

When father Sam gets drunk he gets mean. He beats his family. Sometimes he ties me up to the back of the house. Other times he locks me in the garage. Sam loves to drink blood.

"Go out and kill," commands father Sam.

Behind the house some rest. Mostly young—raped and slaughtered—their blood drained—just bones now. . . .

I feel like an outsider. I am on a different wavelength then everybody else—programmed to kill.

In August 1969, another serial assassin who murdered with a gun—the California killer known only as **Zodiac**—mailed letters to three Bay Area newspapers. Part of each letter was written in code. When these passages were deciphered, they formed one chilling message: "I like to kill people because it is so much fun. It is more fun than killing wild game in the forest, because Man is the most dangerous animal of all. . . . The best part will be when I die. I will be reborn in Paradise, and then all that I have killed will become my slaves. I will not give you my name because you will try to slow or stop my collecting of slaves for my afterlife." The following month, Zodiac sent another letter to the *San Francisco Chronicle,* threatening to "wipe out a school bus full of children"—a threat which, thankfully, he never carried out.

"Zodiac" letter

The tradition has continued in recent years in the case of Wichita's **BTK** Strangler. During a murder spree in the late 1970s, this Midwestern psycho-killer fired off a series of letters that followed the usual pattern. The culprit used the correspondence to supply his own sinister **nickname** (an acronym based on his sadistic MO: Bind, Torture, Kill), as well as to generate media attention. And like a sulky child, he grew petulant when his tactics didn't work. When a newspaper failed to respond quickly enough to one of his letters, he wrote back and demanded: "How many do I have to kill before I get my name in the paper or some national attention?"

In one way, though, BTK was different from his predecessors. As with **Jack the Ripper** and the **Zodiac** killer, his murders came to an abrupt halt. Unlike those earlier psychos, however, BTK suddenly piped up again years later in 2004 with a whole new stream of correspondence. The reason? Perhaps he was starving for recognition again. After all, the Green River Killer had just been captured and was garnering nationwide attention. It's possible that BTK was feeling neglected.

Or maybe he just wanted to get caught. That would explain why one of his new packages contained a computer disk which could be traced to the machine that had housed it—a clue that helped police arrest Dennis Rader, who was quickly charged with the stranglings that had happened nearly thirty years before.

> "I am deeply hurt by your calling me a wemon hater,
> I am not. But i am a monster.
> I am the 'son of Sam.' I am a little brat."
>
> **DAVID BERKOWITZ**

The Sickest Letter Ever Written?

Undoubtedly the most ghastly letter ever written by a serial murderer is the one that cannibalistic child killer Albert **Fish** mailed to the mother of his twelve-year-old victim Grace Budd. Fortunately, Mrs. Budd was functionally illiterate and so was spared the horror of reading this unspeakable document. The original of this letter is now part of the collection of artist Joe Coleman:

My dear Mrs. Budd,

In 1894 a friend of mine shipped as a deck hand on the Steamer Tacoma, Capt. John Davis. They sailed from San Francisco for Hong Kong China. On arriving there he and two others went ashore and got drunk. When they returned the boat was gone. At that time there was a famine in China. Meat of any kind of was from $1–3 Dollars a pound. So great was the suffering among the very poor that all children under 12 were sold to the Butchers to be cut up and sold for food in order to keep others from starving. A boy or a girl under 14 was not safe in the street.

Albert Fish in custody *(New York Daily News)*

You could go to any shop and ask for steak—chops—or stew meat. Part of the naked body of a boy or a girl would be brought out and just what you wanted cut from it. A boy or girls behind which is the sweetest part of the body and sold as veal cutlet brought the highest price. John staid there so long he acquired a taste for human flesh. On his return to N.Y. he stole two boys one 7 and one 11. Took them to his home stripped them naked tied them in a closet. Then burned everything they had on. Several times every day and night he spanked them—tortured them—to make their meat good and tender. First he killed the 11 yr old boy, because he had the fattest ass and of course the most meat on it. Every part of his body was Cooked and eaten except head—bones and guts. He was Roasted in the oven (all of his ass), boiled, broiled, fried, stewed. The little boy was next, went the same way. At that time, I was living at 409 E. 100 St. near—right side. He told me so often how good Human flesh was I made up my mind to taste it. On Sunday June the 3—1928 I called on you at 406 W 15 St. Brought you pot cheese—strawberries. We had lunch. Grace sat in my lap and kissed me. I made up my mind to eat her. On the pretense of taking her to a party. You said Yes she could go. I took her to an empty house in Westchester I had already picked out. When we got there, I told her to remain outside. She picked wildflowers. I went upstairs and stripped all my clothes off. I knew if I did not I would get her blood on them. When all was ready I went to the window and Called her. Then I hid in a closet until she was in the room. When she saw me all naked she began to cry and tried to run down stairs. I grabbed her and she said she would tell her mamma. First I stripped her naked. How did she kick—bite and scratch. I choked her to death, then cut her in small pieces so I could take my meat to my rooms, Cook and eat it. How sweet and tender her little ass was roasted in the oven. It took me 9 days to eat her entire body. I did *not* fuck her tho I could of had I wished. She died a *virgin*.

LIPSTICK

As a general rule, serial killers are not eager to get caught. Their atrocities are a source of unspeakable pleasure, and—as psychopathic personalities—they are immune to guilt or remorse.

Every so often, however, a serial murderer comes along who does feel bad about his behavior. He may even make an effort to stop. At one point, for example, Jeffrey **Dahmer**—who fantasized about having a zombielike sex object under his total control—stole a department store dummy in the hope that the mannequin might serve as a substitute for a human victim. Unfortunately (if predictably), the tactic didn't work. Psychos like Dahmer are in the grip of an irresistible compulsion and find it impossible to kick the murder habit on their own. Sometimes, they will resort to suicide (see **Death Wish**). On other, rare occasions—knowing that they are powerless to prevent themselves from committing future horrors—they will beg for someone else to intervene.

The most famous instance of this latter phenomenon occurred in the case of William Heirens. Raised by sexually repressive parents who filled him with the belief that "all sex is dirty," Heirens grew up to be a fetishist who achieved sexual climax from breaking into women's homes and stealing their underwear. Intellectually gifted, he won admission to the University of Chicago in 1945 at the tender age of sixteen. Even while leading a stereotypical collegiate existence—dating, hanging out with buddies, cutting classes—he continued to pursue his clandestine life as a cat burglar and panty fetishist.

On June 5, 1945, a forty-three-year-old Chicago woman, Josephine Ross, surprised an intruder who was looting her bedroom. She was found that afternoon, sprawled across her bed, her throat slashed, her dress wrapped around her head.

Six months later, on December 10, the naked corpse of a petite, thirty-three-year-old brunette named Frances Brown was found in the bathroom of her Chicago apartment not far from the scene of the earlier crime. She had been shot in the head, a butcher knife protruded from her neck, and her housecoat was draped over her head. Scrawled in lipstick on the living room wall was a cry for help that would become the single most famous serial-killer message of the century: "For heavens sake catch me before I kill more. I cannot control myself."

The "Lipstick Killer" (as he was instantly dubbed by the press) committed his last—and most heinous—crime in early January, when he abducted six-year-old Suzanne Degnan from her bedroom, strangled her, dismembered her body with a hunting knife, and dumped the pieces into the sewer.

Heirens was captured the following June, after the largest manhunt in Chicago's history. Drugged with sodium pentothal—"truth serum"—he initially claimed that the killings had been committed by an evil alter ego named "George Murman," short for "Murder Man" (see **Multiple Personality**). To avoid the chair, he agreed to confess to all three slayings in exchange for life in prison. On the day of his formal sentencing, he tried to commit suicide by hanging himself with a bedsheet but was saved by a quick-acting guard. Since the day he entered prison, Heirens—who has recanted his confession and stoutly maintains his innocence—has been a model prisoner, earning a college degree in 1972.

(Fritz Lang's 1956 thriller, *While the City Sleeps*, features a teenaged "Lipstick Killer" modeled on Heirens and played by a young John Drew Barrymore, future father of the actress Drew Barrymore.)

Of course, not all lipsticked messages left by serial killers have been desperate pleas for help. Richard **Ramirez**—the "Night Stalker," who terrorized Los Angeles in 1985—used a victim's lipstick to inscribe an inverted pentagram on the inside of her thigh: a further desecration of her body and a vicious taunt to his pursuers.

Unlike Heirens, Ramirez wasn't crying out to heaven but invoking the devil.

LOVERS' LANE MANIACS

Driving home from the movies one Saturday night, a high school boy and his date pulled into their favorite lovers' lane to do some necking. The boy turned on the radio for a little mood music. Suddenly, an announcer came on to say that a crazed killer with a hook in place of his right hand had escaped from the local insane asylum. The girl became scared and begged the boy to take her home. He got angry, stepped on the gas, and roared off. When they reached her house, the boy got out of the car and went around to the passenger side to let her out. There, hanging from the door handle, was a bloody hook!

So goes the story of the "Hookman"—a homicidal maniac who preys on adolescents as they make out inside a parked car. Teenagers—who have been telling some version of this story for at least forty years—often accept it as the gospel truth. Folklore scholars, on the other hand, see it as an "urban legend" that reflects the anxieties of adolescent boys and girls who are just confronting the tricky issues of grown-up sexuality. While the folklorists make a valuable point, there may be more reality to the story than they realize. The fact is that the terrifying figure of a lovers' lane maniac is not purely a figment of the teenage imagination.

World War II had barely ended when the tiny southwestern town of Texarkana found itself under siege from a night-prowling gunman whose favorite targets were young, unwary lovers. In early March 1946, this masked maniac snuck up on a couple, ordered them out of the car, then—after pistol whipping the young man—subjected the girl to such vicious sexual torture that she begged to be killed. Precisely three weeks later, he struck again, this time shooting both young victims in the back of their heads. Following another three-week hiatus, the "Moonlight Murderer"—as the press dubbed him—killed yet another pair of sweethearts as they returned from a dance at the VFW hall. A massive manhunt was launched, involving local sheriffs, Texas Rangers, and homicide detectives disguised as teenage lovers. But the phantom gunman was never caught.

Equally elusive was the diabolical gunman known as **Zodiac,** whose victims included several young couples killed on deserted country roads. A third notorious couple killer, David "Son of Sam" **Berkowitz,** was eventually apprehended—but not before he had shot more than a dozen victims as they sat in their cars on the darkened streets of New York City.

Teen Terror Legends

Young people love to give each other the chills with supposedly true stories about psychokillers. Though "The Hookman" is the most famous of these urban folktales, it's only one of many. Another is "The Boyfriend's Death," a story that the teller invariably swears is absolutely, positively true, since she heard it from an unimpeachable source, such as the next-door neighbor of her best friend's cousin. Typically, the story deals with a teenage couple whose car runs out of fuel one night as they are driving through some remote wooded area. The boy decides to hike into town for gas, telling the girl to make sure to keep the car doors locked, since there is a psycho on the loose. Huddling alone in the car, the girl waits anxiously for her boyfriend's return. But as the night passes, there is no sign of him. After a while, she hears a strange, scratching noise on the car roof. The next morning, a police cruiser arrives. As the girl is helped out of the car, she looks up and sees her boyfriend's butchered corpse, swinging upside-down from a tree branch, his fingernails scraping the roof!

A similar folktale, "The Roommate's Death," tells of two young women sharing a suite in a college dorm. Hearing that there is a serial killer at large, they lock themselves into their separate bedrooms. That night, one of the girls hears someone scratching ominously on the connecting door between the two bedrooms. In the morning, she musters up the courage to open the door—and discovers her murdered roommate, her throat cut from ear to ear. The scratching sound had been the victim's dying effort to get help.

Other teen folktales about psychokillers include "The Assailant in the Backseat"—about unwary women who discover that they have been driving along with a homicidal maniac hiding in the car—and "The Baby-sitter and the Man Upstairs," which tells of a baby-sitter who gets menacing calls from a homicidal stranger, only to discover that the calls are coming from the upstairs telephone.

Anyone who hasn't heard these stories firsthand may have encountered them in another form, since many of them have been recast as low-budget horror movies like *Halloween, When a Stranger Calls,* and *Friday the 13th.* They have also been retold by folklorist Jan Harold Brunvand in his popular collections of urban legends, beginning with *The Vanishing Hitchhiker.*

Henry Lee Lucas

Portrait of Henry Lee Lucas
by Chris Pelletiere

Henry Lee Lucas might be America's most prolific serial killer. On the other hand, he might be the biggest liar since Baron von Münchhausen. After experiencing a self-described "religious conversion" in prison, he decided to bare his soul and confess to an astronomical number of murders. Later, however, he recanted most of his testimony. Among law enforcement officials, the exact number of his crimes remains a matter of debate. Still, even if Lucas's final body count falls far short of the five hundred victims he originally claimed, he nevertheless ranks as one of the most depraved serial killers in history.

Subjected to untold horrors by his insanely abusive mother (see **Upbringing**), Lucas began indulging in sadistic depravity while still a child. By thirteen, he was engaging in sex with his older half-brother, who also introduced Henry to the joys of bestiality and **Animal Torture.** (One of their favorite activities was slitting the throats of small animals, then sexually violating the corpses.)

One year later, he committed his first murder, strangling a seventeen-year-old girl who resisted his efforts to rape her. In 1954, the eighteen-year-old Lucas received a six-year prison sentence for burglary. Soon after his release in 1959, he got into a drunken argument with his seventy-four-year-old mother and stabbed her to death. (He also confessed to raping her corpse, though he later retracted that detail.)

Receiving a forty-year sentence for second-degree murder, Lucas ended up in a state psychiatric facility. In spite of his own protestations—"When they put me out on parole, I said I'm not ready to go. I told them all, the warden, the psychologist, everybody, that I was going to kill"—he was released after only ten years. Eighteen months later he was back in prison for molesting two teenage girls.

Lucas was discharged from the state pen in 1975. Not long afterward, he met Ottis Toole, a vicious psychopath who became Lucas's partner in one of the most appalling killing sprees in the annals of American crime. For the next seven years, this deranged duo roamed the country, murdering and mutilating an untold number of victims. Like Lucas, the profoundly depraved Toole also had a taste for **Necrophilia.** He also indulged in occasional **Cannibalism** (an atrocity that Lucas tended to shun, since he found human flesh too gamy). For much of their odyssey, they were accompanied by Toole's preadolescent niece, Frieda "Becky" Powell, who became Lucas's lover, common-law wife, and—ultimately—victim.

Lucas was picked up on a weapons charge in 1983. A few days later, after apparently being stricken by an uncharacteristic attack of bad conscience, he summoned his jailer. "I done some pretty bad things," he muttered. With that, he began spilling his guts, admitting to a staggering number of murders. Some of these have been confirmed, others have proven false, many remain open cases. According to certain investigators, Lucas may have killed as many as sixty-nine victims; others put the number at eighty-one or possibly even higher. At his 1985 trial, he was convicted of ten homicides—more than enough to get him the death sentence.

In the end, Lucas's life would be spared. The state of Texas's leniency came from the most unlikely source. Then-governor George W. Bush, who allowed one hundred fifty-two people to be executed during his term, used his power to commute a death sentence only once—and that was for Lucas in 1998. He based his decision on the findings of the State Board of Pardons and Parole, which indicated Lucas might have been in Florida at the time one of his supposed victims—a female hitchhiker whose corpse was clad in nothing but a pair of orange socks—was killed. But Lucas's unexpected reprieve did not extend his life for very long. In 2001, three years after eluding a lethal injection, he died in prison of a heart attack.

Lucas's nine other murder convictions were never challenged. His prosecutor did not go along with the more extravagant estimates of Lucas's body count, but still maintained that he had killed anywhere between three and a dozen people. Whatever the actual total, the horrific nature of Lucas's life and crimes was summed up in one of his own statements: "Killing someone is just like walking outdoors. If I wanted a victim, I'd just go and get one."

Viewers interested in subjecting themselves to a singularly disturbing cinematic experience should rush right out and rent *Henry: Portrait of a Serial Killer,* John McNaughton's brilliant (if harrowing) fictionalization of the Lucas-Toole story.

> "Sex is one of my downfalls. I get sex any way I can get it. If I have to force somebody to do it, I do. . . . I rape them; I've done that. I've killed animals to have sex with them, and I've had sex while they're alive."
>
> **HENRY LEE LUCAS**

LUSTMORD

For unexplained reasons, possibly having to do with their national character, Germans have a knack for coining colorful, descriptive words for nasty human behavior. The same folks who came up with the term *schadenfreude* (meaning "to take pleasure in another person's misfortune") also invented the word *lustmord:* to kill for joy, for the sheer, sexy fun of it.

Lustmord, in short, is really another, catchier name for sexual homicide. The classic lust murderer doesn't just kill his victims (usually women). He derives intense erotic pleasure from maiming and mutilating their bodies—gutting or beheading them, cutting out their vulvas, slicing off their breasts. "The presumption of a murder out of lust is always given when injuries of the genitals are found," writes Dr. Richard von Krafft-Ebing in his classic study, *Psychopathia Sexualis,* "and still more, when the body has been opened or parts (intestines, genitals) torn out."

Not only did the Germans invent the term *lustmord,* they pioneered its actual practice—at least according to one crime expert, Colin Wilson, who maintains that the earliest documented lust murderer in history was a sixteenth-century German named Nicklaus Stüller. Among his other atrocities, Stüller killed and cut open the bellies of three pregnant women, one of whom was carrying twins.

In our own century, Germany has continued its tradition of producing some of the world's most appalling lust murderers. During the years between the two world wars, no fewer than four of these monsters were at large in Germany: Fritz **Haarmann,** the "Vampire of Hanover," responsible for the slaughter of as many as fifty young men; Georg Grossmann, the "Berlin Butcher," charged with murdering and cannibalizing fourteen young women; Karl Denke, the "Mass Murderer of Münsterberg," another cannibal who butchered at least thirty people and stored their pickled flesh in the basement of his inn; and Peter **Kürten,** the "Monster of Düsseldorf," who murdered, raped, and mutilated a minimum of thirty-five victims, mostly women and children.

For a scholarly discussion of lust murder as a major theme in German art and literature during the years between the wars, readers are referred to Maria Tartar's book, *Lustmord: Sexual Murder in Weimar Germany* (Princeton: Princeton University Press, 1995).

LYCANTHROPY

Serial murder has always existed, but the terminology used to describe this most heinous of crimes has changed over the centuries. Four hundred years ago, killers roamed the European countryside, slaughtering their victims with a bestial ferocity. But back then, they weren't known as "sociopaths" or "homicidal maniacs" or "lust murderers." They were known as "lycanthropes," a term that derives from two Greek words—*lykos* (meaning "wolf") and *anthropos* (meaning "man"). In short, these maniacs were thought to be literal wolfmen or werewolves.

Some of these psychos were so deranged that they themselves might have actually believed they were supernatural monsters. The peasants they preyed on certainly did. So did the authorities, who openly believed in lycanthropy and regarded it as one of the most pressing social problems of the day.

In old-time movies like the 1941 classic *The Wolf Man,* lycanthropy is depicted as a terrible curse. Lon Chaney Jr. doesn't enjoy turning into a werewolf, but whenever the moon is full, he begins to sprout hair, claws, and fangs whether he likes it or not. Sixteenth-century people had a different view of things. Werewolves were regarded as malevolent men who had deliberately entered into a bargain with the devil. They *wanted* to turn into monsters.

In the late 1500s, a French hermit named Gilles Garnier was rumored to have cut just such a demonic deal. In exchange, he received a black-magic ointment that allowed him to turn into a ravenous, man-eating wolf. At roughly the same time, a German named Peter Stübbe supposedly peddled his soul for an enchanted belt that endowed him with lycanthropic powers.

The methods of transformation might have differed, but the killings committed by these two maniacs were remarkably similar and equally stomach churning—far more gruesome than the make-believe horrors in any wolfman movie. Both Garnier and Stübbe were lust murderers and cannibals who preyed primarily on children. In two months, Garnier attacked and tore apart four little victims, using his bare hands and teeth. During a much longer period, Stübbe ravaged at least fifteen victims—including his own son. After ripping out the boy's throat, Stübbe allegedly cracked open his skull and devoured his brains.

Modern-day psychiatry has given us concepts like "antisocial personality disorder" to replace the medieval notion of lycanthropy. Even in the twentieth century, however, a killer occasionally came along whose crimes were so appalling that they seemed like the work of a supernatural monster. Back in the late 1920s, for example, the cannibal-killer Albert **Fish** lured a twelve-year-old girl to an abandoned house known as Wisteria Cottage, then killed her, cut her to pieces, and removed several pounds of her flesh, which he turned into a stew. When this crime was discovered, tabloid writers wracked their brains to come up with sensational names for its perpetrator.

Among other lurid labels, they called him the "Werewolf of Wisteria."

M

> "Look down on me, you will see a fool.
> Look up at me, you will see your lord.
> Look straight at me, you will see yourself."
>
> **CHARLES MANSON**

Charles Manson

Manson is unique among homicidal maniacs. The killings that brought him lasting notoriety—the 1969 Tate-LaBianca murders, the most shocking crimes of the 1960s—were actually committed by others; he himself never fired a pistol or wielded a knife. But that's precisely the source of his dark fascination—the Svengali-like power he exerted over his slavish followers, who were prepared to do his most blood-crazed bidding. Though Manson

Charles Manson trading card from *Bloody Visions*

(© & ™ 1995 M. H. Price and Shel-Tone Publications. All rights reserved.)

29. CHARLES MANSON: Murderous Manipulator

was little more than a clever con artist with a knack for occult babble, he made himself into an evil messiah, a malevolent guru, an embodiment of the darkest impulses of an era that began by preaching peace, love, and flower power and ended up awash in the satanic fantasy of *Rosemary's Baby, The Exorcist,* and "Sympathy for the Devil."

The illegitimate son of a dissolute mother who reportedly once tried to swap him for a pitcher of beer, Manson endured a nightmarish childhood of abandonment and abuse. His adolescence was essentially a continuous cycle of petty crime, arrest, incarceration, and escape. ("Truth is," Manson once said in a rare moment of insight, "I ain't never been anything but a half-assed thief who didn't know how to steal without getting caught.") At eighteen, he sodomized a fellow inmate at knifepoint, a deed that earned him a stint in a federal reformatory. Paroled in 1954, he spent the next dozen years in and out of various prisons for crimes ranging from check forgery to pimping. By the time he was released in 1967—against his own objections—the thirty-three-year-old Manson had spent the bulk of his life behind bars.

He emerged during the heady days of the so-called Summer of Love, when the counterculture was at its euphoric peak. In San Francisco's

Haight-Ashbury district—the hotbed of hippiedom—Manson discovered psychedelic drugs, free love, and Aquarian Age occultism. Before long, his sinister charisma had attracted a "family" of drifters and dropouts.

Living with his followers on a dusty ranch outside LA, Manson developed a bizarre apocalyptic theory, partly inspired by—of all things—the Beatles' *White Album,* one of the most benign and whimsical rock and roll albums ever recorded. In particular, he interpreted the song "Helter Skelter" (which referred to an amusement-park kiddie ride) as a prophecy about an impending race war, during which blacks would rise up and exterminate all white people, except for Manson and his chosen few, who would eventually rule the world. To instigate the war, Manson sent his followers on a deranged mission, ordering them to slay some prominent white people in a way that would implicate black revolutionaries. On the night of August 9, 1969, five of Manson's "family" members broke into the home of film director Roman Polanski and savagely butchered his pregnant wife, actress Sharon Tate, along with four other people. Before leaving, they used the victims' blood to scrawl incendiary graffiti on the walls. The following night, Manson himself led a party of his "creepy crawlers" to the home of a couple named LaBianca, who were similarly slaughtered and mutilated.

The killings set off a panic in Los Angeles and sent shock waves throughout the nation. Ultimately, Manson was arrested when one of his female followers—in jail on an unrelated charge—boasted of the murders to a cell mate.

Manson turned his 1970 trial into a circus (see **Courtroom Theatrics**), but the jury was not amused. He and four of his followers were slated for the gas chamber, but their sentences were commuted to life imprisonment in 1972, when the California Supreme Court abolished the death penalty.

"Wow, what a trip!"

Manson "family" member Susan Atkins,
after licking Sharon Tate's blood off her hands

MARRIAGE

That some of the most notorious serial killers in history have been husbands and fathers is a striking testament to the grotesquely divided personalities of these psychopaths—their ability to lead outwardly "normal" lives while secretly engaged in the most depraved activities imaginable. The roster of homicidal family men includes Albert **Fish**, John Wayne **Gacy**, Albert **DeSalvo**, and Andrei **Chikatilo**. It comes as no surprise to learn that their marriages weren't exactly made in heaven.

Though DeSalvo's wife never divorced him, his unslakable sex drive (reputedly, he insisted on lovemaking as often as six times a day) turned her life into an unremitting ordeal. Other women haven't displayed Mrs. DeSalvo's tolerance. After being driven to distraction by his incessant sexual demands, Earle Leonard **Nelson**'s sixty-year-old wife finally kicked him out of the house (at which point he began venting his libido by raping and strangling elderly landladies from coast to coast).

Three wives abandoned Angelo Buono—one of the "**Hillside Stranglers**"—in rapid succession because of his brutal sex habits (one wife alleged that Buono sodomized her in front of the children). After putting up with his "peculiarities" for almost twenty years—such as his tendency to stroll around the house naked while screaming, "I am Christ!"—Fish's first wife, Anna, finally ran off with a young lover. Fish proceeded to woo and wed a string of desperate widows, each of whom dumped him the moment she discovered his fondness for such nuptial pastimes as flagellation and coprophagy.

Gacy's first wife filed for divorce on the day he was sentenced to prison on sodomy charges. His second marriage likewise fell apart after it became clear that Gacy's preferred form of sex involved young male pickups. His wife had no idea, of course, that the crawl space beneath their suburban home contained the corpses of several dozen of these victims. She herself escaped unscathed. The wife of British sex slayer John Reginald Christie wasn't as lucky. She ended up as one of his victims, her body stashed beneath the dining room floorboards of their London flat (see **Homebodies**).

By contrast, some serial killers actually manage to remain contentedly married to women who never suspect that their husbands are anything other than ordinary, if slightly eccentric, individuals. This was true of Peter

Kürten, one of the most appalling lust murderers of the twentieth century, whose devoted wife had no inkling that her husband was the infamous "Monster of Düsseldorf."

Even more unbelievable are those cases in which the wives are not only aware of their husbands' depravities but also actively participate in them. Gerald Gallego's seventh wife, Charlene, helped lure young female victims into his clutches by promising them free marijuana. And the British sex slayer Rosemary West allegedly helped her husband, Fred, torture and murder ten people—including their own sixteen-year-old daughter (see **Killer Couples**).

MASK OF SANITY

The Mask of Sanity is the title of a classic 1976 study of the psychopathic personality by psychiatrist Hervey Cleckley. The phrase itself refers to the psychopath's most chilling characteristic: his ability to appear perfectly ordinary, to conceal his cold-blooded nature beneath a normal facade.

Not all psychopaths are criminals. Some are highly successful people. After all, they are masters of manipulation. They can make you believe that they are the most caring, sensitive, charming people in the world. But it's all a show. Under the surface, they're hollow to the core—complete egocentrics who care about nothing except their own greedy desires.

The serial killer is the most frightening of all psychopaths. The most basic human emotions—empathy, conscience, remorse—are completely missing from his emotional makeup. Behind his "mask of sanity," he is utterly evil. And yet, he's so good at dissembling that it's almost impossible to see his true, monstrous face.

Not, at any rate, until it's too late.

For more on this phenomenon, see **Jekyll/Hyde.**

========== **Psychopathic Checklist** ==========

Is someone you know—a neighbor, relative, or possibly your spouse—a criminal psychopath? Are you one yourself? Dr. Robert Hare—a professor emeritus at the University of British Columbia in Vancouver and author of

Without Conscience: The Disturbing World of the Psychopaths Among Us (1999)—has devised a twenty-item checklist identifying the main character-istics of the psychopathic personality. See how many you or your loved ones possess!

1. *Glib and superficial charm*—the tendency to be smooth, engaging, charming, slick, and verbally facile. A psychopath never gets tongue-tied.

2. *Grandiose self-worth*—a grossly inflated view of one's abilities and self-worth. Psychopaths are arrogant people who believe they are superior human beings.

3. *Need for stimulation or proneness to boredom*—an excessive need for novel, thrilling, and exciting stimulation; taking chances and doing things that are risky.

4. *Pathological lying*—can be moderate or high.

5. *Conning and manipulativeness*—the use of deceit and deception to con, cheat, or defraud others for personal gain.

6. *Lack of remorse or guilt*—a lack of feelings or concern for the losses, pain, and suffering of victims.

7. *Shallow affect*—emotional poverty or a limited range or depth of feelings.

8. *Callousness and lack of empathy*—a lack of feeling toward people in general; cold, contemptuous, inconsiderate, and tactless.

9. *Parasitic lifestyle*—an intentional, manipulative, selfish, and exploita-tive financial dependence on others.

10. *Poor behavioral controls*—expressions of irritability, annoyance, im-patience, threats, aggression, and verbal abuse.

11. *Promiscuous sexual behavior*—a variety of brief, superficial rela-tions, numerous affairs, and an indiscriminate selection of sexual partners.

12. *Early behavioral problems*—a variety of behaviors prior to age thir-teen, including lying, theft, cheating, vandalism, bullying, sexual activity, fire-setting, glue-sniffing, alcohol use, and running away from home.

13. *Lack of realistic long-term goals*—an inability or persistent failure to develop and execute long-term plans and goals.

14. *Impulsivity*—the occurrence of behaviors that are unpremeditated and lack reflection or planning; inability to resist temptation.

15. *Irresponsibility*—repeated failure to fulfill or honor obligations and commitments.

16. *Failure to accept responsibility for own actions*—as reflected in low conscientiousness, an absence of dutifulness, denial of responsibility, and an effort to manipulate others through this denial.

17. *Many short-term marital relationships*—a lack of commitment to a long-term relationship.

18. *Juvenile delinquency*—behavior problems between the ages of thirteen and eighteen.

19. *Revocation of conditional release*—a revocation of probation or other conditional releases due to technical violations.

20. *Criminal versatility*—a diversity of types of criminal offenses; taking great pride in getting away with crimes.

MASS MURDER

Although some people use the terms "mass murder" and "serial killing" synonymously, there are major differences between the two types of homicide. These differences have to do with matters of *time, place,* and *manner of killing.*

Serial killers typically commit their atrocities over a considerable span of time—sometimes years. Between each killing there is an emotional **Cooling-off Period,** similar to the sated lull that follows sex. Having satisfied his blood lust, the serial killer subsides into a more or less ordinary existence—at least for a while. Eventually, his monstrous cravings begin to grow again until they build into an unbearable need. At that point, he sets out in search of a fresh victim.

Though some serial killers limit themselves to a favorite hunting ground (like the prostitute killer who haunts a particular red-light district), others range freely over a wide territory. Earle Leonard **Nelson,** Ted **Bundy,** and Henry Lee **Lucas,** for example, all murdered women from coast to coast. Once he manages to capture his prey, the serial killer often subjects the victim to unspeakable acts of **Sadism.**

By contrast, the mass murderer is a man or woman who suddenly goes completely berserk, slaughtering a large number of random victims (at least four, according to an **FBI** criterion) in a single eruption of violence that takes place in one location (like a post office or fast-food restaurant). In short, if the most apt image for a serial killer is the "hunter of humans," the appropriate analogy for a mass murderer is the "human time bomb." He detonates without warning, destroying everyone in the vicinity (including himself, since most mass murderers either kill themselves to avoid capture or are gunned down by police in climactic shoot-outs).

The "classic" case of mass murder is that of Charles Whitman, the twenty-five-year-old architecture student who barricaded himself in a bell tower at the University of Texas in August 1966 and began firing at everyone within rifle range, slaying twenty-one people and wounding another twenty-eight.

As Whitman's case shows, mass murderers often claim more victims than serial killers (Jeffrey **Dahmer,** for example, slew seventeen people as compared to Whitman's twenty-one). And yet, the serial killer is an infinitely more terrifying figure. This is largely because we tend to perceive the mass murderer in human terms—as a deeply disturbed individual who snaps because of a crisis at home or on the job and goes on a wildly destructive rampage.

By contrast, the serial killer—the **Jekyll/Hyde** monster who coolly stalks his prey and derives his deepest pleasure from torture, mutilation, and butchery—seems like something straight out of a nightmare. Something hardly human.

MEDIA

See **X-Rated**.

MODELS

At least one notorious serial killer—Harvey Murray Glatman, who enjoyed taking pictures of his terrified victims before killing them—specialized in preying on photographic models (see **Photographs**). But that's not the kind of models we mean. We mean the plastic, assemble-it-yourself kind. Yes, for those hobbyists who wish to add handsome serial-killer figurines to their collection of hand-painted polystyrene airplanes, automobiles, and battleships, a company called Von Then Productions (497 Westside Avenue, Suite 140, Jersey City, NJ 07304) offers both Charles **Manson** and Ed **Gein** model kits.

Anyone inclined to condemn these products as a symptom of the total breakdown of moral values in this country might keep in mind that back in the 1960s the Aurora company—America's premier manufacturer of model kits—put out a line of monster figures (Dracula, Frankenstein, the Wolfman, the Mummy) that proved enormously popular. In fact, these kits were so successful that Aurora followed up with a line of do-it-yourself torture and execution devices (starvation cages, gallows, guillotines, etc.), provoking so much parental outrage that the company was forced to withdraw them from the marketplace—much to the distress of horror-happy boomer boys everywhere.

Advertisement for
Charles Manson
model kit
(Courtesy of Damon Fox)

The Moors Murderers

Myra Hindley

Ian Brady

Myra Hindley and Ian Brady; from *52 Famous Murderers* trading cards
(Courtesy of Roger Worsham)

The most shocking crimes in modern British history were committed by a
pair of perverted lovebirds named Ian Brady and Myra Hindley, aka the
"Moors Murderers." Not since Saucy Jack prowled the backstreets of
Whitechapel had a series of killings provoked such outrage and horror
in England.

A child of the tough Glasgow slums, Brady (whose young, unwed mother
had little time for him) was in trouble with the law by the age of thirteen.
His sadistic tendencies also showed themselves early on. One boyhood
acquaintance recalled the time that little Ian dug a deep pit in a graveyard,
tossed in a live cat, then sealed up the opening with a stone. Brady wanted
to see how long it would take the animal to die of starvation.

In his early twenties, Brady developed an obsessive fascination with
Hitler and the Marquis de Sade. Before long, he was collecting Nazi paraphernalia and indulging in fascistic fantasies and sadistic daydreams. Only

one thing was needed to make those daydreams come true—a slavish, masochistic follower.

He found her in Myra Hindley, an attractive twenty-four-year-old working girl who—until she fell under Brady's sway—had showed no signs of deviancy. Soon after they started dating, however, her puppy dog devotion turned into complete emotional submission. In obedience to Brady's needs, the quiet, seemingly well-adjusted young woman transformed herself into a Nazi fetishist's wet dream, a jack-booted dominatrix/sex slave who loved to wield—and submit to—the whip and to strike pornographic poses for the delectation of her führer. Brady's pet name for her was "Myra Hess" (an homage to Hitler's henchman Rudolph Hess), and he fondly compared her to Irma Grese, the notorious female guard at Belsen concentration camp who took keen delight in torturing inmates.

But acting out Nazi-inspired sex fantasies wasn't enough for Brady. He had other—and far worse—things in mind.

For several years from the early to mid-1960s, the depraved couple abducted and killed at least four children, ranging in age from ten to sixteen. Generally, it was Hindley who lured the victim into her car. Exactly how much she participated in the actual killing remains a matter of debate, though Brady clearly took the more active role. Their final murder was, in many ways, the most appalling. After snatching a ten-year-old girl named Lesley Ann Downey, they brought her back to Hindley's house, bound and stripped hor, oompollod hor to poco for pornographic pictures, and then—before killing her—tape-recorded her heart-wrenching screams, cries, and pleas for mercy. Like their other victims, Downey's corpse was buried on the moors.

The "Moors Murderers" were finally caught when Brady attempted to recruit a second follower, his teenage brother-in-law, David Smith. In the fall of 1965, Brady picked up a young homosexual, brought him home, and bludgeoned him to death in front of Smith. In effect, this was an act of ritual slaughter—a blood initiation intended to bring Smith into Brady's murderous fold. But the plan backfired. Smith was so horrified that he notified the police.

At their 1966 trial, Brady and Hindley had to sit behind bulletproof shields to protect them from an outraged public. When the tape recording of Lesley Ann Downey's final moments was played in court, not only the jury and spectators but hardened police officers as well wept openly.

The "Moors Murderers" were sentenced to life in prison, where Hindley died of respiratory failure in November, 2002, at the age of sixty.

MOTIVES

In Shakespeare's tragic masterpiece *Othello*, the villainous Iago sets out to destroy the noble hero for no apparent reason. After all, Iago has nothing to gain from wrecking Othello's life. And he isn't really acting out of either envy or revenge. In attempting to explain this character's vicious behavior, one famous scholar coined the memorable phrase "motiveless malignity." Iago does terrible things for one reason only—because he's the embodiment of absolute evil.

Some people tend to see serial murder in the same way—as pure, unprovoked malignity. And indeed—in terms of such traditional, easily identifiable causes as jealousy and greed—serial killing does appear to be a "motiveless" crime.

In actuality, however, there is no such thing as a motiveless murder. Everyone has his reasons—even if those reasons are not immediately obvious. What drives the serial killer are dark psychological impulses—perverted passions and monstrous lusts. The twisted needs that dominate his psyche are every bit as real and compelling as more "objective" motives, such as the coveting of wealth or the desire to punish an unfaithful lover.

Insofar as serial killing is synonymous with lust murder, the primary motive, according to some experts in the field, is rage against women and the desire to inflict pain and suffering on them—in short, sexual sadism. Other specialists, however, insist that the dominant motive behind serial murder is not sex but power—even when the murder involves extreme sexual cruelty. As one sadistic serial killer explained to Special Agent Roy Hazelwood of the **FBI**'s Behavioral Science Unit: "The wish to inflict pain on others is not the essence of sadism. One essential impulse: to have complete mastery over another person, to make him/her a helpless object of our will, to become the absolute ruler over her, to become her God. The most important radical aim is to make her suffer, since there is no greater power over another person than that of inflicting pain on her."

For this reason, some criminologists have begun to regard Ted Kaczynski, the so-called Unabomber, not as the antitechnological terrorist he claims to be but as a genuine serial killer. According to John Douglas, former head of the BSU, the Unabomber's demands—as expressed in the lengthy manifesto he sent to the media—suggest a "desire for manipulation, domination, and control typical of serial killers."

> "The most important radical aim is to make her suffer, since there is no greater power over another person than that of inflicting pain on her."
>
> *A serial killer, explaining his motives*

MOVIES

People have always been intrigued by the kind of homicidal maniacs we now call serial killers, and every time a new mass medium has been invented, it's been used to gratify this primal fascination. In pre-electronic days, the "penny press" dished up wildly lurid accounts of grisly crimes, complete with graphic engravings of the murder victims. One of the earliest recordings produced for the Edison phonograph featured an actor reading the shocking confessions of H. H. **Holmes,** the notorious nineteenth-century "Torture Doctor." When radio became popular, listeners thrilled to such programs as Arch Obler's *Lights Out* (which also paid tribute to Holmes in a famous episode called "Murder Castle"). And ghoulish killers began stalking the screen virtually from the moment that motion pictures were invented.

Ever since the enormous commercial and critical success of Jonathan Demme's cinematic version of *The Silence of the Lambs,* Hollywood has churned out a slew of slick and, for the most part, instantly forgettable serial-killer movies—so many that a whole book could be written on the subject. As a matter of fact, a whole book *has* been written on the subject: Robert Cettl's *Serial Killer Cinema* (McFarland Publishers, 2003), an indispensable reference volume for any hardcore slasher fan.

With almost a century's worth of maniac movies to choose from, narrowing the list down to a mere handful is a thankless task. But if we were organizing our annual Serial Killer Film Festival, here—in alphabetical order—is the baker's dozen we'd select:

Deep Red (1976). A truly unsettling gore film from Italian horror maestro Dario Argento. David Hemmings (looking highly dissolute) stars as a

British pianist on the trail of a deranged killer in Rome. The soundtrack alone is scary enough to give you nightmares for a week.

Fear City (1984). A shamefully underrated thriller by director Abel Ferrara, about a serial killer stalking topless dancers in the sleazy heart of Manhattan. The first-rate cast includes Tom Berenger, Billy Dee Williams, Melanie Griffith, Rae Dawn Chong, Michael Grasso, and Maria Conchita Alonso.

Frenzy (1972). After a severe falling off with such turkeys as *Torn Curtain* and *Topaz,* Alfred Hitchcock returned to form in his penultimate film, a witty, stylish, and genuinely shocking thriller about a British serial killer loosely modeled after the real-life psycho known as "Jack the Stripper."

Halloween (1978). John Carpenter draws on every teen horror legend ever told in this brilliant low-budget chiller that was followed by various lesser sequels and countless rip-offs.

Henry: Portrait of a Serial Killer (1990). Very possibly the most deeply disturbing—not to say harrowing—serial-killer movie ever made. A cinematic tour de force, but definitely not for everyone. Based on the ostensible exploits of Henry Lee **Lucas.**

M (1931). Fritz Lang's riveting masterpiece about a serial child killer terrorizing Weimar Berlin. Loosely based on the career of Peter **Kürten,** the movie made an international star of Peter Lorre as the pudgy personification of psychopathic evil who is hunted down and tried by the criminal underworld.

Maniac (1980). A truly repulsive movie but—for that very reason—worth seeing, since it does such an effective job of capturing the sickening, sordid reality of serial murder. Starring the late lamented Joe Spinnell as a Norman Bates-like character who decks out his private collection of mannequins with the bloody scalps of his murder victims. Tom Savini served up the stomach-churning effects.

Peeping Tom (1960). The movie that effectively ended the career of British director Michael Powell (best known for his ballet fantasy, *The Red Shoes*). A young, psychopathic voyeur films his victims while impaling them with a blade concealed in his camera tripod. Vilified upon release, the movie is now considered a classic of psychocinema.

Psycho (1960). Not only a certified cinematic masterpiece but the seminal work from which the entire genre of so-called slasher movies springs. The crème de la crème of psychofilms.

Se7en (1995). From the opening credits to the climactic scene, director David Fincher creates an atmosphere of unsurpassed creepiness in this grim, grueling thriller about the kind of high-concept psycho-killer only a Hollywood screenwriter could dream up: a madman whose murders are based on the Seven Deadly Sins.

The Silence of the Lambs (1991). Jonathan Demme's deluxe, Oscar-winning version of Thomas Harris's brilliant bestseller. Anthony Hopkins's portrayal of Hannibal "the Cannibal" Lecter became such a crowd pleaser that the actor reprised the role in a 2001 sequel, *Hannibal*, and a 2002 prequel, *Red Dragon* (a remake of Michael Mann's 1986 *Manhunter*, in which Lecter was played by Brian Cox). Like *Psycho* and *The Texas Chainsaw Massacre, Silence* owes a large debt to the true-life atrocities of Wisconsin ghoul Ed **Gein.**

The Texas Chainsaw Massacre (1974). The *Citizen Kane* of dismemberment movies. Tobe Hooper—who, sadly, has never been able to duplicate (or even approximate) his greatest achievement—creates the scariest interpretation of the Ed Gein story ever put on film. The movie achieves its shocks through a potent combination of relentless brutality, sickening atmosphere, rampaging sadism, and even a dash of black humor (which first-time viewers tend to miss, since they are generally covering up their eyes with their hands). The 2003 remake has much slicker production values but only a fraction of the scares.

The Vanishing (1988). A gripping, low-key chiller from (of all places) Holland. Don't look for splashy Hollywood-style effects, hyperkinetic action, or graphic gore—just one of the most creepily effective serial-killer stories ever filmed, with an absolutely shattering climax. *Viewer Warning:* Do not confuse with the lame 1993 American remake, starring Kiefer Sutherland and Jeff Bridges.

> ## "Watching him act like a psychopathic killer with a mommy complex is like watching someone else throw up."
>
> New York Times *film critic Vincent Canby on Joe Spinnell's performance in* Maniac

MULTIPLE PERSONALITY

Ever since a mild-mannered motel keeper named Norman Bates became possessed by the evil spirit of his dear, departed mother, people have associated serial killers with split personalities. In reality, however, multiple personality disorder (or MPD, as it's known in the psychology biz) is an extremely rare condition. Still, that hasn't kept a whole string of serial killers from trying to blame their crimes on their ostensible alter egos.

William Heirens—the "Lipstick Killer," who is best known for the desperate message he scrawled on the bedroom wall of one murder scene ("For heaven's sake catch me before I kill more")—claimed that an alternate personality named George Murman was responsible for the three vicious sex murders he committed in 1945 and 1946. Likewise, John Wayne **Gacy** insisted that his thirty-three torture killings were actually the work of an evil personality he called "Jack."

Kenneth Bianchi—one of the "**Hillside Stranglers**"—was so convincing in inventing a second homicidal personality (named "Steve") that he managed to bamboozle several psychiatrists before being exposed as a fraud.

Indeed, despite all claims to the contrary, there hasn't been a single authenticated case of a split-personality serial killer (see **Insanity**). Crime maven Colin Wilson, however, does describe the apparently genuine case of a serial *rapist* named Billy Milligan who suffered from MPD. Sexually brutalized in childhood by his stepfather, Milligan's traumatized psyche responded by splitting itself into no fewer than twenty-two separate personalities—including a sixteen-year-old painter named Tommy; a fourteen-year-old boy named David (who claimed that he had once been buried alive); a twenty-two-year-old Englishman named Arthur who spoke fluent Arabic; a Serbo-Croatian thief called Regan; and a nineteen-year-old lesbian named Adalana, who took responsibility for the rapes.

"MURDERABILIA"

See **Cards, Comics, and Collectibles.**

MURDER RINGS

For the most part, serial killing is a solitary business, though simpatico psychos will occasionally bond in lethal pairs (see **Killer Couples** and **Partners**). Much rarer, though not entirely unheard of, are cases where three or more killers join together to commit murder for fun and profit.

For Dr. Morris Bolber and his confederates, Paul and Herman Petrillo, murder was strictly business. Operating in Philadelphia's Italian ghetto during the Great Depression, these enterprising reprobates found a way of turning bodies into bucks by persuading disgruntled housewives to take out hefty life-insurance policies on their hubbies. Then—after orchestrating the "accidental" deaths of the insured—Bolber & Co. split the proceeds with the widows. Between 1932 and 1937, Dr. Bolber and his associates were responsible for the deaths of at least a dozen victims.

While the Bolber-Petrillo organization was driven by good old-fashioned greed, other, far more unsettling motives lurked behind one of the most bizarre murder rings in the annals of crime. Though historically factual, the case has all the earmarks of a classic horror story—a kind of *Stepford Wives* in reverse, involving a quiet little town where the housewives were really homicidal maniacs.

Between 1919 and 1929, at least twenty-six women in the small Hungarian town of Nagyrev found a novel way to rid themselves of tiresome relatives. Led by a murderous midwife named Julia Fazekas—who taught them how to obtain arsenic by boiling flypaper and skimming off the poisonous residue—these fatal females disposed of boorish husbands, sickly children, ailing parents, obnoxious siblings—at least forty-five victims in all before the "Angel-Makers of Nagyrev" (as the newspapers dubbed them) were finally brought to trial.

Nazi Buffs

Critics of media violence complain that hardcore "splatter" films like *I Spit on Your Grave* and *Maniac* put bad ideas into the minds of budding psychopaths. But aspiring serial killers don't need movies to inspire them. All they have to do is open a history book.

Published accounts of Nazi atrocities were a common source of inspiration for killers who came of age in the post–World War II era. Graham Young, a British sociopath born in 1947, was a boyhood admirer of Hitler and his genocidal policies. Young also loved to read about the notorious English **Poisoners** of the nineteenth century. When Young was just fourteen, he set about poisoning his own family with all the dispassion of a concentration camp commandant. After a nine-year stint in a mental asylum, Young took a job at a photographic supply firm and immediately reverted to his old exterminative ways, poisoning a bunch of his co-workers before being caught.

Another postwar Briton who embraced Nazi philosophy was Ian Brady, the male half of the notorious **Killer Couple** known as the "**Moors Murderers.**" Captivated by the concept of the Aryan Übermensch—the "superman" who is entitled to exert his will on lesser mortals—Brady recruited a willing sex slave, Myra Hindley, who played obedient storm trooper to his two-bit führer. Together this vile pair abducted and murdered four children and left their mangled bodies buried on the moors.

In America, a tormented Chicago teenager named William Heirens was similarly infatuated with Nazism. Both an honor student and a compulsive burglar, Heirens nursed a simmering obsession with violence, sex, and totalitarian power. Besides a stockpile of firearms and a stash of stolen female panties (which he liked to wear around the house), he collected photographs of Hitler, Himmler, and other Nazi bigwigs. In 1945 and 1946, Heirens's obsessions finally boiled over. He murdered two women and a six-year-old girl, leaving an infamous lipstick-scrawled message on the bedroom wall of one crime scene: "For heaven's sake catch me before I kill more. I cannot control myself."

At roughly the same time in Wisconsin, Edward **Gein** was feeding his own demented fantasies with magazine stories about Nazi atrocities. A deranged do-it-yourselfer, Gein was inspired by accounts of concentration camp officials who turned human skin into lampshades. When investigators broke into Gein's horror house in 1957, they found a staggering collection of similarly constructed ghastly artifacts—chair seats, lampshades, wastebaskets, and more—all crafted from the flesh of corpses Gein had been stealing from local graveyards.

NECROPHILIA

In *Psychopathia Sexualis,* his classic study of aberrant behavior, Richard von Krafft-Ebing calls necrophilia the most monstrous of all perversions. Since necrophilia (from the Greek, meaning "love of the dead") is the practice of having sex with corpses, this is not a surprising assessment. Nor is it surprising that this most monstrous of acts should be common among the most monstrous of criminals—serial killers.

Many infamous psychopaths, from Earle Leonard **Nelson** to Ted **Bundy,** occasionally raped the bodies of their freshly slain victims. Still, some experts in the field of criminal psychology distinguish between this type of outrage—which is motivated by the malevolent desire to completely dominate and violate a victim—and the behavior of the "true necrophiliac," the man who is deeply infatuated with death, who derives his greatest sexual satisfaction from making love to a cadaver. This sort of necrophiliac is much rarer among serial killers. But there have been some notable cases.

Jeffrey **Dahmer**'s love affair with dead things began as a child, when his favorite hobby was collecting and dissecting roadkill. By the time he was a grown-up, this morbid obsession had metastasized into an unspeakable perversion. Dahmer told psychiatrists that he routinely cut open the abdomens of his murder victims and masturbated into their viscera. He also confessed to anally raping the corpses. His British counterpart, Dennis **Nilsen,** was also driven by necrophiliac urges, though he tended to treat his victims more tenderly, masturbating as he snuggled beside them in bed.

The most infamous of all American necrophiliacs is Ed **Gein.** Like all classic necrophiliacs, Gein was completely uninterested in living women. He found his sex partners in local cemeteries, which he plundered periodically for more than a dozen years. In general, necrophiliacs are regarded as less of a menace than serial killers because the victims they prey on are already dead. Gein was no exception. He was more ghoul than serial killer. Still, he was not, by any means, harmless. When the local graveyards ran low on available females, he simply went out hunting for a likely looking prospect and turned her into the kind of woman he loved best—a dead one.

> **"I took her bra and panties off and had sex with her. That's one of those things I guess that got to be a part of my life—having sexual intercourse with the dead."**
>
> **HENRY LEE LUCAS,**
> *describing his reaction to the death of his beloved common-law wife, twelve-year-old Becky Powell, whom he had just stabbed in the chest during an argument*

Earle Leonard Nelson

Earle Leonard Nelson; from
Bloody Visions trading cards

In the annals of U.S. crime, Earle Leonard Nelson—aka the "Gorilla Man"—
holds a historic position. He was the first American serial sex killer
of the twentieth century. In February 1926, he began a frenzied, eighteen-
month odyssey that took him from one end of the country to the other and
up into Canada. Along the way, he slaughtered no fewer than twenty-two
women—a grisly record that would remain unbroken for another fifty years.

Orphaned in infancy when his young parents both died of syphilis, Nelson was taken in and raised by his mother's family. He was a withdrawn,
moody child with bizarre personal habits. (Among his other peculiarities, he
would regularly set off for school in neat, freshly laundered garments and
return in foul rags, as though he'd swapped clothes with a derelict.) As a result of a severe head injury—sustained when his bicycle collided with a
cable car—his behavior became even more erratic.

By his early teens, he was already a habitué of the brothels and bars of
San Francisco's Barbary Coast. He had also taken to petty thievery. In
1915—just a few months after his eighteenth birthday—he was arrested
for burglary and sentenced to two years in San Quentin. America had just

entered World War I when Nelson emerged. He enlisted in the navy, but—
after refusing to do anything but lie on his cot and babble about the Great
Beast of Revelations—he was confined to a mental institution. He remained there for the duration of the war.

Discharged in 1919, the twenty-two-year-old Nelson met and married
a sixty-year-old spinster and proceeded to make her life a daily hell.
Shortly after she left him, he attacked a twelve-year-old girl and was
returned to the mental asylum. Discharged in 1925, he soon embarked
on his deadly career.

He started in San Francisco, working his way up the Pacific Coast to
Seattle, then headed eastward. At first, the tabloids dubbed him the "Dark
Strangler"; later, he became known as the "Gorilla Man"—a nickname that
had less to do with his appearance (he was actually quite ordinary-looking)
than with the savagery of his crimes. For the most part, his targets were
middle-aged or elderly landladies who had placed "Rooms to Let" ads in
their local papers. Nelson—who could be ingratiating when he wanted to—
would show up at their homes and ask to see a room. Once alone with his
victims, he would undergo a **Jekyll/Hyde**–like transformation.

Typically, he would choke the women to death, commit postmortem
rape, then conceal the corpses in bizarre hiding places. One of his victims
was stuffed into an attic trunk. Others were crammed behind the basement
furnaces. His final victim was discovered when her husband knelt to say his
evening prayers and found her body shoved under the bed.

With the police departments of a dozen different cities on the alert, Nelson headed into Canada, where he finally reached the end of his corpse-
strewn trail. After killing two more victims, he was captured in Manitoba.
He managed to escape from jail, setting off a widescale panic and massive
manhunt. Twelve hours later, he was back in custody—this time for good.

Several months later, Earle Leonard Nelson went to the gallows. His
final words were: "I forgive those who have wronged me."

NICKNAMES

With the advent of tabloid newspapers in the 1800s, crime reporters began wracking their brains to come up with catchy nicknames for sensational killers—a tradition that continues to this day. (When a co-ed was
murdered in New York City in early 2006 and her brutalized corpse found

heavily wrapped in packing tape, the papers immediately dubbed her killer "The Mummy Maniac.") Following is a list of notorious serial murderers along with their sinister pseudonyms:

Richard Angelo, "The Angel of Death"
Elizabeth Bathory, "The Blood Countess"
Kenneth Bianchi and Angelo Buono, "The Hillside Stranglers"
William Bonin, "The Freeway Killer"
Ian Brady and Myra Hindley, "The Moors Murderers"
Gary Carlton, "The Stocking Strangler"
Harvey Louis Carnigan, "The Want-Ad Killer"
David Carpenter, "The Trailside Killer"
Andrei Chikatilo, "The Mad Beast"
Douglas Clark, "The Sunset Strip Slayer"
Albert DeSalvo, "The Boston Strangler"
Theo Durrant, "The Demon of the Belfry"
Albert Fish, "The Moon Maniac"
John Wayne Gacy, "Killer Clown"
Ed Gein, "The Plainfield Ghoul"
John Wayne Glover, "The Granny Killer"
Cleo Green, "The Red Demon"
Vaughn Greenwood, "The Skid Row Slasher"
Fritz Haarmann, "The Butcher of Hanover"
William Heirens, "The Lipstick Murderer"
H. H. Holmes, "The Torture Doctor"
Edmund Kemper, "The Coed Killer"
Richard Macek, "The Mad Biter"
Earle Leonard Nelson, "The Gorilla Man"
Thierry Paulin, "The Monster of Montmartre"
Heinrich Pommerencke, "The Beast of the Black Forest"
Dennis Rader, "BTK"
Richard Ramirez, "The Night Stalker"
Melvin Rees, "The Sex Beast"
Vicytor Szczepinski, "The Doorbell Killer"
Peter Sutcliffe, "The Yorkshire Ripper"
Coral Eugene Watts, "The Sunday Morning Slasher"

Thomas Harris acknowledges this tradition in his bestselling thrillers, *Red Dragon* and *The Silence of the Lambs,* whose **FBI** heroes are on the hunt for two terrifying figures: a serial killer nicknamed the "Tooth Fairy" (because he bites his victims with a special set of dentures) and another dubbed "Buffalo Bill" (because he "always skins his humps").

Dennis Nilsen

DENNIS NILSEN

Dennis Nilsen; from *True Crime Trading Cards Series Two: Serial Killers and Mass Murderers;* art by Jon Bright

(Courtesy of Jon Bright and Valarie Jones)

Nilsen—the "British Jeffrey **Dahmer,**" responsible for the grisly murders of fifteen young men—never fit the standard profile of a serial killer. As a child, he recoiled from cruelty to animals. Even bird hunting seemed wrong to him. In his adult life, he devoted himself to helping the downtrodden in his work for the Manpower Services Commission. Even his murders were motivated less by psychopathic rage than by a grotesque form of love. In the phrase of writer Brian Masters, Nilsen "killed for company."

From early adolescence onward, Nilsen's sexuality was marked by a necrophiliac strain. As a teenager, he liked to stretch out in front of a mirror and masturbate while imagining that the body reflected in the glass was a corpse. During a brief homosexual affair in 1972, he took home movies of his lover—an eighteen-year-old army private—while the young man pretended to be dead.

During his eleven-year stint in the military, Nilsen worked for a time as a butcher (an occupation that provided him with skills he would later put to appalling use). After leaving the army in 1972, he joined the London police, lasting just a year. Before long, he had begun his civil service career at a government-run Job Centre. For a time, he had a contented relationship with another young man, but when it finally broke up, the reclusive Nilsen was plunged into a despairing loneliness. He reverted to bizarre autoerotic rituals. Applying powder and paint to his naked body—to make it look like the corpse of a gunshot victim—he would masturbate while regarding his own ghastly flesh in a mirror.

A few days after Christmas, 1978, Nilsen began to kill. After picking up a teenage boy in a pub, Nilsen brought him back to his apartment in the Cricklewood section of London. Frantic for companionship, Nilsen did not want the young man to leave. While the teenager slept, Nilsen garroted him with a necktie, then finished the job by submerging the boy's head in a bucketful of water. Afterward, Nilsen stripped the corpse, gave it a tender, ritual bath, and laid it out on his bed. He kept it around the flat for the next few days, caressing it, cleaning it, masturbating over it. Eventually, he stashed it under the floorboards.

Over the next three years, the same ghastly pattern repeated itself another eleven times in Nilsen's Cricklewood apartment. The accumulating bodies posed a problem, which Nilsen dealt with in increasingly sickening ways. At first, he stored the corpses in and around his flat—in his cupboard or under the floorboards or in a garden shed. Eventually, however, he was compelled to dismember the decaying bodies and incinerate them in a backyard bonfire. He tossed an old tire onto the blaze, hoping that the smell of burning rubber would disguise the stench of burning flesh.

In 1981, Nilsen moved to a different apartment, where he murdered three more young men and got rid of the bodies by chopping them up and flushing the chunks down the toilet. (To remove the flesh from the skulls, he boiled the heads in a big soup pot.) Eventually, this method of **Disposal** led to his downfall. When the toilets in the entire building became clogged up, neighbors called a plumber, who discovered human bones and gobs of decomposed flesh blocking the pipes.

Inside his fetid flat, police found a ghastly assortment of human remains—heads and limbs, torsos, bones, and viscera. Nilsen, who confessed freely to fifteen murders, was sentenced to life imprisonment at his 1983 trial.

> **"I wished I could stop but I could not.
> I had no other thrill or happiness."**
>
> **DENNIS NILSEN**

NOMADS

Here's a sobering statistic: nearly three-quarters of all known serial killers in the world—74 percent to be exact—come from the United States (as opposed to a measly 19 percent for all of Europe). Clearly, there is something about American culture that is conducive to serial murder. Theories range from our puritanical attitudes about matters of the flesh—which presumably produce all kinds of sexual pathology—to our steady diet of media violence.

Whatever other factors are involved, one aspect of our cultural life surely exacerbates the problem: the extreme mobility of Americans. Ever since the time of the early pioneers, we've been a people on the go. While this cultural characteristic has undoubtedly been a source of strength (our unique freedom of movement has helped our nation develop at an extraordinary pace), it has also contributed to our notoriously high crime rate. From the days of John Wesley Hardin and Billy the Kid, highly mobile outlaws have been able to get away with murder for years by staying a few steps ahead of the law.

As early as the 1920s, however, a new and even more frightening phenomenon appeared on the criminal scene: the nomadic killer who exploited modern modes of transportation (primarily cars and trains) to keep constantly on the move, leaving behind a trail of corpses (and little else in the way of traceable clues). Earl Leonard **Nelson**—the "Gorilla Man" who strangled nearly two dozen women during an eighteen-month, coast-to-coast killing spree—was one of the first of this deadly breed. Another was Carl **Panzram,** the globe-trotting sociopath who bragged of having committed more than one thousand homosexual rapes and twenty-one murders in the course of his extraordinarily hard-bitten life. Twenty years later, a homicidal drifter named Jake Bird racked up an even higher body count during his career of peripatetic **Axe Murder.**

It wasn't until the late 1970s and early 1980s, however, that Americans began to perceive nomadic serial murder as a growing public menace, thanks largely to the crimes of monsters like Ted **Bundy** (who committed his lust killings in four different states) and—even more unnervingly— Henry Lee **Lucas,** who may have slaughtered as many as one hundred people during his life of aimless travel. In our mobile, fast-paced society, such itinerant psychopaths can go on killing for years, depositing corpses in quiet stretches of woods, along deserted coastlines, and beside isolated highways—preying on hitchhikers, roadside hookers, casual pickups, and other easy victims as rootless (and often as difficult to trace) as the killers themselves.

For a contrast to the nomadic style of serial murder, see **Homebodies.**

NURSERY RHYMES

As everyone knows, little children are fascinated by violence and horror (if you want to read something *really* scary, check out *The Complete Grimm's Fairy Tales*). So it's not surprising that homicidal maniacs frequently pop up in children's verse.

An anonymous **Axe Murderer** is the subject of this cheerfully grisly nursery rhyme:

> *Here comes a candle to light you to bed.*
> *Here comes a chopper to chop off your head.*

A different "chopper"—the one belonging to the infamous German lust murderer and cannibal, Fritz **Haarmann**—features in this German nursery rhyme:

Just you wait 'til it's your time,
Haarmann will come after you,
With his chopper, oh so fine,
He'll make mincemeat out of you.

The bloody deeds of other real-life killers have also been celebrated in nursery rhymes. Everyone, of course, knows the one about Fall River's most notorious daughter:

Lizzie Borden took an axe
And gave her mother forty whacks.
And when she saw what she had done,
She gave her father forty-one.

Lizzie's near contemporary, the British "Queen Poisoner," Mary Ann Cotton (see **Black Widows**), was also immortalized in a kiddie rhyme:

Mary Ann Cotton
She's dead and she's rotten.
She lies in her bed
With her eyes wide oppen.

The English, in fact, seem to specialize in turning lurid crimes into nursery rhymes. Two of the most notorious murderers in British criminal history were the nineteenth-century miscreants Thomas Burke and William Hare. Up until 1832, British law forbade the dissection of human corpses, except for those of executed murderers. As a result, there was a serious shortage of medical school cadavers. To fill this scientific need, some physicians turned to professional body snatchers, who would plunder fresh graves and peddle the bodies. Burke and Hare added a new twist to the body-peddling business by murdering lodgers in the boardinghouse they ran, then selling the corpses to an Edinburgh surgeon named Robert Knox. Their story has been retold many times and in various forms, from street ballads to Robert Louis Stevenson's "The Body Snatcher" (made into a 1945 Boris Karloff movie). It also inspired this little rhyme:

Burke's the murderer, Hare's the thief,
And Knox the boy who buys the beef.

And, of course, there's this whimsical couplet about the legendary "Butcher of Whitechapel":

> **Jack the Ripper** *stole a kipper,*
> *Hid it in his father's slipper.*

More recent British murderers have also served as the subject for children's verse. In the mid-1930s, a physician named Buck Ruxton murdered his wife, Isabella, and a witness to the crime, his housemaid, Mary Rogerson. Then he dismembered both corpses and dumped the remains in a ravine near Moffat, Scotland. Before long, British schoolchildren were chanting this little ditty:

> *Red stains on the carpet, red stains on your knife.*
> *Oh Dr. Buck Ruxton, you murdered your wife.*
> *The nursemaid she saw you, and threatened to tell.*
> *Oh Dr. Buck Ruxton, you killed her as well.*

Today, of course, we live in less poetic times. Instead of verse, horrific crimes tend to be transformed into grisly jokes. Still, every now and then some humble versifier will compose a tribute to a serial killer. The atrocities of Edward **Gein,** for example, inspired not only a spate of sick riddles (see **Jokes**) but also these immortal lines:

> *There once was a man named Ed*
> *Who wouldn't take a woman to bed.*
> *When he wanted to diddle,*
> *He cut out the middle,*
> *And hung the rest in a shed.*

NURSES

It's bad enough when a law student (like Ted **Bundy**) or a policeman (like G. J. Schaefer, the Florida "Sex Beast" linked to twenty sadistic murders) turns out to be a serial killer. It seems even worse when the psycho is affiliated with the healing arts—someone who has pledged his or her professional life to the care of other human beings. Deadly **Doctors** fall into this category. So do lethal nurses—those homicidal health-care workers who prey on the sick and the helpless, administering not succor and comfort but suffering and death.

In Cincinnati during the 1930s, a German immigrant named Anna Marie Hahn made a reputation for herself as a kindly, devout nurse, an angel of mercy who looked after sickly old men—all of whom happened to have very healthy bank accounts. In one way or another, Hahn managed to get her hands on their money, either by asking for "loans," getting herself written into their wills, or stealing it outright. Then she dispatched her patients with a dose of lethal medication. Over five years, she poisoned at least eleven of the trusting old souls. She became the first woman ever electrocuted in Ohio.

While Hahn was in it strictly for the money, other lethal nurses have been motivated by even darker impulses. The notorious turn-of-the-century multi-murderer Jane **Toppan** declared that her deepest desire was to become the most prolific killer of her day. Though Toppan was accused of eleven murders, she claimed to have committed thirty-one, and some crime buffs believe that the real total was closer to one hundred. If so, then Toppan certainly achieved her ambition.

Much more recently, in the late 1980s, a sociopathic nursing-home aide named Gwendolyn Graham and her lesbian lover, Catherine Wood, devised a demented game. They decided to smother six elderly patients, selecting victims whose last initials, when strung together, spelled out the word *murder*. As it happened, the "game" became too complicated to complete, but Graham and Wood kept killing old people anyway, largely because it provided the two depraved lovers with such a powerful sexual thrill.

Not all lethal nurses are women. Richard Angelo—Long Island's "Angel of Death"—had perhaps the weirdest rationale of all for multiple medical murder. Obsessed with the need to be recognized as a hero, the one-time Eagle Scout and volunteer fireman got his degree as a registered nurse, then went to work in the intensive-care unit of Good Samaritan Hospital, where (aptly enough) he worked the graveyard shift. Before long, postoperative patients began dropping like flies. Eventually, the authorities discovered the cause of the mysterious deaths. Between mid-September and late October

1987, Angelo had injected an average of two patients per week with Pavulon and Anectine, drugs that induced paralysis and heart failure. His reason? So that he could rush to their rescue and prove that he was a hero. Unfortunately, his plan had its flaws: out of the nearly forty patients he injected, at least ten—perhaps as many as twenty-five—died.

Beginning in 1987, another malevolent male nurse, Charles Cullen, embarked on a killing spree that would outdo Richard Angelo's. Working in nursing homes and hospitals throughout New Jersey and Pennsylvania, Cullen dispatched as many as forty people by injecting them with various medications, such as the heart drug digoxin. When arrested in 2003, he insisted that he was simply helping to put old, terminally ill patients out of their misery—a claim seriously undercut by the fact that his victims included a twenty-one-year-old college student recovering nicely after surgery.

Dubbed "the worst serial killer in New Jersey history," Cullen avoided the death penalty by agreeing to help prosecutors identify his victims. At his sentencing hearing in March 2006, he was denounced as "Satan's son." "Maybe some days he actually believes he was an angel of mercy," said the daughter of one of his elderly victims. "Let us correct that. He is a demon from the lowest depths of hell." He was sentenced to eleven consecutive life terms.

ORCHARDS

Back in the early 1800s (according to legend) a wandering folk hero named Johnny Appleseed roamed across the land, turning empty fields into fertile orchards. Of course, fertility isn't the only quality connected with apple orchards. Ever since the days of Adam and Eve, the apple tree has also symbolized sin and corruption. In real life as in myth, orchards have been associated with both goodness and crime—not only with the delicious fruits of God's earth but also with the deadly fruits of man's evil.

In the spring of 1873, the citizens of Labette County, Kansas, were concerned about the alarming number of travelers who had vanished while passing through the region. A posse investigating the recently abandoned farmstead of a family named Bender noticed something peculiar about the apple orchard behind the house. Depressions in the soil between the blossoming seedlings were rectangular in shape—and approximately the size of human graves. By the time the posse finished digging up the orchard, they had uncovered the bodies of a dozen people. Most of them were men, their skulls crushed with a sledgehammer. One was a baby girl who had been buried alive with her father's corpse. As it turned out, the "Bloody Benders" had been preying on unwary travelers for years, having turned their ram-shackle farmhouse into a kind of hotel-from-hell where overnight guests rarely survived to see the light of day (see **Clans**).

An apple orchard also featured prominently in the most sensational crime of the 1920s, the Hall-Mills murder case. On a September morning in 1922, a young couple out for a stroll in New Brunswick, New Jersey, stumbled upon two corpses, male and female, lying side by side in a crabapple orchard. The woman's throat had been slashed so ferociously that she was nearly decapitated. She had also been shot three times in the face at point-blank range. Though the dead man had not been subjected to the same mutilations, he had been killed with chilling deliberation—executed with a single bullet to the brain. What made the murders especially lurid was the identity of the victims: the Reverend Edward Wheeler Hall, pastor of New Brunswick's most fashionable Episcopal church, and his choir-girl mistress, Mrs. Eleanor Mills. The subsequent trial of the reverend's betrayed wife and her two eccentric brothers was the O. J. Simpson affair of its day—a frenzied, three-ring media circus followed with prurient fascination by the whole country. (As in the O.J. case, the defendants were acquitted and the case remains officially unsolved.)

The orchard where the bodies had been found turned into a major tourist attraction, where vendors hawked soft drinks and popcorn to the curious hordes, who stripped every leaf and crabapple from the branches as morbid souvenirs.

Fifty years later, orchards of another kind—the peach orchards surrounding Yuba City, California—became the site of one of the most gruesome discoveries in American criminal history. In May 1971 a farmer discovered a hacked-up corpse buried between two fruit trees. Other discoveries in nearby orchards soon followed. One by one, the corpses of migrant workers and male transients were unearthed until the body count reached a staggering twenty-five. All of the victims had been savagely slashed with a knife and a machete, and a number of them bore the signs of sexual assault. Evidence eventually led police to someone very familiar with the orchards of Yuba City, a farm labor contractor named Juan Corona, whose conviction on twenty-five counts of murder in 1973 marked him as the nation's most prolific serial killer. Unfortunately for America, that record has since been eclipsed several times.

Organized/Disorganized

See **Profiling**.

Ovens

Few fairy tales are more chilling to children than "Hänsel and Gretel"—the story of a cannibal witch who plans to feast on two fattened children but ends up incinerated in her own oven. Perhaps that's what adds a special dimension of horror to serial killers who use ovens to dispose of their victims. The whole situation seems like something from a childhood horror story—a real-life, exceedingly grim fairy tale.

Henri Landru, the "Bluebeard of Paris," even *looked* like a fairy-tale villain, with his bald head, bristling brows, and spiky red beard. In spite of his unprepossessing appearance, however, he became infamous as one of the world's leading lady-killers, marrying and murdering no fewer than ten women (see **Bluebeards**). Believing (incorrectly) that without a corpse, the authorities could not convict him of murder, he reduced all his victims to ash in an outdoor oven. Even without a single identifiable body, however, the authorities were able to assemble enough circumstantial evidence to send Landru to the guillotine.

Dr. H. H. **Holmes**—the turn-of-the-century serial killer and another notorious lady-killer—disposed of dozens of victims in the same way. When

Perhaps the most appalling of Holmes's many crimes was the murder of two young girls, Alice and Nellie Pitezel, who were gassed to death inside a steamer trunk—an atrocity portrayed in this nineteenth-century book illustration

investigators finally broke into his rambling "Horror Castle" in a suburb of Chicago, they discovered both a basement crematorium and an oversized office stove that still contained the charred remnants of one of his ill-fated mistresses. Holmes's most heinous crimes, however, were the cold-blooded murders of three young siblings—the children of his accomplice, Ben Pitezel. Two of these little ones were asphyxiated and buried in a basement crawl space. The blackened remains of the third, a ten-year-old boy, were found in the belly of a coal-burning oven.

Of course, disposing of victims isn't the only use to which ovens have been put by deranged psychokillers. When German police arrested the cannibalistic sex killer Joachim Kroll in 1976, they found something cooking on his stove: the chopped-off hand of a four-year-old girl, simmering in a saucepan with sliced potatoes and carrots.

Carl Panzram

During his final prison stretch in the late 1920s, Carl Panzram confessed to twenty-one murders, countless felonies, and more than one thousand acts of sodomy. "For all these things," he declared, "I am not the least bit sorry." It was a typical statement by one of the most incorrigible criminals in American history. Some sociologists have blamed Panzram's vicious nature on the penal system, which subjected him to countless brutalities in an effort to break his spirit, but only filled him with a hatred for all humankind. Others have a different explanation: that he was simply born bad.

Whether Panzram's badness was acquired or innate is a matter of debate. One thing is certain: his criminal career started early. His first conviction was for drunk and disorderly conduct—when he was eight years old. Three years later, a string of burglaries landed him in reform school. During his time there, he torched one of the buildings, causing an estimated $100,000 worth of damage. The thirteen-year-old Panzram was released from the institution in 1904 with knowledge that would last him a lifetime—"how to steal, lie, hate, burn, and kill" (as he would write in his autobiography).

Portrait of Carl Panzram by Joe Coleman

Paroled to his mother's custody, he promptly ran away to lead the life of a hobo. While hitching a ride in a boxcar, he was gang-raped by four "burly bums," who taught him another lesson he would continue to live by: "Force and might make right."

He joined the army at sixteen, but military discipline was not Panzram's long suit. He was court-martialed and sentenced to three years in Leavenworth. Following his release, he embarked on a career of spectacular brutality. Traveling around the world—to South America, Europe, Africa, and finally back to the United States—he left a trail of corpses in his wake.

In the 1920s, Panzram committed two of his most infamous crimes. With the proceeds from an especially profitable heist, he purchased a yacht and lured ten sailors aboard with the promise of free bootleg liquor. After the sailors drank themselves into a stupor, Panzram raped them, shot each one in the head, then dumped their bodies in the ocean.

Later, after shipping out as a merchant seaman to West Africa, he hired eight native bearers, presumably to help him hunt crocodiles. Panzram ended up killing and raping the Africans, then feeding their corpses to the crocs.

By 1928, Panzram was back in America, where he was arrested for a series of burglaries in the vicinity of Washington, D.C. Sentenced to twenty years in Leavenworth, he announced that he would "kill the first man that bothers me." He made good on his threat the following year, smashing in the skull of a laundry foreman. It was this crime that finally got Panzram a long-overdue death sentence. He was hanged on September 5, 1930. Consistent to the end, he went to his death with a curse on his lips. "Hurry it up, you Hoosier bastard," he snarled as the executioner prepared the noose. "I could hang a dozen men while you're fooling around!"

For a flawed but intriguing film about Panzram, check out *Killer* (1996), with the always watchable (if somewhat miscast) James Woods in the title role.

> "I sat down to think things over a bit. While I was sitting there, a little kid about eleven or twelve years old came bumming around. He was looking for something. He found it, too. I took him out to a gravel pit about one-quarter mile away. I left him there, but first committed sodomy on him and then killed him. His brains were coming out of his ears when I left him, and he will never be any deader."
>
> **CARL PANZRAM**

PARAPHILIA

Paraphilia—which literally means "abnormal love"—is the technical term for sexual deviation or perversion. It need hardly be said that when it comes to paraphiliac behavior, serial killers are as sick as they come.

The average foot fetishist, for example, might assemble a sizable collec-

Painting of Albert Fish
flagellating himself with a
nail-studded board; art by
Michael Rose

tion of stolen spike-heeled shoes. By contrast, at least one serial killer grati-
fied his fetish by cutting off the feet of his victims and storing them in his refrigerator. Clipping and saving tufts of female pubic hair is another
common fetish. Serial killers, on the other hand, are just as likely to remove
the entire vulvas of their victims.

Voyeurism is another paraphilia that serial killers practice with a singular
malevolence. The typical Peeping Tom enjoys spying on people who are having sex. Voyeuristic serial killers, on the other hand, like to watch while their
partners or accomplices rape, sodomize, and torture helpless victims.
Among the other paraphilias favored by serial killers are bestiality, S-M, and
exhibitionism.

Undoubtedly the single most perverted serial killer in the annals of
American crime was Albert **Fish.** According to the psychiatric experts who
examined him, Fish had spent his lifetime indulging in every known paraphilia, plus a few no one had ever heard of before. (For example, he liked
to insert long-stemmed roses into his penis and look at himself in the

mirror. Then he would remove the roses and eat them.) His more common-place paraphilias included: sadism, masochism, flagellation, exhibitionism, voyeurism, piquerism (deriving sexual pleasure from jabbing himself with sharp objects), pedophilia, analingus (oral stimulation of the anus), co-prophagia (eating feces), undinism (sexual preoccupation with urine), fetishism, and cannibalism.

PARTNERS

Serial killers have their own special form of male bonding. Instead of bowl-ing with a buddy, they will occasionally link up with a partner and go prowl-ing in pairs. It is estimated that approximately 28 percent of all serial homicides in this country are committed by such deadly duos.

Though the bisexual Henry Lee **Lucas** and his homosexual partner, Ottis Elwood Toole, were occasional lovers, the true basis of their friendship was not sex but a shared passion for serial slaughter. Shortly after meeting in a Florida soup kitchen, they launched into a life of random, nomadic vio-lence, traveling the highways and preying on an untold number of victims—hitchhikers, vagrants, women with car trouble. They killed with appalling cruelty. (In one typical instance, they attacked a forty-six-year-old woman in her mobile home, Lucas raping her while Toole strangled her with a tele-phone cord; after she was dead, Toole ripped off her nipples with his teeth.) When the pair ran low on cash, they would knock over a convenience store and kill the clerk (whose corpse was generally raped by the necrophiliac Toole).

Both Lucas and Toole had committed homicide before hooking up with each other. Other cases, however, are examples of what the French call a **Folie à Deux**—a shared psychopathology that only operates when the two individuals come together. Separately, each man—however potentially vio-lent—might never commit murder; together, they bring out each other's most monstrous impulses. This was the case, for example, not only with the "**Hillside Stranglers,**" but also with Leonard Lake and Charles Ng, a pair of ex-marines with a common interest in automatic weapons and sado-masochistic pornography. In the early 1980s, this depraved duo abducted at least three women and kept them as "sex slaves" in an underground bunker on Lake's remote, wooded compound in Calaveras County, California. The victims were videotaped while being subjected to extreme sexual torture, then murdered when their captors grew tired of them. (Ng awaits trial on these charges and maintains his innocence to this day.) Other depraved two-somes include Lawrence Bittaker and Roy Norris (a pair of degenerates who cruised the California roads in a van they called Murder Mack, abducting, torturing, and killing a string of young girls), Dean Corll and Wayne Henley (who conspired to lure dozens of young males to Corll's home in Pasadena, Texas, where the boys were drugged, shackled, tortured—sometimes for days—then killed), and Theodore Simmons and Milton Jones of Buffalo, New York (who teamed up to torture and kill Catholic priests).

Some serial-killer teams have more in common than their psychopathology—they are actually related by blood. This was true of the "Hillside Stranglers," Kenneth Bianchi and Angelo Buono, who were cousins; the Haley brothers of Los Angeles, who committed no fewer than five hundred burglaries, sixty rapes, and eight murders in the early 1980s; and the wildly psychotic Joseph Kallinger, who enlisted the aid of his own twelve-year-old son in his six-month campaign of murder and mutilation.

Of course, even the closest of companions can sometimes disagree. Rudolph Pleil—arguably the most monstrous German lust murderer of the post–World War II era—had a voracious appetite for rape, mutilation, and murder but objected when an accomplice insisted on beheading a victim. Though Pleil slaughtered at least two dozen victims with hammers, hatchets, and knives, he evidently drew the line at decapitation. And Lucas disapproved of his partner's cannibalistic proclivities, refusing to participate when Toole indulged his taste for human flesh.

Marcel Petiot

The smoke spewing from the chimney of 21 Rue Le Sueur on March 11, 1944, was so thick, black, and foul smelling that it might have been coming from a Nazi crematorium. A neighbor telephoned the Parisian authorities. When firemen broke into the building, they made an appalling discovery—a stack of dissected and dismembered human bodies, more than two dozen in all. These would later prove to be the remains of Jewish men and women. Inside the furnace, the firemen found a pile of burning limbs—the source of the billowing stench.

There was a good reason why the chimney smoke carried the stench of a Nazi crematorium. In effect, that's what the building's owner—a physician named Marcel Petiot—had turned his basement furnace into.

When Petiot was confronted with the evidence of his crimes, however, he had a ready explanation. A psychopath of unusual—even flamboyant—audacity, he insisted that far from being a criminal, he was actually a patriot. The remains, he claimed, were those of Nazi collaborators, killed by the Resistance and entrusted to himself for disposal. The gullible gendarmes swallowed this whopper whole and released Petiot, who immediately fled Paris with his wife.

He remained at large for seven months, during which time he sent regular, pseudonymous letters to the newspaper *Resistance,* repeating his claim that the bodies were those of Nazis and traitors. In Paris, however, police were entertaining a different theory: that Petiot himself was a collaborator who had been murdering patriots on behalf of the Gestapo.

The truth finally came to light when Petiot was arrested after seven months on the lam. Though perceived by his Parisian neighbors as a prosperous, benevolent physician, the forty-seven-year-old Petiot had a history of criminal behavior going back to World War I, when he was convicted of black marketeering. Later, as mayor of the town of Villeneuve, he had been arrested for drug peddling. He was also a suspect in the mysterious disappearance of a pregnant servant girl. But nothing in his past compared to the outrages he had been perpetrating in his Rue Le Sueur residence.

The murders, it turned out, had nothing to do with politics at all. The victims were neither Nazis nor French patriots. Greed was the sole motive behind Petiot's atrocities. The victims were wealthy Jews desperate to flee occupied France. Posing as a Resistance leader, Petiot offered to smuggle them out of the country—for a fee. When the unsuspecting victims showed up at his house—laden with all their valuables—Petiot administered a "typhoid inoculation" that was spiked with strychnine. Then he placed them in a sealed chamber. After observing their death agonies through a peephole, he disposed of their remains in his furnace. The valuables he netted through this unspeakable swindle amounted to nearly a million English pounds.

Petiot's 1946 trial was one of the most sensational in modern French history. The defendant himself—by turns witty and withering, charming and arrogant—put on quite a show, though his histrionics failed to beguile the judge and jury. The "greatest criminal affair of the century" (as the

French papers dubbed it) ended on May 26, 1946, when Marcel Petiot, still maintaining his innocence, went to the guillotine.

For an interesting (if overly arty) dramatization of the case, curious viewers might check out the 1992 French movie *Docteur Petiot,* starring Michel Serrault.

> "There is a legend that you all know well: the story of the shipwreckers. Cruel men placed lanterns on the cliffs to lure ashore ships in distress. The sailors, confident, never suspecting that such evil deceit could exist, sailed onto the reefs and died, and those who had pretended to lead them to safety filled their coffers with the spoils of their foul deeds. Petiot is just that: the false savior, the false refuge. He lured the desperate, the frightened, the hunted, and he killed them by turning their instincts for self-preservation against them."
>
> **PIERRE VERON,**
> *lawyer at the trial of Dr. Marcel Petiot*

PHASES

The step-by-step pattern that the typical serial killer follows—from the time he first starts brooding on his crime through the inevitable letdown of its aftermath—has been charted by Dr. Joel Norris, one of the country's leading experts on the subject. According to Norris, the seven "key phases" of serial murder are as follows:

1. *The Aura Phase.* The process begins when the potential killer starts to withdraw into a private world of perverted fantasy. From the outside,

he may appear to be perfectly normal. Inside his head, however, he exists in a kind of twisted twilight zone. His grasp on reality loosens as his mind becomes increasingly dominated by daydreams of death and destruction. Gradually, the need to act out his demented fantasies becomes an overwhelming compulsion.

2. *The Trolling Phase.* Like a fisherman casting out his line and trolling for a catch, the killer now begins to seek out a victim, focusing on those places where he is most likely to encounter the precise kind of person that his sick needs require. He may stake out a schoolyard, cruise a red-light district, patronize a popular pickup spot, or stalk a local lovers' lane. Eventually, he will zero in on a target.

3. *The Wooing Phase.* In some cases, the killer will simply strike without warning—snatching a victim off the street or breaking into a house and slaying everyone inside. Often, however, the killer will derive a depraved satisfaction from luring his victims into his clutches— lulling them into a false sense of security, tricking them into lowering their defenses. Ted **Bundy** seemed so disarmingly clean-cut and normal that he had no trouble talking young women into his death car. Other killers, like John Wayne **Gacy**, seduce their victims with the promise of money or a job or a place to spend the night. In November 1995, a drifter named Glen Rogers allegedly committed five murders during an interstate killing spree. According to those who knew him, Rogers was a master at wooing his victims. "He could talk a person into anything," one acquaintance told the police. "A ride home from the bar. A place to crash for a few days. A woman's affections." (Rogers has not yet been tried and denies the charges.)

4. *The Capture Phase.* The next step is to spring the trap that the killer has set for his victims. Seeing their terrified reactions as the true horror of their situation suddenly hits home is part of his sadistic game. This is the moment when—having accepted a lift from an affable stranger who has offered you a ride home—you suddenly notice that the car is headed in the wrong direction and that the door handle on the passenger side has been removed, so that there is no possibility of escape. Or when the handsome one-night stand who has handcuffed

you to the bedposts for some kinky fun and games smilingly tells you that he has no intention of releasing you—ever.

5. *The Murder.* If killing is a substitute for sex, as it is for so many serial murderers, then the moment at which they put a victim to death is the climax, the acme of pleasure toward which the whole process has been building ever since they began fantasizing about the crime. (Indeed, it's not uncommon for sexual psychopaths to experience an orgasm while murdering their victims.) And just as normal people have their particular sexual pleasures—their favorite positions or ways of being touched—serial killers have their own homicidal preferences, some enjoying strangulation, others bludgeoning or slashing or death by slow torture.

6. *The Totem Phase.* Like a sexual climax, the murder is an intense but transient pleasure for the serial killer. To prolong the experience and help him relive it in fantasy during the fallow period before his next crime, he will often remove a souvenir or "totemic" object associated with the victim. This may be anything from a wallet to a body part (see **Trophies**).

7. *The Depression Phase.* In the aftermath of the murder, the serial killer often experiences an emotional letdown that is the equivalent of what the French call postcoital *tristesse.* This state can be so severe that the killer may actually attempt suicide. Unfortunately, a more common response is a renewed desire to commit murder again—a growing need for a fix of fresh blood (see **Post-Homicidal Depression**).

PHOTOGRAPHS

In his chilling 1971 book, *The Family,* Ed Sanders reveals that Charles **Manson** and his creepy-crawly followers allegedly made snuff movies with stolen super-8mm cameras—real-life splatter films depicting human sacrifice, decapitations, and other atrocities. Though Sanders was never able to confirm this story (he was offered a reel of reputed Manson porn by one unnamed source but couldn't come up with the $250,000 asking price), the rumor itself embodies an unnerving truth about serial killers. In the same way that ordinary people like to record life's special moments on film (weddings, birthday parties, family vacations) many serial killers enjoy taking pictures of their victims, dead and alive, to keep as twisted souvenirs—morbid mementoes to help them relive the thrill of their murders.

When police entered the squalid apartment of Jeffrey **Dahmer,** they were staggered to find a cache of Polaroid pictures showing male corpses in various stages of dismemberment. One photo was of a body slit from breastbone to groin like a gutted deer. Another showed a corpse eaten away by acid from the nipples down. Perhaps the most shocking of all was described by Milwaukee journalist Anne E. Schwartz: a photograph of "a bleached skeleton [with] the flesh on the head, hands, and feet . . . left perfectly intact."

In the mid-1960s, the British **Killer Couple** Ian Brady and Myra Hindley—aka the **Moors Murderers**—kidnapped a ten-year-old girl and forced her to pose for pornographic snapshots before strangling her to death. They also made an audiotape of the child's piteous pleas for mercy—a recording so heart wrenching that when it was played in court during the murder trial, even hardened policemen wept openly.

As technology has progressed over the years, the recording techniques of serial killers have become increasingly sophisticated. Twenty years after the "Moors Murders" case, Leonard Lake and Charles Ng began kidnapping women and imprisoning them in an underground bunker in Northern California (see **Partners**). The bunker was outfitted with a set of state-of-the-art video equipment, which Lake had stolen from the home of a San Francisco photographer named Harvey Dubs. Lake and Ng used the equipment to record the rape, torture, and murder of three young women—including Dubs's wife, Deborah.

Harvey Murray Glatman, Snuff Photographer

In 1960, the distinguished British director Michael Powell—renowned for his beautiful ballet fantasy, *The Red Shoes*—released a film that so incensed both the public and critics that it effectively ended his career. It was called *Peeping Tom,* a movie about a sadistic voyeur who films his victims as he is stabbing them to death with a lethal camera tripod (see

Harvey Murray Glatman;
from *52 Famous Murderers*
trading cards
(Courtesy of Roger Worsham)

Movies). What sort of sick mind—asked the outraged reviewers—could have dreamed up such a story? But, in fact, just a year before *Peeping Tom* came out, an American psycho named Harvey Murray Glatman had been put to death at San Quentin for crimes shockingly like the ones depicted in the film.

Even as an adolescent, Glatman showed twisted sexual tendencies. His favorite form of masturbation was autoerotic asphyxiation—achieving sexual release while dangling by his neck from a rope tied to an attic rafter. A family physician assured Glatman's mother that her son would outgrow this bizarre practice. As Glatman matured, however, he continued to be obsessed by fantasies of bondage, sadism, and strangulation. At the age of twenty-nine, he set about making his depraved dreams come true.

Posing as a professional photographer, he managed to persuade a series of struggling young models that he was going to take their photos for the covers of the kind of sleazy detective magazines that were so popular back in the 1950s. Since these covers typically featured bound and helpless young women, the models allowed Glatman to truss them up and gag them. They were further disarmed by his appearance—Glatman looked like a creepy but essentially harmless nerd. (If a movie were ever made about his case, Rick Moranis would be the inevitable casting choice.)

Once he had the women in his power, Glatman proceeded to strip and photograph them, rape them at gunpoint, and take more photos of their terrified looks as the true horror of their situation finally dawned on them. Then he strangled them with a length of rope and disposed of their bodies in the desert.

Altogether, Glatman murdered three young women in this way. He tried to set up a fourth deadly photo session—but this time, the intended victim proved to be more than he could handle. When Glatman pulled his pistol on her in his car, she lunged at him, wrestled the weapon away, and held him at gunpoint until the police arrived.

In custody, Glatman confessed in lengthy detail. He was convicted after a three-day trial in November 1958 and received his death sentence with a philosophical shrug. "It's better this way," he remarked.

Few people would have argued with him.

PIED PIPERS

According to German legend, the Pied Piper lured the rats out of the medieval town of Hamelin by playing a magical tune on his flute. When the townspeople refused to pay him, he piped his siren song again, this time leading all the children away and (as one especially disturbing version of the story goes) sealing them up in a cave where they were entombed forever.

Over the years, scholars have tried to discover a historical basis for the tale. In his 1992 book *A World Lit Only by Fire,* for example, author William Manchester argues that the real-life model for the legendary figure was a fifteenth-century lust murderer who kidnapped and killed 130 children. It's impossible to judge the validity of this claim. Still, there's reason to believe that there might have been a true-life Pied Piper. Certainly, our own era has produced a number of flesh-and-blood examples—strangely charismatic misfits who have used some sort of intoxicating enticement to lead young people horribly astray.

The most infamous of these characters is Charles **Manson.** At the height of the flower-child era, this psychopathic ex-con managed to mesmerize a group of young hippie followers with a seductive mix of drugs, sex, and occult mumbo-jumbo. Like the mythical Pied Piper, he was a musician (of sorts). And—also like the Piper—he believed he had been cheated of his just reward for his musical talents.

Determined to become a rock star, he toadied his way into contact with such industry insiders as the Beach Boys' Dennis Wilson and even saw one of his songs performed on a Beach Boys album. But he failed to land the lucrative recording contract that he craved. After this snub, Manson began to formulate his murder plans—partly to realize his deranged apocalyptic visions, and partly, some say, to get revenge against music producer Terry Melcher, whom he blamed for his failures.

Manson prepared his "family" to go on a homicidal rampage. Once again, music played a part. To Manson's unhinged mind, the songs from the Beatles' *White Album*—especially "Helter Skelter"—were actually coded messages relating personally to him. Manson used his wacko interpretations of the songs to help program his disciples to carry out his plans. When he was done, seven people were dead, all of them hacked to death.

Another modern-day Pied Piper was Dean Corll, nicknamed the "Candy Man" for his habit of handing out free treats to neighborhood children while working at his family's confectionery company. Behind that innocent veneer, Corll was an insanely sadistic gay sex killer who employed a teenage accomplice named Elmer Wayne Henley to procure male victims. Enticed to Corll's apartment in suburban Houston with the promise of glue-sniffing parties, the unwitting young men would be overpowered by Corll, then subjected to hours of unspeakable sexual torture and mutilation before being killed. Corll himself was eventually murdered by Henley, who then led police to the moldering remains of twenty-seven young men, victims of the abominable "Candy Man."

Another modern murderer was explicitly compared to the old German legend by the press. This was Charles Schmid, a mid-1960s thrill killer dubbed the "Pied Piper of Tucson."

In the eyes of most of those who knew him, Schmid was just plain bizarre. He dyed his hair jet black and shaped it into a towering pompadour (like his idol, Elvis), wore heavy pancake makeup over his unwashed face, painted his mouth with white lipstick, and sported a fake "beauty mark" fashioned from a quarter-inch circle of dark putty. And then there was his walk—an odd, staggering gait that resulted from his habit of stuffing his boots with rags, cardboard, and crumpled beer cans to boost his undersized stature.

For the bored and restless teens who cruised the Tucson strip known as the Speedway, however, the twenty-two-year-old "Smitty" was a charismatic rebel. He enticed them into his crackpot little orbit with booze and sex and tantalizing (if totally fictitious) tales of his secret life involving the Hell's Angels, drug-running, and the Mafia.

He led his teenage followers into a deadly nightmare in mid-1964, when he convinced two of his acolytes to help him lure a fifteen-year-old girl out into the desert. There he raped the girl and crushed her skull with a rock. A year later he murdered his girlfriend and her thirteen-year-old sister. Some of his followers knew about these murders but for months refused to tell the police, so devoted were they to their psychopathic leader. Eventually, however, Smitty was turned in by a guilt-ridden accomplice. While awaiting execution in the Arizona penitentiary, he was fatally stabbed in the face and chest by another inmate.

Shortly after his arrest at the end of 1965, a pop tune hit the charts that seemed to be an eerie reflection of the Schmid phenomenon. Titled, appropriately enough, "The Pied Piper," and sung by Crispian St. Peters, its chorus went: "Hey, c'mon, babe, follow me/I'm the Pied Piper, follow me/I'm the Pied Piper/And I'll show you where it's at."

The Lure of the Piper

Given her fascination with the Gothic and grotesque, it's no surprise that author Joyce Carol Oates was attracted to the Schmid case, using it as the basis for her classic 1966 short story "Where Are You Going, Where Have You Been?" In Oates's version, an ineffably creepy character named Arnold Friend—obviously modeled on Schmid—shows up at the home of a teenaged girl named Connie one Sunday afternoon while her family is away and spirits her off to a nameless, but clearly awful, fate.

In 1985, Oates's tale was made into a handsome film called *Smooth Talk,* starring Treat Williams as Arnold and Laura Dern as Connie. Though the film is an intelligent adaptation of its source, horror buffs are likely to find it disappointingly artsy.

The opposite problem afflicts two other films based on the Schmid story, both of which are hopelessly schlocky affairs: *The Todd Killings,* a low-budget 1971 shocker that changes Schmid into a character named Skipper

Todd but otherwise hews fairly close to the facts; and *Dead Beat* (1994), which focuses on a lonely high-schooler named Rudy who moves to Albuquerque, where he gets involved with a Schmid-like figure named Kit.

PLUMBING

Clogged pipes have proven to be the undoing of more than one serial killer. In February 1983, residents of a small North London apartment house complained that their toilets wouldn't flush. When a plumber showed up to check out the problem, he opened a nearby manhole and descended into the sewer. As expected, he found a blocked drainpipe leading from the building. What he couldn't possibly have anticipated was the nature of the obstruction—a reeking mass of putrefying flesh, mixed with human finger bones. It didn't take long for police to discover the source of this nightmarish glop. It had come from the upstairs flat of a thirty-seven-year-old **Civil Servant** named Dennis **Nilsen,** who—just several days earlier—had murdered and butchered his fifteenth homosexual victim, then flushed the remains down his toilet.

A similar grisly discovery had been made in West Germany seven years earlier. In July 1976, police in the city of Duisburg were conducting a door-to-door search for a missing four-year-old girl. In the course of interviewing one old man, they heard a bizarre story. According to the old man, a fellow tenant of his apartment building—a lavatory attendant named Joachim Kroll—had warned him not to use the communal bathroom on their floor because the toilet was backed up. What made the story so weird was Kroll's explanation of the plumbing problem. He had casually mentioned that the toilet was blocked "with guts."

The police summoned a plumber, who applied a plunger to the clogged toilet. Up came a mass of human entrails and other viscera. Inside Kroll's apartment, police found several freezer bags full of human flesh and a child's hand simmering in a saucepan. Like his British counterpart, Dennis Nilsen, Kroll had been murdering for a long time—since 1955. In all, the German cannibal and sex killer was responsible for fourteen homicides.

POETRY

Among the ranks of infamous serial killers there have been some rather creative individuals. John Wayne **Gacy** was a prolific painter whose works have become trendy collectibles (see **Art**). Charles **Manson** has composed dozens of **Songs,** some of which have been recorded by bands like Guns N' Roses and the Lemonheads. Ed **Gein** crafted everything from belts to wastebaskets to soup bowls out of the exhumed and dismembered corpses of middle-aged women. So it's not entirely surprising that some serial killers have tried their hands at poetry. It's also not surprising that their poetry is really bad.

Dennis **Nilsen** wrote a whole slew of verse in homage to the young men he strangled, dismembered, and flushed down the toilet. Here's a typical example, addressed to one of his dead victims: "I try to smile / Despite the vengeance looking at me, / Covered in your tomato paste, / A man of many parts / I try to forget. / Even the perfume of your passing / Lingers on. / More problems now / With all your bits and pieces. . . ."

As a teenager, Long Islander Joel Rifkin—who murdered and dismembered at least seventeen prostitutes—obviously saw himself as some sort of knight in shining armor, as this scrap of adolescent doggerel suggests: "A siren temptress calls me near / a stranger beyond darkness haze / pleading from within the shadows / and though I be helpless to help her / help her I must." And the ever-romantic Ted **Bundy** beguiled his lovers with greeting-card verse like: "I send you this kiss / deliver this body to hold. / I sleep with you tonight / with words of love untold."

What woman could resist such lyrical power?

If the verse written by serial killers has been invariably awful, the case is very different when it comes to poetry *about* serial killers. Some outstanding writers have produced powerful works that delve into the twisted minds of psychopathic killers. This tradition extends at least as far back as Robert Browning's 1842 "Porphyria's Lover," whose demented speaker conveys his love for his girlfriend by winding her long blond hair around her "little throat" and strangling her to death. More recent poets have also explored the psychology of sociopathic murderers in their work. These include Ai's "The Good Shepherd: Atlanta, 1981" (about the Atlanta Child Murders) from her 1986 book, *Sin;* Frank Bidart's profoundly unsettling "Herbert

White," which can be found in his 1991 collection, *In the Western Night;* and Thom Gunn's "Troubadour: Songs for Jeffrey **Dahmer**" from his 2001 volume, *Boss Cupid.*

A Perverse Verse

Dr. J. Paul de River's classic forensic text, *The Sexual Criminal* (1949), includes a chapter called "The Poetic Nature of the Sado-Masochist," which reprints a number of works by convicted sex offenders. Reprinted below is one example, entitled "Uncensored Exotics." As poetry it's no "Gunga Din," but it does offer insight into the workings of one psychopathic mind:

> *Vainly I crouch at the fireside,*
> *For the flames on the hearth cannot warm me.*
> *Vainly I put on coats*
> *Against the cold of the star winds . . .*
>
> *And my bones are chilled within me*
> *And my blood is become as water.*
> *And now from the void behind me*
>
> *Comes the piping of the piper,*
> *That senseless, complaining piping,*
> *That tuneless, high, thin piping. . . .*
>
> *Then, with a shout, I surrender*
> *And leap to do the bidding.*
> *From the wall I snatch my weapons*
> *And rush from the house to the forest.*
> *Where the road winds down the mountain,*
> *Panting I lie in ambush,*
> *Waiting for some poor traveller*
> *Who shall bring me my release.*
> *When he comes with laggard footsteps,*
> *Sudden and fierce is my onslaught.*
> *Like a beast I overcome him*
> *And utterly destroy him.*
> *And I cut out his heart and eat it,*
> *And I guzzle his blood like nectar,*

And I cut off his head and scalp him,
And hang his scalp at my belt.
Homeward I walk through the snowdrifts,
And my heart is warm within me,
And my blood and bones are new again
And the star winds cease to chill me. . . .

POISONERS

Compared to the average lust murderer who goes in for torture, mutilation, and evisceration, serial killers who quietly dispatch their victims with poison seem like models of refinement. When it comes to racking up bodies, however, serial poisoners can be every bit as deadly as any blood-crazed psycho.

Particularly back in the 1800s—when forensic pathology was still in its infancy—poisoners could get away with murder for years, since their victims appeared to drop dead of natural causes. Homicidal **Housekeepers** like Anna Zwanziger and Helene Jegado knocked off dozens of people by serving them arsenic-spiked food. As late as the 1930s, a sociopathic **Nurse** named Anna Marie Hahn was dishing out lethal doses of arsenic to her patients in Cincinnati's German community, murdering as many as eleven elderly men over a five-year period. (In 1938, Hahn became the first woman to die in Ohio's electric chair.)

Though women have a particular preference for poison, they certainly don't have a monopoly on this insidious murder method. In the latter half of the nineteenth century, England was home to a trio of men who left a trail of poisoned corpses in their wake: Dr. William Palmer (who used antimony tartrate and strychnine to get ride of bothersome relatives and insistent creditors); George Chapman (who poisoned a succession of lovers, also with antimony); and Dr. Thomas Neill Cream (who prescribed strychnine pills to four London prostitutes and claimed he was **Jack the Ripper**).

The deadly tradition of these Victorian villains was carried on by a twentieth-century British youth named Graham Young. Curious about the effects of antimony tartrate on the human body, the fourteen-year-old chemistry buff (and psychopath) began lacing his family's food with the deadly substance, eventually killing his stepmother. Found guilty but insane in 1962, he spent the following nine years in a mental asylum. No sooner was he released in 1971 than he took a job at a photographic supply firm and began poisoning fellow employees with thalium. By the time investigators figured out what was going on, five of Young's co-workers had fallen violently ill and two of them had died after days of agony. "I could have killed them all if I wished," Young told the arresting officers.

Young's crimes were the basis of *The Young Poisoner's Handbook,* a 1996 film praised by *New York Times* movie critic Janet Maslin for its "assured style, malevolent wit, and uncompromising intelligence."

POLITICAL CORRECTNESS

Since PC etiquette requires language and behavior that are completely inoffensive, serial killers are about as *in*correct as it's possible for people to be. Bizarrely enough, however, at least one multiple murderer—a young Californian named John Linley Frazier—acted out of his own demented sense of political correctness. From his warped point of view, he was killing to protect the environment.

A high school dropout who worked as an auto mechanic, Frazier evolved into an ecological zealot, apparently under the influence of the psychedelic drugs he began ingesting in the late 1960s. Quitting his job (because he believed that cars contributed to "the death cycle of the planet"), he began drifting from commune to commune. His fierce, obsessive rants against environmental destruction, however, clashed with the mellowed-out sensibilities of his newfound hippie friends, and Frazier soon found himself living like a hermit in a six-foot-square shack in the Northern California woods.

About half a mile away from the shack stood the home of an eye surgeon named Victor Ohta. In the fall of 1970, Frazier broke into the Ohtas' house and—in his paranoia—decided that the family was the evil personification of American materialism in its most pernicious form. Returning shortly afterward with a .38 revolver, Frazier managed to tie up the entire family (father, mother, and two sons), plus Dr. Ohta's secretary. After lecturing them on the damage done to the environment by capitalistic society, Frazier shot and killed all five people and dumped their bodies in the swimming pool. Next, he typed out a note promising death to all those who would "ruin the environment," set the house on fire, and fled.

With the help of local hippies—who recognized the crackpot ideas in the note as Frazier's—police quickly nabbed the suspect. During his 1971 trial, Frazier showed up in court with one side of his head shaved completely bald, the other side sporting shoulder-length hair and half a beard. In spite of his flagrantly bizarre behavior, he was ruled sane and sentenced to the gas chamber. Frazier appeared to welcome the decision, since, as he said, he preferred death to spending his life under the control of "fascist pigs." When the Supreme Court abolished capital punishment, however, his sentence was commuted to life imprisonment.

PORNOGRAPHY

See **X-Rated.**

POST-HOMICIDAL DEPRESSION

Sick as it sounds, the fact is that for many serial killers murder is a substitute for sex. The act of plunging a sharp, pointed object into the writhing body of another person is the equivalent of intercourse. Many lust murderers actually achieve orgasm while stabbing (or beating or strangling) their victims to death. So it's not surprising that following a murder, many serial killers experience the equivalent of postcoital depression—the emotional letdown that sometimes descends after sex.

Indeed, so common is this experience among lust murderers that one expert on the subject, Dr. Joel Norris, actually describes depression as one of the standard **Phases** of serial murder. According to Dr. Norris, many serial killers suffer severe bouts of dejection following a murder because the killing fails to live up to their fantasies. Moreover, even the most cold-blooded killers can sometimes be hit with a belated sense of horror and guilt after perpetrating a particularly vicious crime. Occasionally, they suffer such intense despair that they actually attempt suicide (see **Death Wish**).

Whatever the cause of their depression, the response is often a binge of drinking or drug taking, which dulls their sense of emptiness and despair. Soon their inner compulsions rise up again. Like addicts who can't stop getting high—even though they know that they will suffer an inevitable crash—they go prowling for their next "fix" of blood.

POWER TOOLS

The chain saw is the favorite weapon of serial killers. At least that's what you'd think if your concept of serial killers came entirely from the movies. During the 1970s, Hollywood churned out a spate of low-budget splatter films with titles like *Driller Killer, The Toolbox Murders, The Bloody Mutilators,* and *The Ghastly Ones.* The psychos in these movies wielded more power tools than Tim Allen on *Home Improvement:* drills, bucksaws, chain saws, you name it. The power-tool motif made it to the big time in a pair of Brian De Palma movies from the early 1980s—*Body Double* (featuring an electric drill bit large enough to qualify for *The Guinness Book of World Records)* and *Scarface* (which contains what is arguably the most harrowing chain-saw mutilation sequence in cinematic history).

Though the very first chain-saw murder movie was Wes Craven's pioneering splatter film *The Last House on the Left* (1971), the film that made this particular piece of equipment de rigueur for cinematic psychos was Tobe Hooper's 1975 cult classic, *The Texas Chainsaw Massacre.* Like *Psycho* and *The Silence of the Lambs,* Hooper's masterwork was inspired by the horrific deeds of the Wisconsin ghoul, Edward **Gein.** Indeed, the original advertisements for the film claimed that it was entirely factual. "What happened is true! Now see the movie that is just as real!" The real truth, however, is that Hooper's film is only loosely—*very* loosely—based on reality. Among other things, Ed Gein didn't even *own* a chain saw. The only tools he is known to have employed were his trusty spade (for exhuming female corpses) and a big-bladed hunting knife (for dismembering them).

It's easy to see why the makers of in-your-face splatter movies are attracted to chain saws—they are big, loud, and exceptionally scary-looking (the chain saws, that is, though the description undoubtedly applies to some of the filmmakers, too). For those same reasons, however, chain saws do not make very suitable weapons for real-life serial killers. After all, it's hard to sneak into a house in a nice residential neighborhood and quietly dismember an entire family with a chain saw. Chain saws also make notoriously poor concealed weapons.

There is, however, at least one serial killer who used a power saw on his victims, albeit posthumously. In the 1980s, a Swedish physician named Teet Haerm, who worked as a medical examiner for the Stockholm police, was accused of the serial murder of seven prostitutes. But his outrages didn't stop there. After killing his victims, he beheaded and dismembered their bodies with a power saw.

Then—like another serial-killer physician, the fictional Hannibal "the Cannibal" Lecter—Dr. Haerm devoured portions of their flesh.

PROFILING

During the 1950s, New York was terrorized by an anonymous psycho— dubbed the "Mad Bomber" by the press—who planted dozens of home-made explosives around the city. Stymied in their investigation, police turned to a psychiatric whiz named James Brussel. After studying all the available evidence, Dr. Brussel deduced that the unknown madman would turn out to be a middle-aged paranoiac of Eastern European descent who lived in Connecticut with a maiden aunt or sister, was afflicted with a serious physical illness like tuberculosis, attended church regularly, went out of his way to behave in a polite, soft-spoken manner, and would be wearing a double-breasted suit (buttoned) when arrested.

Thanks in large part to Brussel's description, police were able to trace the bomber, who turned out to be a well-mannered, fifty-four-year-old bachelor of Polish immigrant stock named George Metesky, who lived in Connecticut with his unmarried sisters, was a weekly churchgoer, had been treated for TB, and suffered from severe paranoia. When Metesky was led off by police, he was dressed in a blue, double-breasted suit. Buttoned.

Brussel's amazing prediction is universally acknowledged as the pioneering example of a technique that now stands as one of the most potent weapons in the war against serial killers: the psychological profiling of "unsubs" (police slang for "unknown subjects"). Building on Brussel's groundbreaking work, agents of the **FBI** Behavioral Science Unit began visiting prisons in the late 1970s. They interviewed several dozen of America's most infamous killers in an effort to figure out what makes these monsters tick. The agents found that serial murderers can be roughly divided into two categories. The *organized* type is a methodical killer who carefully plans his crimes, stalks his prey, brings along his weapon of choice, then—once he has his victim in his power—engages in slow, sadistic murder. By contrast, the *disorganized* killer tends to be subject to sudden, overwhelming impulses, chooses his victims spontaneously, then quickly overpowers and kills them with whatever weapons are at hand.

Beyond these broad classifications, each case taken on by the FBI's crack team of "mind hunters" receives highly individualized attention. When local law officers are faced with a particularly savage and baffling crime, they can—as an ultimate resort—submit a request to the FBI's Criminal Personality Profiling Program. If the Bureau decides to accept the case, a profiler will make a close study of all the facts he receives, then send back a highly detailed, multipage report containing his analysis of the unsub. Since profiles are a form of highly educated guesswork, involving as much intuition as science, they sometimes miss their mark. But when they are accurate—which is surprisingly often—they can seem uncanny.

Stumped by the brutal murder of a twelve-year-old girl, for example, police in a small Southern town contacted renowned FBI profiler John Douglas, who came up with this sketch of the unsub: a divorced white man who drove a black or blue car, worked at a "macho laborer's job," was dishonorably discharged from the military, knew the victim, and had a previous record of sex crimes. Following through on this lead, police soon arrested the culprit—a divorced white male who drove a blue Pinto, cut tree limbs for a living, had been kicked out of the army, had done work at the victim's house, and was implicated in an earlier rape case.

Sherlock Holmes couldn't have done it any better.

PROSTITUTES

It comes as no surprise to learn that prostitutes are prime targets of serial killers. For one thing, hookers have no compunctions about going off to isolated places with strange men (indeed, it's part of the job description). For another, since so many working girls are runaways, drifters, and druggies, nobody becomes very concerned—or even notices—when they disappear or turn up dead. Finally—for those twisted, often impotent lust killers who see all women as "sluts"—prostitutes epitomize everything they most hate and fear about sex. In the demented view of these psychos, these prostitutes "deserve to die."

From the very beginning of modern serial murder, killers have seized on the vulnerability of prostitutes. In the 1880s, **Jack the Ripper** set the pattern for future generations of night-stalking butchers by slaughtering a series of harlots. His deadly descendants include Dr. Thomas Neill Cream (who deviated from the usual pattern by poisoning his victims instead of slashing them to pieces), the still-unidentified "Jack the Stripper," and Peter Sutcliffe, who believed he was doing the Lord's work in ridding the world of whores. Dr. Teet Haerm of Sweden also believed that he was engaged in a righteous cause. During the 1980s, he killed, dismembered, and occasionally cannibalized a string of Stockholm hookers in order—so he claimed—to clean the streets of sin.

One of the more sensational cases of the serial murder of prostitutes in recent years occurred in 1990, when a forty-five-year old man named Arthur Shawcross was accused of the mutilation and murder of ten hookers in Rochester, New York. According to Shawcross, he killed one woman because she bit him, another because she made too much noise during sex, a third for trying to steal his wallet, and a fourth because she called him a "wimp." Like a number of other serial killers, Shawcross insisted that he had **Multiple Personalities,** and was possessed by the reincarnated spirit of a thirteenth-century English cannibal named Ariemes, who had taught him to dine on human flesh. (Shawcross claimed to have eaten the body parts of several of his victims.)

Not all of Shawcross's victims were prostitutes; he also preyed on children. So did another psycho-killer, the South African serial murderer Stewart Wilken, whose victims were more or less equally divided between pubescent boys and female prostitutes. During a seven-year span between February 1990 and January 1997, Wilken murdered ten victims in the coastal town of Port Elizabeth, usually by strangulation. He also routinely engaged in necrophiliac sex, sometimes returning to a dump site to have sex with the victim's decomposing corpse. In at least one case, he engaged in cannibalism, slicing off the nipples of a forty-two-year-old prostitute and eating them on the spot. And to top off the list of his enormities, he murdered his own ten-year-old daughter, stripped her naked, and slept beside the corpse until it mummified. When finally arrested, he offered a self-assessment that stands as one of the greatest understatements on record.

"I am sick," he told his interrogators.

> "The women I killed were filth—bastard prostitutes who were littering the streets.
> I was just cleaning up the place a bit."
>
> PETER "YORKSHIRE RIPPER" SUTCLIFFE

PSYCHOTICS

Thanks in large part to the Alfred Hitchcock 1960 horror masterpiece, the word *psycho* is routinely used in reference to serial killers. There are two very different mental conditions, however, that use *psycho* as a prefix: *psychotic* and *psychopath*.

The first of these terms refers to an extreme form of personality disintegration: basically what clinicians call paranoid schizophrenia. People afflicted with this severe mental illness have lost touch with reality. They suffer from bizarre visions, grotesque delusions, and a variety of terrifying hallucinations—visual, auditory, even olfactory. They see, hear, even smell things that exist only inside their own deeply disordered minds. Ed **Gein,** for example, saw flocks of buzzards squatting in tree limbs, heard laughter emanating from dead leaves, and smelled the stench of rotting flesh wafting up from the ground. Another psychotic, Herbert Mullin, committed a string of random murders in obedience to a voice that commanded him to kill in order to stave off a cataclysmic earthquake.

The vast majority of psychotics are not prone to violence, however, and only a small minority of serial killers fall into this category.

Most are not psychotics but *psychopaths.* (See **Mask of Sanity.**)

PYROMANIA

Along with **Animal Torture** and protracted **Bed-Wetting,** starting fires is one of the three early warning signals of future homicidal mania (see **Triad**). So it's not surprising that some serial killers continue their pyromaniac activities as grown-ups. After all, destruction is the serial killer's raison d'être. Human beings are his ultimate target, but when a living victim isn't readily available, an inanimate object will do. Torching a building or two is a common way for a serial killer to satisfy his urge to annihilate.

Back in the late 1800s, Thomas Piper—the "Boston Belfry Murderer," who fatally bludgeoned and raped four victims (including a five-year-old girl)—confessed that in between his frenzied outbursts of lust murder, he was fond of setting fire to some of the city's most prominent buildings, including Concord Hall. Since then, arson has been a favorite form of amusement for a long line of serial killers, from turn-of-the-century killer-nurse Jane **Toppan,** to the "Monster of Düsseldorf," Peter **Kürten,** to such recent psychos as David "Son of Sam" **Berkowitz** and Ottis Toole (Henry Lee **Lucas**'s partner in crime).

The ferociously nihilistic Toole might have been speaking for all killers of this kind when he explained why he felt compelled to burn down houses. "I just hated to see them standing there," he said.

QUAKER

Partly because the term *serial killer* came into common usage only within the last twenty or so years—and partly because human beings have a natural tendency to romanticize the past—people tend to assume that serial homicide is a strictly contemporary phenomenon. In point of fact, America had plenty of multiple murderers in the good old days. They just weren't called serial killers—or even necessarily regarded as criminals.

A case in point can be found in the 1837 bestselling novel *Nick of the Woods* by Robert Montgomery Bird. The title character—whose real name, aptly enough, is Nathan Slaughter—is, of all things, a Pennsylvania Quaker. Despite belonging to a religion that promotes pacifism, Nathan is a confirmed Indian hater, who has come to the Kentucky wilderness for the express purpose of conducting a bloody campaign against Native Americans. Throughout the novel, he engages in gruesome acts of violence, all described in loving detail. At one point, for example, he attacks a chief named Wenonga. After burying a tomahawk in his enemy's brain, he grabs a knife and scalps the chief. Then—still not satisfied—Nathan proceeds to draw "the knife over the dead man's breast, dividing skin, cartilage, and even bone, so sharp was the blade and so powerful the hand that urged it."

To be sure, Nathan is a fictional character. But he reflects a historical reality. Many Americans believe that we are living in a time of unprecedented violence. But bloodshed and mayhem were no less endemic to our society a hundred years ago than they are today. On the contrary. The history of the American frontier—with its appalling record of lynchings, massacres, shootings, and other everyday barbarities—makes our own time seem like a Golden Age. Back in the 1800s, a man with a taste for human blood could go out into the wilderness and satisfy his sadistic cravings to his heart's content—as long as his victims weren't white. He might even be regarded as a hero. Certainly that was how nineteenth-century readers viewed Nathan Slaughter. To modern eyes, however, he looks somewhat different. As one critic puts it, he resembles a "Quaker serial killer."

QUARRY

An obsessed big-game hunter—who has bagged everything from Bengal tigers to Alaskan grizzlies—grows bored of ordinary prey. He seeks an exciting new challenge, the ultimate thrill. He buys a small South American island and stocks it with castaways and shipwreck survivors. He begins to hunt the only animal that possesses courage, cunning, and the ability to reason: man.

This is the premise of Richard Connell's prizewinning short story, "The Most Dangerous Game." At the time of its publication in 1924, the tale was perceived as an exercise in sardonic imagination, its kill-crazed villain—a Russian count named Zaroff—as a chilling embodiment of the hunting instinct gone mad.

Unfortunately, the hunting of humans has become an all-too-common reality, as serial killers stalk, trap, and butcher their human quarry with all the methodical madness of Connell's fictitious monster.

Serial killers of the so-called organized type (see **Profiling**) pursue their quarry in a frighteningly systematic way. Arming themselves with their chosen weapons, they stalk their favorite hunting grounds in search of the easiest prey—unescorted women, female hitchhikers, prostitutes of either sex, unsupervised children. Then they pounce, snaring their victims by force or deception.

Perhaps the most unnerving parallel between serial killers and big-game hunters is their shared fondness for taking **Trophies.** Though some serial killers are satisfied with saving mementoes like the wallets or photographs of their victims, others collect and preserve body parts. Edward **Gein**—the most notorious of all human-trophy hunters—kept the flayed, stuffed, and mounted faces of women hanging on his bedroom walls (very much in the manner of Connell's crazy Count Zaroff, who decorates his trophy room with the heads of his human victims).

Between 1973 and 1983, an Alaskan outdoorsman named Robert Hansen indulged in his own depraved version of "The Most Dangerous Game." Abducting prostitutes to the wilderness outside Anchorage, he would strip and rape them, then force them to flee through the woods while he stalked them with a knife, bow and arrow, or hunting rifle. Hansen was ultimately convicted of four savage murders, though his actual tally may have been as high as seventeen.

> " 'Oh,' said the general, 'it supplies me with the
> most exciting hunting in the world. No other
> hunting compares with it for an instant.
> Every day I hunt and never grow bored now,
> for I have a quarry with which I can match my wits.' "
>
> **RICHARD CONNELL,**
> *"The Most Dangerous Game"*

QUICKLIME

When Indiana police dug up the farmyard of Belle Gunness in April 1908, they uncovered more than a dozen bodies—the grisly record of years of profit-motivated murder, mostly of prospective husbands (see **Black**

Widows). Most of the corpses were drastically decomposed. A chillingly practical woman, Gunness had devised a way to expedite the putrefaction process. She had chopped each of the bodies into six sections, then treated the pieces with quicklime, a highly caustic substance that eats away at organic matter. If the search of her farmyard had occurred any later, the bodies would have been decomposed beyond the possibility of identification.

Other murderers have employed quicklime for the same purpose—eliminating the corpus delicti. Dr. H. H. **Holmes** kept a vat of the stuff in the dungeon of his Chicago "Horror Castle," where untold victims disappeared at the tail end of the nineteenth century. Fifty years later, Dr. Marcel **Petiot**—who murdered dozens of would-be refugees during the Nazi occupation of Paris—used quicklime to dissolve the corpses buried in his backyard. (Only later did he turn to another method—cremation—as a more efficient means of disposal.) John Wayne **Gacy** periodically sprinkled lime into the crawl space beneath his house to dampen the stench of the rotting male bodies accumulating in the muck.

Of course, if you're going to use quicklime for this ghoulish purpose, it helps to know something about its chemical properties. In the mid-1980s, a sixty-year-old woman named Dorothea Puente began renting rooms in her San Francisco boardinghouse to elderly welfare recipients, who subsequently vanished without a trace. Alerted by suspicious social workers, police launched an investigation and eventually discovered seven headless corpses planted in Puente's backyard garden. Though Puente had taken care to sprinkle the bodies with quicklime, she was undone by her faulty knowledge of chemical reactions. Unless lime is mixed with water, it actually acts as a kind of preservative, slowing down instead of accelerating the decomposition process. As a result, medical examiners had no trouble discovering that the victims had died from massive doses of Valium and Dalmane—evidence that helped convict the lethal landlady and send her to prison for life.

RACE AND RACISM

Say the phrase "serial killer" to most people and they will immediately conjure up mental images of Jeffrey **Dahmer**, John Wayne **Gacy**, Ted **Bundy**, Charles **Manson**—or perhaps Hannibal Lecter. In other words, white guys.

It's true that a significant majority of American serial killers are white. But there's a simple explanation for this—namely, that whites make up the majority of the U.S. population. But there have been plenty of African-American serial killers, too. According to the *New York Times*, "black serial killers occur in roughly equal—or even slightly greater—proportion to the number of blacks in the population." Recent studies show that between 13 and 22 percent of U.S. serial killers are African-American.

Among the most notorious are Coral Watts, who killed an indeterminate number of women in Houston in the early 1980s (he confessed to thirteen homicides, though he's suspected of as many as forty); Henry Louis Wallace, who strangled nine young women in North Carolina in the early 1990s; Cleophus Prince Jr. (aka the "Clairemont Killer"), who butchered a half-dozen women in San Diego during a nine-month spree beginning in January 1990; and Kendall Francois, who murdered eight women in the upstate

New York town of Poughkeepsie in the late 1990s and stashed their corpses in his attic crawl space.

Given the significant number of black psycho-killers in the U.S., why do most people assume that serial murder is an all-white phenomenon? The likeliest explanation is deep-rooted racial prejudice. Serial killers tend to stick to their own race. White psychos generally prey on white victims; blacks on black. And the sad fact is that white America isn't particularly interested in crimes involving minorities. Even the most horrific murders get far less attention from the mainstream media—and often from the police as well—when the victims are people of color.

Indeed, some serial killers have counted on this very fact in order to get away with their crimes. In the 1920s, for example, the cannibalistic pedophile Albert **Fish** prowled the inner-city slums because he knew that the police wouldn't exert themselves to investigate the disappearance of black children. More recently, Jeffrey **Dahmer** preyed mostly on African-American and Asian young men for the same reason. The discovery of Dahmer's atrocities set off major protests among black and Asian Milwaukeeans, outraged at the perceived racism of the city's police department.

Fish and Dahmer may have been exploiting the prevailing prejudices of society, but their crimes were motivated by extreme sexual depravity, not racism. The case has been otherwise with a small minority of serial murderers. The late 1970s and early 1980s in particular were a boom time for serial murders based on race, as a handful of self-styled "Aryan warriors" launched homicidal crusades against minorities. In Cleveland, a Nazi transvestite named Frank Spisak killed one black man and two whites he believed were Jews. In western New York State, white supremacist Joseph Christopher hunted down and murdered a dozen African-Americans over a three-month period (cutting out the hearts of two of his victims), while Hitler-worshipping Joseph Franklin roamed from state to state, slaughtering blacks, Jews, and interracial couples—more than thirteen victims in all.

Of course, racially inspired serial murder (like the sexually motivated variety) is not strictly a white phenomenon. In the early 1970s, a Black Muslim splinter group known as the "Death Angels" required that prospective members prove their zeal by murdering white people and taking Polaroids of their corpses. San Francisco's "Zebra" killings (so called because the victims were white and the perpetrators black) were the horrific result: fifteen men and women slain in six months. A few years later, the Chicago area was the scene of a similar string of random killings. Calling themselves "De Mau Mau," the culprits were a group of black Vietnam veterans who vented their rage against white society by slaughtering ten people, including two entire families.

The Atlanta Child Murders

Though crimes involving African-American victims often receive scant attention in the press, a notable exception was the appalling series of child murders that took place in Atlanta in the late 1970s and early 1980s. The case, which generated nationwide outrage and horror, was covered extensively by the mainstream media. Indeed, it was in a May 1981 *New York Times Magazine* article on the then-unsolved case that the recently coined term "serial killer" first appeared in a major publication.

In a two-year period between 1979 and 1981, the killer claimed twenty-nine victims. Most were children, most were male, and all were African-American. What made the investigation especially difficult was the lack of a clear pattern. Like the infamous Peter **Kürten,** the killer didn't seem to have any particular homicidal preference—usually strangling his victims, but sometimes stabbing them or bludgeoning them to death.

As the months went by and the body count rose, both the public and the media demanded a solution to what seemed to be a case of racial terrorism. Civil rights groups led the way, and President Reagan responded by setting aside federal funds to track down the killer. Meanwhile, celebrities from Muhammad Ali to Burt Reynolds offered private financial assistance. Many perceived the murders as a deranged political act, probably committed by the Ku Klux Klan. When investigators finally made an arrest, however, the suspect turned out to be not a homicidal white racist, but a young black male who fit the classic profile of a psychopathic loner.

The turning point in the case was a mysterious incident on a bridge that seemed to come straight out of the ominous 1967 ballad "Ode to Billie Joe." On the night of May 22, 1981, police officers heard something splash beneath the bridge spanning the Chattahoochee River. Moments later, they stopped a car leaving the bridge and questioned the driver, a young African-American named Wayne Williams. He became the prime suspect in the Atlanta Child Murders when police discovered the body of one of the victims in the river. Over the next month, more evidence emerged, including fibers found on the victims that matched furnishings in Williams's car and house, and animal hairs that matched his pet dog.

Also implicating him were odd personality traits reminiscent of other psychopaths. He often lied, for instance, to exaggerate his own importance, and he was fond of impersonating police officers, a favorite tactic of serial killers to win the trust of their victims. The police arrested him in June. Eventually, Williams was convicted of two counts of murder and received a life sentence for each.

Despite the convictions, many people have claimed that authorities railroaded Williams through a combination of questionable circumstantial evidence and inconclusive fiber matches. More than twenty years later, in May 2005, these skeptics got an opportunity to prove their point when police chief Louis Graham of DeKalb County reopened the investigation of the four Atlanta Child Murders in his jurisdiction. Graham, a police officer at the time of Williams's arrest, has always believed that the true culprit was the KKK.

These developments, however, may be less significant than they seem. Even if Williams is cleared of the four DeKalb County homicides, he will not be released, since the cases in Graham's jurisdiction don't include the two murders that sent Williams to prison in the first place. And the new investigation will also have to answer one crucial question: Why did the child killings suddenly stop after Williams was arrested?

RAILROADS

In the 1800s, the railroad was regarded as one of the wonders of the age, a glorious achievement celebrated in story and song. In one of his most famous poems, the great American bard Walt Whitman rhapsodized about the railroad:

> I see over my own continent the Pacific Railroad,
>   surmounting every barrier;
> I hear the locomotives rushing and roaring,
>   and the shrill steam-whistle,
> I hear the echoes reverberate through the
>   grandest scenery in the world.

For Whitman, the transcontinental railroad was a symbol of America's greatness and glory. Of course, he couldn't possibly foresee the day when it would serve as the preferred mode of transportation for roving psychopathic killers.

Carl **Panzram**—the Jazz Age drifter who eventually confessed to twenty-one murders and more than a thousand acts of sodomy—began riding the rails shortly after finishing a stint in reform school. He was still in his teens when four hoboes gang-raped him in a boxcar. The experience taught him a lesson that would serve as his credo for the remainder of his incorrigible life: "Force and might make right."

It was a lesson he put into practice every chance he got. For a while, he worked as a train guard for the Illinois Central Railroad—a job that offered him a prime opportunity for beating the brains out of practically everyone he could lay his hands on, whether union agitators, scabs, or even other guards.

The rails also figured in an especially spectacular (if undocumented) episode from his misbegotten life. From time to time, Panzram claimed, he would place a bomb in a railroad tunnel, blow up an oncoming train, then shoot anyone who happened to survive the explosion.

Though Panzram was as vicious as they come, his story about massacring whole trainloads of passengers was probably just a homicidal fantasy. The terrible crimes of "Railway Killer" Angel Maturino Resendez, however, were all too real. A modern railway hobo, Resendez was a migrant worker from Mexico who hitched rides on freight cars from one temporary job to another. He was also a rage-filled psychokiller who preyed upon his victims along the railroad right-of-way.

After committing his first murder in Lexington, Kentucky, in 1997, Resendez bummed his way by rail from one random destination to the next, killing as he went. Typically, he broke into people's homes and savaged his victims with whatever weapon was handy—shotgun, kitchen knife, sledgehammer, or gardening tool—then slipped back to the tracks and moved on. The "Railway Killer" struck several times in Texas and ventured as far north as Illinois. Placed on the **FBI**'s "Ten Most Wanted List," he finally surrendered in July 1999. The following year, he received a death sentence for one murder, though he may have killed as many as nine people in all.

For one serial killer, trains were not a means of moving from one murder to another. Nor were they a breeding ground for abuse and homicidal rage. They were a target. Panzram might have spun yarns about blowing up trains and trying to kill everyone inside, but the mad Hungarian, Sylvestre Matuschka, actually did it.

A World War I veteran and a successful businessman, Matuschka went for years without acting upon the bizarre obsessions that festered inside him. Then in 1930, at the age of thirty-nine, he attempted to derail two trains by setting up obstructions on the tracks. Neither act of sabotage produced any significant casualties, which only prodded him into devising a more devastating approach.

After methodically teaching himself the art of setting explosives, he blew up a set of tracks in Germany and sent an oncoming train careening off course. Matuschka was not satisfied. The crash injured seventy-five passengers but killed no one. His next explosion, in his native Hungary, was more to his liking. Twenty-two people were killed. This made him so happy, according to one account, that he experienced an orgasm as he watched the disaster unfold.

In court, Matuschka offered a series of wild explanations for his crimes, presumably to support an insanity defense. An evil hypnotist made him do it. He believed his train wrecks would stop the spread of atheism. He was controlled by a bunch of demons named Leo.

But the explanation he gave at the time of his arrest was far simpler. "I wrecked trains because I like to see people die," he said. "I like to hear people scream."

Richard Ramirez

They called him the "Night Stalker"—a shadowy fiend who would slip into darkened houses and savage the sleeping occupants. During his six-month rampage in the spring and summer of 1985, no one in Los Angeles felt safe.

Often, he would kill the husband first, then turn his depraved attentions to the woman. His victims—who ranged in age from thirty to eighty-three—were shot, slashed, bludgeoned, and viciously mutilated. In one case, he carved out the eyes of a forty-four-year-old woman and carried them off as

Richard Ramirez; from
Murderers! trading card set
(Courtesy of Roger Worsham)

Trophies. Sometimes, he daubed satanic pentagrams on the bodies before fleeing into the night.

By early August 1985, he was officially credited with more than a dozen homicides. A few weeks later, after attacking another couple— shooting the man in the head and raping the woman—he fled in their car. After recovering the stolen vehicle, police were able to lift a clear set of fingerprints, which turned out to match those of a small-time hood named Richard Ramirez. An all-points bulletin was issued for the suspect, and his mug shot was broadcast on local TV.

On August 31, Ramirez tried to yank a woman from her car in a Hispanic neighborhood in East LA. Her screams drew the attention of passersby, who recognized Ramirez and pounced on him. Only the timely arrival of the police saved the "Night Stalker" from the enraged mob.

At his trial, Ramirez (who had also been involved in numerous sexual assaults, including the abduction-rape of several small children) indulged in various bizarre antics. He enjoyed playing Satan, inscribing a pentagram on his left palm and flashing it to photographers, and making devil's horns with his fingers while intoning, "Evil, evil, evil . . ." He was ultimately convicted of thirteen murders and sentenced to death. "Big deal," he said with a sneer when the judge handed down the sentence. "Death comes with the territory. See you in Disneyland."

According to his own estimate, the "Night Stalker" (who remains on death row) was responsible for even more murders than the thirteen he was convicted of. "I've killed twenty people, man," he told a fellow inmate. "I love all that blood."

> "You maggots make me sick. I will be avenged.
> Lucifer dwells within all of us!"
>
> **RICHARD "NIGHT STALKER" RAMIREZ,**
> *addressing the court after being convicted of thirteen murders*

RECOMMENDED READING

Though the popularity of true-crime books has boomed in recent years, the genre itself dates back at least as far as 1621, when one of the bestselling tomes in England was a collection of real-life crime stories called *God's Revenge Against Murder and Adultery*. Clearly, a comprehensive history of crime books would require a lot more space than we have at our disposal. Even a history of books dealing only with American serial killers is beyond the scope of this entry. As long ago as 1896, Frank P. Geyer—the Philadelphia detective who followed the trail of the notorious "multi-murderer" Dr. H. H. **Holmes**—published an account of his investigation, *The Holmes-Pitezel Case*. Since that time, virtually every serial killer of note has been the subject of at least one book. Covering all of them would take a book of its own.

Still, there are some volumes that anyone interested in serial killers should be aware of. Some of these deal with the phenomenon as a whole. These include: Thomas S. Duke's *Celebrated Criminal Cases of America* (1910); L. C. Douthwaite's *Mass Murder* (1928); Eric Hickey's *Serial Murders and Their Victims* (1991); Jack Levin and James Alan Fox's *Mass Murder: America's Growing Menace* (1988); Elliott Leyton's *Hunting Humans* (1988); Michael Newton's *Serial Slaughter* (1992); Colin Wilson and Donald Seaman's *The Serial Killer* (1990); and the volume *Serial Killers* (1992), part of the "True Crime" series of Time-Life Books.

Capsule biographies of infamous serial killers are included in a number of encyclopedia-style collections. Jay Robert Nash's sweeping *Bloodletters and Badmen* (1973) is the best known of these, but it has to be approached with a certain amount of caution, since it is rife with inaccuracies. Others include: Michael Newton's *Hunting Humans* (1990); Brian Lane and Wilfred Gregg's *The Encyclopedia of Serial Killers* (1992); and David Everitt's *Human Monsters* (1993).

In terms of full-length studies of individual serial killers, the following is an alphabetical list of selected world-class psychos and the books that examine their crimes.

The Axeman of New Orleans
Robert Tallant and William Kimber, *Murder in New Orleans* (1953)

Martha Beck and Raymond Fernandez
Paul Buck, *The Honeymoon Killers* (1970)

David Berkowitz
David Abrahamsen, *Confessions of Son of Sam* (1985)

Kenneth Bianchi and Angelo Buono
Ted Schwartz, *The Hillside Strangler* (1981)

Ian Brady and Myra Hindley (The "Moors Murderers")
Emlyn Williams, *Beyond Belief* (1967)

Ted Bundy
Ann Rule, *The Stranger Beside Me* (1988)

Andrei Chikatilo
Richard Lourie, *Hunting the Devil* (1993)

John Reginald Christie
Ludovic Kennedy, *Ten Rillington Place* (1961)

The Cleveland Torso Killer
Steven Nickel, *Torso* (1989)

Juan Corona
Tracy Kidder, *The Road to Yuba City* (1974)

Jeffrey Dahmer
Anne E. Schwartz, *The Man Who Could Not Kill Enough* (1992)

Albert DeSalvo
Gerold Frank, *The Boston Strangler* (1967)

Albert Fish
Harold Schechter, *Deranged* (1990)

John Wayne Gacy
Tim Cahill, *Buried Dreams* (1986)

Edward Gein
Harold Schechter, *Deviant* (1989)

Harvey Glatman
Michael Newton, *Rope* (1998)

Belle Gunness
Janet L. Langois, *Belle Gunness* (1985)

Gary Heidnik
Ken Englade, *Cellar of Horror* (1988)

William Heirens
Lucy Freeman, *Before I Kill More . . .* (1955)

H. H. Holmes
Harold Schechter, *Depraved* (1994)

Jack the Ripper
Donald Rumbelow, *The Complete Jack the Ripper* (1975)

Jack the Stripper
Brian McConnell, *Found Naked and Dead* (1974)

Edmund Kemper
Margaret Chaney, *The Co-Ed Killer* (1976)

Peter Kürten
Margaret Seaton Wagner, *The Monster of Düsseldorf* (1932)

Leonard Lake and Charles Ng
John Lasseter, *Die for Me* (2000)

Henry Lee Lucas
Joel Norris, *Henry Lee Lucas* (1991)

Charles Manson
Vincent Bugliosi, *Helter Skelter* (1975)

Dennis Nilsen
Brian Masters, *Killing for Company* (1985)

Carl Panzram
Thomas Gaddis, *Panzram: A Journal of Murder* (2002)

Marcel Petiot
John V. Grombach, *The Great Liquidator* (1982)

Jesse Pomeroy
Harold Schechter, *Fiend* (2000)

Richard Ramirez
Clifford Lindecker, *Night Stalker* (1991)

Joel Rifkin
Robert Mladinich, *The Joel Rifkin Story* (2001)

Dr. Harold Shipman
Brian Whittle and Jean Ritchie, *Prescription for Murder* (2000)

Charles Starkweather
Michael Newton, *Waste Land* (1998)

Peter Sutcliffe ("The Yorkshire Ripper")
David A. Yallop, *Deliver Us from Evil* (1980)

Jane Toppan
Harold Schechter, *Fatal* (2003)

Fred and Rosemary West
Colin Wilson, *The Corpse Garden* (1998)

Aileen Wuornos
Sue Russell, *Lethal Intent* (2002)

Zodiac
Robert Graysmith, *Zodiac Unmasked* (2003)

Psycho Fiction

One of the many things that distinguish Hannibal Lecter from real-life serial killers is that—while passionate about classical music, Renaissance literature, and fine Italian wines—he seems to care nothing about sex. Certainly we never see him indulge in anything as mundane as erotic activity. He appears to be a singularly celibate serial killer, who derives his deepest pleasure from dining on a perfectly sautéed human liver while savoring a first-rate Barolo and listening to the latest recording of Mozart's *The Magic Flute.*

For a seemingly asexual man, however, Lecter has produced a prodigious number of offspring: namely the hundreds (if not thousands) of make-believe serial killers who have pervaded popular fiction since the runaway success of Thomas Harris's *Red Dragon* and *The Silence of the Lambs.* Thanks to Harris—the first pop novelist to hit the jackpot by tapping into America's obsessive fascination with psycho-killers—the serial murderer has become the favorite monster of modern-day thriller writers, who wrack their brains dreaming up ever more diabolical homicidal maniacs with fantastically elaborate MOs. By now, there are far too many books in this genre to list here, though Professor Martin Kich of Wright State University has compiled an excellent bibliography, available online at www.wright.edu/~martin.kich.

Here are a dozen of our personal favorites (a few of them golden oldies):

1. *Psycho.* The granddaddy of psycho-killer novels. This pulp classic by the late great Robert **Bloch** transformed the real-life atrocities of Ed **Gein** into genuine myth and inspired one of the masterworks of American cinema.

2. *American Gothic.* A lesser-known (but in certain ways even more suspenseful) novel by Bloch, based on the crimes of Chicago's nineteenth-century **Bluebeard,** Dr. H. H. **Holmes.**

3. *American Psycho.* Bret Easton Ellis's notorious bestseller—which set off a feminist firestorm when it was originally published—is actually a savagely dark comedy about Yuppie consumerism, though its scenes of stomach-churning sadism often obscure its basically satirical intent.

4. *Red Dragon.* Hannibal Lecter made his debut appearance in this nail-biter by Thomas Harris. One of the most sheerly suspenseful thrillers of modern times with a knockout ending that, bizarrely, Hollywood has failed to get right in both cinematic versions, Michael Mann's 1986 *Manhunter* and Bret Ratner's 2002 *Red Dragon.*

5. *The Silence of the Lambs.* The *Gone with the Wind* of psychokiller

novels. A tour de force of horror-suspense, this novel by Harris—the second to feature Hannibal Lecter—stands as the yardstick against which all other fiction in the serial-killer genre must be measured.

6. *The Killer Inside Me.* The narrator of Jim Thompson's pulp classic—a small-town sheriff who torments people by speaking in mind-numbing clichés when he isn't committing horrendous acts of homicide—is not, strictly speaking, a serial killer. Still, this powerfully unsettling, darkly hilarious novel is one of the best psychological portraits of a psychopath in print.

7. *Zombie.* Joyce Carol Oates crawls into the mind of a Jeffrey **Dahmer**-like psycho who dreams of creating his own personal **Zombie** by using ice picks to perform lobotomies on living victims. Not for the squeamish!

8. *The Alienist.* An intensely evocative historical thriller by Caleb Carr about a psychiatrist tracking down a serial killer in turn-of-the-century New York City. The novel features a cameo appearance by the real-life "Boy Fiend," Jesse Pomeroy (see **Juveniles**).

9. *Child of God.* Written in the trademark lyrical style of author Cormac McCarthy, this haunting novel tells the story of an Eddie **Gein**-like necrophile named Lester Ballard who holes up in a Tennessee cave with his unholy trophies, emerging periodically to seek new victims.

10. *In the Cut.* Susanna Moore's brutally suspenseful erotic thriller deals with a New York City college professor who finds herself involved in a highly charged sexual affair with a cop who may also be a serial killer. The novel builds to a shattering climax, completely lost in the disappointing 2003 film version starring Meg Ryan.

11. *Darkly Dreaming Dexter.* In this engaging novel, Jeff Lindsay manages the unlikely feat of creating an utterly endearing serial killer. Dexter Morgan, the protagonist of this delightfully offbeat thriller, is a police forensic specialist by day and a sadistic murderer in his spare time. What makes him such an appealing character—besides his wit and self-deprecating humor—is his strict code of serial killer ethics: he preys only on psychos sicker than himself.

12. *13 Steps Down.* Readers looking for hardcore horror and edge-of-the-seat suspense may find this book disappointing. But for those who cherish stylish prose, complex characterization, and psychological subtlety, this novel by acclaimed British mystery writer Ruth Rendell—about an eccentric spinster landlady and her sociopathic tenant, a fitness-equipment repairman obsessed with the legendary serial killer Reg Christie—is a rare literate treat.

For Bibliophiles Only

Patterson Smith, an antiquarian bookseller and social historian, specializes in rare and out-of-print crime volumes. Smith offers everything from hard-to-find reference works (like a reprint of Thomas S. Duke's 1910 classic, *Celebrated Criminal Cases of America*) to oddities like *Killer Fiction,* a collection of absolutely hair-raising stories by convicted sex killer G. J. Schaefer.

For information, contact: Patterson Smith, 23 Prospect Terrace, Montclair, NJ 07402.

RECORDS

No, we're not referring to Guns N' Roses' version of Charlie **Manson**'s "Look at Your Game, Girl" or "**Heidnik**'s House of Horrors" by the Serial Killers (you'll find those catchy numbers covered under **Songs**). We're talking about something much grimmer: killers who can claim the deadly distinction of having slain the most victims.

The serial-murder rate has increased so alarmingly in recent years that some criminologists talk in terms of an "epidemic." One indication of how scary the situation has become is the escalating number of victims attributed to individual killers. In 1888, the Western world was horrified by the deeds of **Jack the Ripper**—but Saucy Jack's total of five victims wouldn't even rate a mention on the national news nowadays.

By 1896, Jack's record had already been eclipsed by Dr. H. H. **Holmes,** who killed a minimum of nine victims (he himself claimed twenty-seven, and some crime historians put the total in the hundreds). Thirty years later, Earle Leonard **Nelson** set the homicidal record in our country, strangling twenty-two women during a savage, cross-country killing spree. His contemporary Carl **Panzram** fell just short of that number, confessing to twenty-one murders (in addition to a slew of other crimes).

During the past twenty-five years, each new record has been broken almost as soon as it was set. In 1973, Juan Corona officially became the most prolific serial killer in American history when he was convicted of slaying twenty-five California transients. But by the end of the decade, Ted **Bundy** had slain at least twenty-eight and John Wayne **Gacy** thirty-three.

And still the numbers kept rising. In Russia, Andrei **Chikatilo** was accused of fifty-two sadistic slayings and suspected of even more. Gary Ridgway—the long-elusive "Green River Killer"—eventually confessed to forty-eight murders, though there may have been as many as sixty. As appalling as these figures are, they pale before the estimated two hundred and fifty murders committed by Dr. Harold Shipman, England's most prolific serial killer (see **Doctors**).

When it comes to killers who have *claimed* the highest total, the all-time champions are America's own Henry Lee **Lucas** and the South American lust slayer Pedro Lopez (aka the "Monster of the Andes"), each of whom confessed to more than three hundred murders. Lucas, however, ultimately retracted his story. As for Lopez—who was convicted in 1980 of fifty-seven homicides—the true number of his victims has never been definitively established.

Henry Lee Lucas; from
Murderers! trading card set
(Courtesy of Roger Worsham)

REFRIGERATORS

Serial killers have been known to use their household appliances for purposes that the friendly folks at Maytag and KitchenAid have never dreamed of—not even in their worst nightmares. Living in a decaying old farmhouse without electricity, Edward **Gein** was forced to rely on time-consuming tanning methods to preserve his collection of anatomical **Trophies.** Other serial killers, however—whose homes were equipped with all the modern conveniences—had a much easier time of it. To preserve a favorite body part, all they had to do was pop it into the fridge.

Douglas Clark—the "Sunset Strip Slayer," who killed a string of Hollywood hookers in 1980—had a particular fetish for decapitated female heads. His girlfriend, Carol Bundy, indulged this perversion by applying makeup to the head of one of Clark's victims, a twenty-year-old streetwalker. Clark stored this grotesque keepsake in his apartment refrigerator, occasionally removing it for the purpose of oral sex.

Seven years later, in March 1987, Philadelphia police raided the home of a maniac named Gary **Heidnik** and discovered a trio of half-starved women chained up to the plumbing in his cellar. Heidnik, as it turned out, had abducted and enslaved a total of six victims altogether, subjecting them to months of rape and torture. Searching the rest of the house, the officers quickly discovered that the horrors were not confined to the so-called Torture Dungeon. In the freezer compartment of the kitchen refrigerator, they found a human arm, intended for a cannibal meal. Among his other atrocities, Heidnik liked to mix chopped-up human flesh with dog food and force his starving captives to devour the unholy meal.

Other serial killers, like the German lust murderer Joachim Kroll, had stocked their refrigerators with human flesh to satisfy their own cannibalistic cravings. The same was true of Jeffrey **Dahmer,** whose refrigerator contained a wide assortment of body parts, including heads, intestines, kidneys, lungs, livers, and a heart.

RELIGION

See **Zealots.**

RIPPERS

According to most crime historians, **Jack the Ripper** is the seminal psychokiller of the modern era—the granddaddy of all serial murderers. So it's only fitting that some of his descendants have been named after him.

His earliest namesake stalked the countryside of southern France: Joseph **Vacher,** the "French Ripper," who savaged almost a dozen victims in the late 1890s. Since that time, most of the killers christened with the Ripper name have been compatriots of the original.

During the London blitz of World War II, while Hitler's Luftwaffe rained terror from the sky, the city was confronted with a very different kind of menace—a homicidal fiend who stalked and slaughtered defenseless women. On February 9, 1942, this bloodthirsty butcher struck for the first time, strangling a female pharmacist in an air-raid shelter. The following day, he picked up a prostitute in Picadilly Circus, then—after accompanying her back to her Soho flat—slit her throat and mutilated her genitals with a can opener. Two more victims followed on succeeding nights, both subjected to hideous mutilations. The perpetrator of these atrocities—who turned out to be a twenty-five-year-old RAF cadet named Gordon Cummins—was caught after two more attempted killings, both of which he botched. His ghastly deeds, so reminiscent of those of the original "Whitechapel Horrors," earned him the moniker the "Blackout Ripper."

Another of Jack's homicidal heirs was Peter Sutcliffe, aka the "Yorkshire Ripper." A thirtyish truck driver and former gravedigger, Sutcliffe—who believed he was acting on orders from God—conducted a five-year campaign of carnage that commenced in the mid-1970s. Using his favorite weapons— ball peen hammer, chisel, carving knife, and screwdriver—he attacked more than two dozen women, killing thirteen. Though some of his victims were coeds, his primary targets were prostitutes. When Sutcliffe was finally arrested in 1981 after the largest manhunt in British history, his younger brother, Carl, asked him why he had done it. "I were just cleaning the streets," Sutcliffe replied.

The crimes of Cummins and Sutcliffe were clearly in the tradition of the original "Whitechapel Horrors." But these two killers differed from Jack the Ripper in one important respect: both of them were eventually caught. One serial killer of **Prostitutes** who eluded the police was the shadowy killer who strangled half a dozen women in the early to mid-1960s. After dispatching his victims, he dumped their naked bodies in various places around London—an MO that inspired his punning tabloid moniker. The killer (who has never been officially identified) was dubbed "Jack the Stripper."

RITUAL

Ritual killings committed by devil-worshipping cultists happen all the time in horror fiction and fantasy but rarely, if ever, in real life. The **FBI** has yet to document a single instance of such ceremonial sacrifice in America (see **Satanism**). On the other hand, bizarre ritualistic patterns are commonplace among serial killers. Though this behavior often appears random to an outside observer, it clearly possesses some deep, terrible significance to the killer himself, who is compelled to repeat it again and again.

Often the pattern involves a particular *way* of killing. Each of **Jack the Ripper**'s crimes culminated in a kind of ritual evisceration—as if he were enacting some primitive sacrifice in which the victim's entrails were removed and offered up to the gods. Another unidentified serial murderer, the 1930s madman known as the "Cleveland Torso Killer," methodically dismembered his victims and made off with their heads, which he apparently kept as ritual **Trophies**—in much the same way that aboriginal warriors collect the scalps and shrunken heads of their foes.

At other times, the killer will perform some compulsive ritual as an integral *part* of the crime. John Wayne **Gacy** turned his hideous murders into a grotesque ceremony by reciting the Twenty-Third Psalm ("The Lord is my shepherd") while slowly garroting his victims. The "Green River Killer"—who murdered a string of young women in the Seattle area during the early 1980s—left weird, pyramid-shaped stones in the vaginas of his victims. Ed **Gein**—in unwitting emulation of those Aztec priests who arrayed themselves in the flayed skin of sacrificial victims—liked to parade around in apparel fashioned from the human flesh of dissected female corpses. And Albert "Boston Strangler" **DeSalvo** ritualistically left his victims looking like grotesque, gift-wrapped holiday presents. After strangling a woman, he would tie the ligature—usually a scarf, stocking, or bathrobe sash—into a big, ornamental bow. In one case, he also left a greeting card propped up against the victim's foot.

RUSSIA

For decades, leaders of the Soviet Union maintained that crime was not a problem in their country. Thievery and murder, they insisted, were symptoms of Western-style capitalistic decadence. The collapse of communism in the early 1980s, of course, revealed all sorts of problems that had been hidden by the Iron Curtain. In particular, the 1992 trial of Andrei **Chikatilo**—the "Rostov Ripper"—demonstrated that while the USSR might not have been able to supply its citizens with basic consumer items, it could certainly produce serial killers every bit as terrifying as any American psycho. Moreover, though Chikatilo was undoubtedly the most savage of Russian sex killers, he was not unique: multiple murderers had been prowling through the Soviet Union from the earliest days of the Communist regime.

In the early 1920s, thirty-three men fell victim to a sociopathic horse trader named Vasili Komaroff, aka the "Wolf of Moscow." After luring a prospective customer to his stable, Komaroff—assisted by his wife—would bludgeon or strangle the victim to death, strip him of his possessions, then truss up the body, stuff it into a sack, and deposit it in an empty lot somewhere in the city. When authorities finally caught up with him, Komaroff claimed that he killed solely for money—an unlikely explanation, since his nearly three dozen murders netted him a grand total of $26.40. Clearly, there were other, darker motives at work—but the Soviet authorities were much less interested in fathoming his psychology than in putting him to death as promptly as possible. Komaroff and his wife were executed by a firing squad in June 1923.

In more recent years, as the serial-murder rate started burgeoning in the West, the Soviet Union also had its share of grisly killers. In 1964, an unemployed Moscow actor named Vladimir Ionosyan butchered five people with an **Axe.** Ten years later, a shadowy killer nicknamed "Ivan the Ripper" slaughtered eleven Moscow women. Authorities eventually arrested a man for the killings, but—in typically secretive Soviet style—they never divulged who the culprit was or how the case was resolved.

In the 1980s—while America was confronted with the gruesome likes of Henry Lee **Lucas** and Gary **Heidnik**—Soviet authorities caught up with Gennadily Mikhasevich, who used his position as an auxiliary policeman to trap and strangle thirty-three women. Another homicidal monster of that decade was Nikolai Dzumagalies—one of the most frightening and ferocious serial killers ever spawned in the USSR (or anywhere else, for that matter). Like Francis Dolarhyde, the terrifying psychocreep in Thomas Harris's novel *Red Dragon*—who savages his victims with a lethal set of dentures—Dzumagalies (or "Metal Fang," as he came to be nicknamed) sported scary, white metal false teeth. Luring women to a lonely riverbank at night, he proceeded to rape them, stab them, and carve up their bodies. Then he roasted the flesh and shared it with friends, who—believing they were partaking of beef—were turned into unwitting cannibals.

SADISM

Some criminologists define serial murder in strictly quantitative terms: three or more homicides committed over an extended length of time, with an emotional "cooling-off" period between each incident (see **Definition**). Other specialists in the field, however, believe that serial murder in the strict sense of the term always contains another element: a powerful streak of sexual sadism.

Certainly, this is the aspect of serial killing that makes it such a uniquely hideous crime—even worse than mass murder. After all, it is one thing to be cut down by a crazed gunman in a convenience store; it is quite another to fall victim to a psycho who calmly explains (as one serial killer actually did): "First, I'm going to torture you in the most horrible and painful manner I can think of. Then I'm going to abuse you sexually in the most degrading way I can possibly think of. Then I'll kill you in the slowest and most painful way I can. Any questions?"

Albert **Fish** liked to castrate teenage boys and watch them bleed to death in agony. Leonard Lake and Charles Ng took videotapes of the slow, sadistic murder of their bound and captive sex slaves. Another serial killer tortured a prostitute for forty-three days before killing her. These are just a few of countless unspeakable examples.

In this regard, serial murder can be seen as a kind of depraved travesty of normal sexual functioning. Instead of looking for a date at a singles bar or dance club, the serial killer goes trolling for victims in some favorite hunting ground—a red-light district, say, or a homosexual hangout. Once he has a victim in his power, he achieves sexual release not through intercourse but through torture, degradation, and finally murder (it is not uncommon for a lust murderer to reach orgasm during his victim's death throes). The so-called cooling-off period corresponds to the contented lull that normally follows sex, while the psychopath's growing need to kill again is the equivalent of building sexual hunger—in effect, the serial killer gets increasingly horny for blood.

Sexual psychopaths of this type tend to be victims of extreme physical and/or emotional childhood abuse (often sexual abuse). Subjected to vicious **Upbringings** that twist their erotic natures completely out of shape, they grow up equating sex not with love and tenderness but with aggression, dominance, and murderous rage. To cite just one of many examples: Joseph Kallinger—who tortured and mutilated a string of young boys (including his own son)—was raised by parents who routinely flogged him with a cat-o'-nine-tails and threatened him with castration. Other serial killers who conform to this pattern are Henry Lee **Lucas,** John Wayne **Gacy,** Edmund **Kemper,** and Jeffrey **Dahmer**—in short, some of the most monstrous criminals of our (or any other) time.

> "I always had a desire to inflict pain on others
> and to have others inflict pain on me.
> I always seemed to enjoy everything that hurt.
> The desire to inflict pain,
> that is all that is uppermost."
>
> **ALBERT FISH**

> "It is probable that he first cut the throats of his victims, then ripped open the abdomen and groped among the intestines. In some instances he cut off the genitals and carried them away; in others he only tore them to pieces and left them behind. He does not seem to have had sexual intercourse with his victims, but very likely the murderous act and subsequent mutilation of the corpse were the equivalents for the sex act."
>
> **RICHARD VON KRAFFT-EBING,**
> *discussing Jack the Ripper*

SATANISM

If you believe everything you hear on *Geraldo*, you might well think that our country is overrun with satanic cultists who regularly indulge in human sacrifice and every other manner of unspeakable perversion. In fact, beyond the highly unreliable testimony of various religious nuts and sexual hysterics, there is little or no evidence that such devil-worshipping covens actually exist, at least not in the United States of America.

On the other hand, since serial killers are inexorably drawn to all that is dark and depraved, they often enjoy embellishing their crimes—and themselves—with a bit of satanic symbolism. Wayne Nance, a Montana truck driver who killed five people in the mid-1980s, used a white-hot coat hanger to brand the number of the Beast—"666"—onto his own flesh. Similarly, John Kogut—a young Long Island landscaper who led a gang that raped and murdered three young women—burned an inverted cross onto his forearm.

Other self-styled devil devotees like to leave satanic markings at the crime scene. After breaking into the suburban home of an eighty-four-year-old Los Angeles woman and beating her to death, Richard the "Night

Stalker" **Ramirez** drew pentagrams on her skin, then painted a few more on the walls before fleeing. At his trial, he kept the press corps entertained by shouting salutations to Satan and flashing a pentagram that he had inscribed on his palm. "You don't understand," he said, sneering at the judge. "You are not expected to. I am beyond good and evil. Legions of the night! Night breed!"

One of the most notorious of all Lucifer-related cases was the savage 1984 mutilation-slaying of Long Island teenager Gary Lauwers by the devil-besotted druggie Rickie Kasso. "Say you love Satan!" Kasso commanded over and over again, while slashing Lauwers to pieces with a pocketknife. Horrific as it was, however, the murder was not—as originally reported—a ritualistic sacrifice but rather a vicious act of revenge over some bags of stolen angel dust.

The only documented case of satanic serial murder occurred in Matamoros, Mexico, where a devil-worshipping drug gang slaughtered fifteen sacrificial victims in a demonic rite designed to ensure supernatural protection (see **Cults**).

SLIPPING THROUGH THE CRACKS

Serial killers tend to possess two characteristics typical of psychopaths. Lacking normal human emotions, they are able to stay absolutely calm under intensely stressful circumstances. They also have the ability to appear so utterly, blandly normal that it is virtually impossible for anyone to conceive of them as crazed, cold-blooded killers (see **Mask of Sanity**). Both of these traits have stood many serial killers in extremely good stead, allowing them to fool even highly trained investigators and elude arrest for years.

For several decades, Albert **Fish** roamed across the country, in search of young prey. During that time, he was frequently in and out of custody for charges ranging from petty theft to public indecency. At no time, however, did authorities suspect that he was capable of insanely violent crime. Only in 1934 did the appalling truth come to light: the gray-haired, grandfatherly old man, who looked so sweet and kindly that strangers would entrust their children to his care, had spent his lifetime torturing, mutilating, and ultimately cannibalizing little boys and girls.

In the mid-1970s, a string of young women were abducted and murdered in Seattle after meeting a man named "Ted." One of the many suspects in the case turned out to be a law student named Ted **Bundy.** When police checked into his background, however, they decided that the bright and ambitious young Republican couldn't possibly be the killer—leaving the sociopathic Bundy free to murder, rape, and mutilate young women for another four years.

One of the most notorious instances in which a serial killer slipped through the hands of police occurred on the night of May 27, 1991, when two Milwaukee cops, alerted by a 911 call, found a naked teenaged boy apparently attempting to flee from an older man. The man—a soft-spoken thirty-year-old named Jeffrey **Dahmer**—explained that he and the boy were gay lovers who had been engaged in nothing more serious than a "domestic dispute." Dahmer was so polite and persuasive that police let him take the teenager back to his apartment—where Dahmer proceeded to strangle him, have sex with the corpse, and dismember the body.

Police are not the only ones who have been known to let real-life monsters go free. In 1978, the world's most prolific serial killer, Pedro Lopez, was caught by a group of Peruvian Indians as he tried to kidnap one of the girls from their village. The outraged Indians were in the process of putting Lopez to a slow, agonizing death, when a female missionary happened onto the scene and persuaded them to desist. Lopez was turned over to the Peruvian police, who simply deported him to Ecuador. As a result of the missionary's misplaced compassion—and the gross negligence of the Peruvian police—the "Monster of the Andes" went on to rape and murder scores of Ecuadorian women.

It is one thing for a Christian missionary, whose faith demands forgiveness, to be fooled by sociopathic evil. It seems much less comprehensible when the sucker is a trained psychiatrist—supposedly an expert in the darker workings of the human mind. In September 1972, an entire panel of state-appointed psychiatrists interviewed Edmund **Kemper** to determine how well he had adjusted to life since his release from a mental hospital three years earlier. The doctors were unanimous in their judgment—Kemper was no longer a threat to society. Kemper drove away from the interview free from any further psychiatric supervision.

Inside the trunk of his car was the head of a fifteen-year-old girl he had decapitated the previous day.

SONGS

Though the crime-ridden lyrics of "gangsta" rap have come in for all kinds of flak, the truth is that people have always enjoyed songs about sex and violence. Moralists who long for the good old days before songs like "Murder Was the Case" ruled the airwaves might keep in mind that one of the biggest hits of the 1950s was the Kingston Trio's "Tom Dooley"—a mournful ditty about a guy who is about to be hanged for slaying his girl-friend ("Met her on the mountain, / There I took her life. / Met her on the mountain, / Stabbed her with my knife"). And indeed—though folk songs are generally thought of as cheery and uplifting—some of the oldest songs in folklore tradition are so-called murder ballads, many of which date back hundreds of years and describe violent crimes in horrifying detail. A popular ballad called "Expert Town," for example, contains lyrics like: "Little attention did I pay, / I beat her more and more; / I beat her till the blood run down— / Her hair was yellow as gold."

In America, songs about serial killers date at least as far back as the nine-teenth century. In her book *American Murder Ballads,* Olive Burt reprints a song about the notorious **Black Widow** killer Belle Gunness whose first few verses go like this:

> Belle Gunness was a lady fair,
> In Indiana State.
> She weighed about three hundred pounds,
> And that is quite some weight.

> That she was stronger than a man
> Her neighbors all did own;
> She butchered hogs right easily,
> And did it all alone.

> But hogs were just a sideline
> She indulged in now and then
> Her favorite occupation
> Was a-butchering of men.

Contemporary songs about psychokillers, in short, are not just a modern-day aberration but a continuation of a genre that extends all the way back to the Middle Ages and probably further.

For teenaged listeners, of course, one of the main functions of rock music is to send their parents into fits of sputtering outrage. Few things can accomplish this time-honored goal more effectively than songs that celebrate serial killers. The members of Marilyn **Manson**'s band pay tribute to their favorite psychokillers in their assumed surnames, which—in addition to their leader's Charlie-inspired moniker—include **Gacy, Gein, Berkowitz,** and **Fish.** The "death metal" band Macabre has recorded such ditties as "The Ted **Bundy** Song," "Gacy's Lot," and "Edmund **Kemper** Had a Terrible Temper," along with an entire concept album dedicated to the depraved doings of Jeffrey **Dahmer.**

The following is a list of twelve memorable recordings dealing with serial murder and mayhem.

1. *Bobby Darin,* "Mack the Knife." At the height of the sixties counterculture, no self-respecting hippie would have confessed to a fondness for the hopelessly out-of-date crooning of Bobby Darin. These days, however, he's widely regarded as the epitome of finger-snapping Sinatraesque cool. In this irresistible rendition of a chilling little ballad from Kurt Weill and Bertolt Brecht's 1928 *Threepenny Opera,* Darin sings of a Jack-the-Ripper-like character named MacHeath. Rarely has serial murder sounded so swingin'.

2. *The Rolling Stones,* "Midnight Rambler." Though the only shocking thing about them now is their age, the Stones were the original bad-boy rock band: the anti-Beatles who sang "Let It Bleed" in answer to the Moptops' "Let It Be." This bluesy paean to the Boston Strangler is belted out by Mick Jagger at his sneering, strutting, pre-geriatric best.

3. *Warren Zevon,* "Excitable Boy." From the sardonic singer-songwriter best known for his hit "Werewolves of London" comes this toe-tapping tune about an "excitable boy" who rapes and murders his high school prom date. After doing ten years in prison, he digs up her grave and builds "a cage with her bones."

4. *Talking Heads,* "Psycho-killer." A catchy musical foray into the mind of a homicidal creep, this is the song that put David Byrne and his band on the map. *Qu'est-ce que c'est?*

5. *Police,* "Murder by Numbers." An ironic commentary on the culture of violence disguised as a paean to the art of murder. Sting's lyrics play a pivotal role in the plot of the 1995 serial-killer movie *Copycat.*

6. *The Beatles,* "Maxwell's Silver Hammer." Not everyone is a fan of this infectious little ditty penned by Paul McCartney about a homicidal maniac. Ian MacDonald, author of the definitive *Revolution in the Head: The Beatles' Records and the Sixties,* calls it a "ghastly miscalculation that represents McCartney's worst lapse in taste."

7. *Slayer,* "Dead Skin Mask." A brain-pummeling tribute to Ed "Psycho" Gein from a band that is one of the leading purveyors of "black metal" rock.

8. *Serial Killers,* "**Heidnik**'s House of Horrors." A rarity. Released on the obscure Suspiria label and pressed on blood-red vinyl, this punk-rock tribute to killer Gary Heidnik features a melody that can best be described as "primitive." But how can you hate a song with lyrics like "He had a basement straight out of hell / Marquis de Sade would think it was swell"?

9. *Bruce Springsteen,* "Nebraska." The haunting title song of Springsteen's 1982 acoustic album is a first-person account of Charles Stark-weather's infamous killing spree across the badlands of Nebraska (see **Killer Couples**).

10. *Alice Cooper,* "I Love the Dead." Not exactly a serial-killer song but—with lines like "I love the dead before they're cold / They're bluing flesh for me to hold"—it's certainly one that serial killers could relate to.

11. *Guns N' Roses,* "Look at Your Game, Girl." This song set off a firestorm of controversy when it appeared on GNR's 1993 *The Spaghetti Incident?* album, even though it has nothing to do with serial killers. The

reason? It was written by none other than Charles **Manson,** who—before he gained notoriety as the kill-crazed leader of a cult of homicidal hippies—was an aspiring songwriter. Manson's own version of "Look at Your Game, Girl" appears on his legendary LP *Lie,* along with such other immortal compositions as "People Say I'm No Good," "Garbage Dump," "Sick City," and "Don't Do Anything Illegal." The Manson discography also includes: *The Manson Family Sings, Charles Manson Live at San Quentin,* and a recent CD called *Commemoration,* which includes his tribute to Hank Williams Sr. and several heartfelt numbers about the environment.

12. *Joe Coleman's Infernal Machine.* Unlike the previous titles in this list, this is an *entire album* of mayhem-related music assembled by the one and only Joe Coleman (see **Art**). Among its many treasures are Red River Dave's yodelling country-western number, "California Hippie Murders," and "Strangler in the Night," with lyrics by Albert "Boston Strangler" **DeSalvo!**

Record sleeve from "Heidnik's House of Horrors";
art by **Liz Pop** *(Courtesy of Larry Kay and Paul Bearer)*

In the realm of serial-killer-related pop music, mention must also be made of the now-defunct punk group Ed Gein's Car; the 1991 album *Too Much Joy* by a group called Cereal Killers (get it?); and the limited edition single "Biter" by the Kansas City band Season to Risk, which features a jacket painting by John Wayne Gacy.

Album cover for *Joe Coleman's Infernal Machine*
(*Courtesy of Joe Coleman*)

SOUVENIRS

See **Trophies.**

Richard Speck

Strictly speaking, Richard Speck was a **Mass Murderer,** not a serial killer, since the crimes that earned him everlasting infamy were all committed in a single night. Still, those crimes were so horrific that they place Speck squarely in the ranks of twentieth-century American monsters.

Richard Speck; from
52 Famous Murderers
trading cards
(Courtesy of Roger Worsham)

A hulking, acne-scarred thug addicted to booze and drugs, Speck had logged nearly forty arrests by the time he was twenty for offenses ranging from burglary to assault with a deadly weapon. Mass murderers are sometimes referred to as "human time bombs"—and the description certainly fits Speck, whose life had been one slow, inexorable buildup to a devastating explosion of violence.

That explosion occurred on the night of July 13, 1966. Speck—who worked as a merchant seaman—was in Chicago, waiting to ship out to New Orleans. He spent the day guzzling booze, popping downers, and ogling the women as they sunbathed in the park behind Jeffey Manor, a town house for student nurses working at a local hospital. At around 11 P.M., Speck returned to the town house and knocked on the door. It was opened by a twenty-three-year-old student nurse named Corazon Amurao, who found herself face-to-face with a pockmarked stranger brandishing a knife and a gun. "I'm not going to hurt you," Speck said as he shoved his way inside. "I need your money to go to New Orleans."

Speck led her upstairs, where he found five more student nurses. Herding them all into one bedroom, he ordered them to lie on the floor. Then, ripping a bedsheet into strips, he proceeded to truss his terrified victims. Over the next hour, three more young women arrived at the town house. They, too, ended up bound and helpless on the bedroom floor.

Toying with his gun, Speck sat on the floor with his nine captives, as

though debating what to do with them. Finally, he came to a ghastly decision. Untying twenty-year-old Pamela Wilkening, he led her into an adjoining
bedroom, where he stabbed her in the breast and strangled her. Mary Ann
Jordan and Suzanne Farris were next. Speck shoved them into another bedroom and savaged them with his knife.

Pausing to wash the blood from his hands, Speck returned to his grisly
work. One by one the young women were led off into different bedrooms
and brutally killed—some had their throats slashed, others were strangled.
The last to die was twenty-two-year-old Gloria Davy. Speck took his time,
raping her twice before sodomizing her with a foreign object and strangling
her to death.

Having dispatched every one of the young women—or so he thought—
Speck shuffled off into the night. But during his rampage, he had lost count
of his victims. One of the student nurses—Corazon Amurao—had managed
to hide herself under a bed. Waiting until five in the morning, she wriggled
out from under the mattress, made her way to the balcony, and began
screaming, "They are all dead! My friends are all dead!"

From Amurao's description, along with other clues—primarily the fingerprints he had left all over the apartment and the telltale knots he had tied,
which were characteristic of a seaman—police quickly identified Speck,
who was arrested in Cook County Hospital after a failed suicide attempt. He
was given the death sentence, but when the U.S. Supreme Court abolished
the death penalty, he was resentenced to consecutive life terms amounting
to four hundred years. He had served only nineteen of them when he died
in prison of a heart attack.

The Speck Tape

In May 1995, the public got its first stunned look at a grainy VHS tape that
gave new meaning to the term "pornographic video." Shot in Stateville
prison in 1988—three years before his death—the tape shows Richard
Speck snorting cocaine, engaging in oral sex with another inmate, and
flaunting his monstrously repulsive body.

Looking unspeakably grotesque in a blond, bobbed hairdo, Speck—
lounging in a cell with his young African-American lover—jokes about his
murders, talks about how much he loves to be anally penetrated by other

men, and brags about the good life he has been enjoying in prison. "If they only knew how much fun I was having in here," he says, laughing, "they would turn me loose."

In what is perhaps the most revolting moment in this thoroughly odious tape, Speck—at the behest of his lover—strips off his clothes to reveal that he is sporting blue silk panties and a floppy set of hormonally induced female breasts. He then proceeds to perform fellatio on the other man.

When this video was shown to Illinois lawmakers, it set off a storm of outrage. "This is the kind of thing that really shakes the public's confidence in the criminal justice system," remarked one state legislator. Indeed, this comment was a significant understatement. The tape was so abhorrent that—after portions of it were broadcast on news stations around the country—even some die-hard opponents of the death penalty found themselves regretting that Speck had escaped execution.

Spree Killers

In its efforts to establish precise criminal classifications, the **FBI** distinguishes between serial killing and spree killing. According to the Bureau's definitions, a serial killer always experiences an emotional "cooling-off" period between his crimes—a hiatus lasting anywhere from days to years. By contrast, a spree killer is someone who murders a string of people in several different locations with no cooling-off period between homicides.

A classic case of spree killing occurred in 1949, when a crazed ex-GI named Howard Unruh strode through his Camden, New Jersey, neighborhood with a 9mm Luger in hand, gunning down everyone who crossed his path. In the space of just twelve minutes, he killed thirteen people and wounded three more. More recently, a twenty-seven-year-old Englishman named Michael Ryan decked himself out like Rambo—complete with an AK-47 Kalashnikov assault rifle—and spent the morning of August 19, 1987, shooting thirty people around the British market town of Hungerford.

Other spree killers, however, commit their crimes over a much more extended period of time. This can make the FBI's distinction between spree killing and serial murder seem a little blurry. In 1984, for example, a homicidal maniac named Christopher Wilder went on a murder spree that left six women dead in a month's time. Perhaps the most famous of all American spree killers, Charles Starkweather, killed ten people during a twenty-six-day rampage through the badlands of Nebraska and Wyoming (see **Killer Couples: A Couple of Crazy Kids**).

Perhaps a more useful distinction between spree killing and serial homicide has to do with underlying motives. Serial killing is, bottom-line, a sexual crime. The serial killer spends a great deal of time (perhaps years) indulging in dark, obsessive fantasies about dominance, torture, and murder. Finally, driven by an overpowering hunger, he goes out in search of a very precise type of victim (women with long dark hair parted in the middle, for example, or Asian teenage boys). Once he has fulfilled his depraved desires, his blood lust subsides for a certain length of time, until it builds again to an irresistible need.

34. CHARLES STARKWEATHER

Charles Starkweather; from *Murderers!* trading card set
(Courtesy of Roger Worsham)

Spree killing, on the other hand, is really a form of mobile **Mass Murder.** While the mass murderer commits his crimes in a single location (for example, the disgruntled employee who suddenly goes berserk and blows away all his co-workers), the spree killer moves from place to place (throughout a neighborhood, around a town, or even across an entire county or state). But his rampage is essentially a single extended massacre (even when it lasts for several weeks).

In short, the spree killer is generally not a sexual psychopath but a deeply unbalanced individual who suddenly snaps and embarks on a murderous jaunt, leaving a trail of corpses in his wake. Spree killers share another trait with mass murderers: they are driven by profoundly self-destructive impulses. Typically, their rampages end with their own deaths, either by suicide or in a barrage of police gunfire. They are walking time bombs who detonate without warning, destroying everyone in sight—themselves included.

That suicidal impulse was clear in the case of Andrew Cunanan, whose cross-country rampage became a worldwide media sensation in the summer of 1997. A charismatic young man who led a glitzy, hedonistic life as the kept boy-toy of a succession of older gay males, Cunanan eventually went into a sudden downward spiral, possibly as a result of drug abuse. By the summer of 1996, the high-living party boy was leading a sordid, desperate existence. Shortly afterward, he embarked on a murderous spree that culminated in the killing of celebrated fashion designer Gianni Versace. With a mammoth manhunt under way, Cunanan took refuge in a Miami houseboat, where, on July 25, 1997, he shot himself in the head with his .40-caliber handgun.

Cunanan perfectly fit the profile of a spree killer: a profoundly embittered individual, full of suppressed rage and resentment, whose world suddenly falls apart. Life having become unendurable, he decides to go out with a bang—but not without taking others down with him. By committing such a high-profile crime, moreover, he seeks to demonstrate that he is someone to be reckoned with after all—not the nonentity he appears to be, but the kind of person who can rivet the attention of the world.

The same psychological syndrome can be seen in the case of another spree killer whose crimes held the nation in thrall: the "Beltway Sniper," John Allen Muhammad. A supremely arrogant man, Muhammad had failed in every area of grown-up life—marriage, fatherhood, business. Seething with resentment, he blamed everyone but himself for his botched life. With the aid of a worshipful, teenaged accomplice, Muhammad—who had honed his shooting skills in the army—set off on a terrifying spree, randomly shooting more than a dozen people in the Washington, D.C., area as they went about their daily routines. As in the case of Cunanan, the crimes were Muhammad's way both of taking revenge on society and of satisfying his own deluded sense of importance.

Unlike Cunanan, Muhammad was taken alive, though he had contrived to end his life just the same. He awaits execution in Virginia, having been condemned to death in March 2004. His teenaged acolyte, Lee Boyd Malvo, received a life sentence.

STATISTICS

If you live in California and you're the kind of person who worries obsessively about encountering a serial killer, you might consider moving to a different place—like Maine. Of all the states in the union, California has the single highest number of serial homicide cases in the twentieth century—fully 16 percent of the national total. Maine, on the other hand, has the lowest—none. Other states to avoid: New York, Texas, Illinois, and Florida. The safest places in America, at least in terms of serial murder, are Hawaii, Montana, North Dakota, Delaware, and Vermont, each of which had only one case of serial murder in of the twentieth century.

For the statistically minded student of serial murder, here are a few other interesting facts and figures:

- The United States is the hands-down leading producer of serial killers, with 76 percent of the world's total. Europe comes in a distant second with a measly 17 percent.
- England has produced 28 percent of the European total. Germany is a very close second with 27 percent, and France is third with 13 percent.
- In terms of demographics, the vast majority of American serial killers—fully 84 percent—are Caucasian and a mere 16 percent black.
- In terms of gender, men constitute the overwhelming preponderance of serial killers—at least 90 percent. Indeed, depending on how the crime is defined, many experts believe that serial murder is an exclusively male activity. (See **Definition** and **Women.**)
- While women constitute, at most, an infinitesimal fraction of serial murderers, they make up the majority of victims—65 percent.
- It is very rare for a serial killer to prey on members of another race. Since most serial killers are white, so are the vast majority of victims—89 percent.

- Serial murder tends to be a young person's crime. Most serial killers—44 percent—embark on their deadly careers in their twenties, with 26 percent starting out in their teens and 24 percent in their thirties.
- If you're seeking a career that will keep you safe from serial killers, you'll want to avoid prostitution, since hookers are prime targets for sociopathic sex slayers. The bad news is that there really isn't any profession that will necessarily protect you from a run-in with a serial killer. In almost 15 percent of serial-murder cases, the victims are chosen entirely at random.

SUICIDE

See **Death Wish.**

THEATER

The kinds of sickos we now call serial killers—bloodthirsty butchers who revel in torture, mutilation, and every conceivable variety of murder—have been portrayed onstage for centuries. During the Elizabethan era, for example, one of the most popular forms of drama was the so-called revenge tragedy, featuring villains who were never happier than when gouging out a rival's eyes or ripping out his entrails or feeding him pies made from the reeking flesh of his own children. Even Shakespeare got in on the act. In his play *Titus Andronicus,* a young girl—after being gang-raped—has her tongue cut out and her hands chopped off to keep her from identifying her attackers.

A few centuries later, Parisians flocked to the Theater of the Grand Guignol, which specialized in insanely sadistic skits with titles like "The Garden of Torture," "The Merchant of Corpses," "The Kiss of Blood," "The Castle of Slow Death," and "The Horrible Experiment." The plots, such as they were, were little more than a flimsy pretext to depict the most outrageous atrocities imaginable, all simulated with shockingly realistic stage effects. Audiences shrieked, swooned, and occasionally lost their suppers as they watched cackling psychos amputate their victims' limbs or tear out their tongues or saw open their skulls or grill their faces on red-hot stoves.

Nowadays, the Grand Guignol tradition of gratuitous gore and stomach-churning effects has largely been taken over by low-budget slasher **Movies** (and the occasional high-end Hollywood production, like Ridley Scott's *Hannibal*). Occasionally, however, a play about serial murder still appears on the Broadway stage. Stephen Sondheim's 1979 "musical thriller" *Sweeney Todd,* for example, resurrects the tale of the legendary "Demon Barber of Fleet Street"—the Victorian madman who slaughtered his customers in his specially designed chair, then (with the help of his landlady-lover) turned them into meat pies. The score, one of Sondheim's best, contains the wittiest paean to **Cannibalism** ever written ("A Little Priest").

There are no songs in Martin McDonagh's *The Pillowman,* which debuted on Broadway in 2005. Like Sondheim's play, however, it contains a potent blend of horror and humor, along with some shocking moments that wouldn't have been out of place on the stage of the Theater of the Grand Guignol. A meditation on the power of storytelling, the play deals with a series of grisly child murders that may or may not have been inspired by the macabre tales written by the main character and committed by his mentally deficient brother.

Another recent, powerfully disturbing play about serial murder is Bryony Lavery's *Frozen,* a harrowing, three-character drama about a British woman, Nancy, whose ten-year-old daughter is abducted and slain by a serial killer; the serial killer himself, a brain-damaged pedophile named Ralph; and an American psychologist, Agnetha, who is studying the causes of serial homicide. Agnetha's theory—that criminal psychopathology is rooted in neurological changes caused by extreme child abuse—closely echoes that of real-life criminal psychiatrist Dorothy Otnow Lewis, co-author of the influential 1999 study *Guilty by Reason of Insanity.* The similarities were not lost on Lewis, who, in 2004, launched a highly publicized plagiarism suit against the playwright, claiming that Lavery had not only ripped off her book but "stolen her life."

They call **Nurses** "angels o
fit that description. Beside
sensitive, sympathetic wo
families. Of course, none
early years. They did not
was just an infant—or ab
pelled him to stitch his e
They weren't aware of Ja
fiancé. Or the morbid ob
years at a Cambridge ho
became a source of dismay to her supervisors.

It wasn't until members of the Davis family began dropping like flies in
the summer of 1901 that the terrible truth about the skilled, seemingly
compassionate nurse finally came to light. Far from being an "angel of
mercy," Jane Toppan turned out to be one of America's most bloodthirsty
"angels of death."

Mrs. Mattie Davis was the first to go, presumably of heart failure. She
died while visiting her old friend Jane Toppan. The elder Davis daughter,
Mrs. Annie Gordon, was so grief-stricken that she turned to Nurse Toppan
for relief. Toppan obliged by administering some injections. Shortly thereafter, Annie Gordon followed her mother to the grave. A few days later, the
patriarch of the family, Captain Alden Davis, was felled, supposedly by a
massive stroke. He, too, had been receiving medication from Nurse Toppan.
That left just one surviving member of the family, another married daughter,
Mrs. Mary Gibbs. Several days after her father's funeral—after placing herself under the care of kindly Nurse Toppan—Mary Gibbs dropped dead, too.

With his wife's entire family wiped out in less than six weeks, Mary
Gibbs's husband demanded an autopsy. Toppan did her best to prevent it,
but Gibbs—suspecting foul play—called in the Massachusetts State Police.
The autopsy on Mary Gibbs's body confirmed her husband's darkest fears.
His wife had been killed with a lethal injection of morphine and atropine, ob-
viously administered by Jane Toppan.

By then, Toppan had fled Boston. She was finally arrested in Amherst,
New Hampshire, on October 29, 1901—though not before she had knocked
off her own foster sister.

At first, Toppan insisted on her innocence, though she admitted to the

PEDIA OF SERIAL KILLERS

troubled with her head." As investigators
covered a string of former patients who had
ious deaths. Questioned by psychiatrists (or
of the day), Toppan finally confessed to poisoning
embers of the Davis family but also seven other people
victims altogether. Later, she would tell her own attorney
total was thirty-one.

1902 trial, doctors testified that Toppan had been "born with a
nd nervous mental condition" and suffered "from a lack of moral
se and defective self-control." There was reason to believe that her
condition was hereditary: not only her father but her sister, too, had ended
up in an insane asylum. Toppan's own testimony helped persuade the jury
of her madness. "That is my ambition," she declared, "to have killed more
people—more helpless people—than any man or woman who has ever
lived." Declared insane, she was confined to a state asylum, where she
died in 1938 at the age of eighty-four.

> "That is my ambition, to have killed more people—
> more helpless people—than any man or woman
> who has ever lived."
>
> **JANE TOPPAN**

TOURIST ATTRACTIONS

Ever since the summer of 1994, one of the most popular sightseeing spots in
Los Angeles has been the Brentwood condo where the late Mrs. O. J. Simpson and her waiter-friend, Ron Goldman, met their brutal ends. What are we
to make of this phenomenon? Are the tourists who come to gape at this celebrated crime scene little more than morbid voyeurs satisfying their prurient fascination? Well . . . yes. And does such fascination reflect something
alarming about the decline of moral values in our violence-obsessed society? Absolutely not. The fact is that for better or worse, intense public

fascination with sensational crimes has always been a feature of human society—and enterprising hucksters have always found ways to exploit it.

One hundred years ago, our nation was riveted by the case of the Chicago "multi-murderer" H. H. **Holmes,** who knocked off an indeterminate number of victims in the labyrinthine depths of his so-called Murder Castle. Much like today's O.J.-crazed public, Americans couldn't get enough of the Holmes story. Perceiving the commercial potential of this mania, an aspiring showman named A. M. Clark leased the "multi-murderer's" notorious residence and announced his plans to turn it into a "murder museum," complete with guided tours by a Chicago homicide detective. The Castle, however, was gutted by a mysterious blaze before Clark could cash in on its gruesome reputation.

Sixty years later, another suspicious fire razed the ramshackle farmhouse of the Wisconsin ghoul, Ed **Gein,** shortly before the property was scheduled to be auctioned. For months, the place had drawn hordes of curiosity seekers. The torching of the house (apparently by outraged townspeople) scotched any plans to turn it into a permanent tourist site. A sideshow exhibitor named Bunny Gibbons, however, came up with another way to capitalize on "Crazy Ed's" notoriety. Successfully bidding on Gein's beat-up Ford sedan, Gibbons equipped the car with a pair of wax dummies—one in the driver's seat, simulating Ed, the other representing a mutilated female corpse. Then he displayed "Ed Gein's Death Car" in county fairs all around the Midwest, charging gawkers two bits apiece for a peek at THE CAR THAT HAULED THE DEAD FROM THEIR GRAVES!

This ghoulish sideshow, however, paled before the carnival atmosphere that prevailed at the property of the infamous **Black Widow** killer Belle Gunness, in the weeks following the discovery of her crimes. Traveling by wagon, automobile, and special excursion train, thousands of Midwesterners flocked to the farmstead where a dozen murder victims had been unearthed. Once there, they could gape at the open graves and peer at the decaying remains on display in the carriage house. After viewing the decomposed body parts, they could settle down for a family picnic, then treat themselves to candy and ice cream peddled by local hawkers. And for those desiring a souvenir of the occasion, there were handsome picture postcards of one of Gunness's dismembered victims.

As the local sheriff cheerfully proclaimed, "I never saw folks have a better time!"

TRANSVESTISM

Homicidal transvestites have been a feature of horror films ever since Anthony Perkins's Norman Bates put on his mother's clothes and carved up Janet Leigh in the shower. In real life, of course, there is no correlation at all between cross-dressing and violence. On the contrary, guys who enjoy wearing angora sweaters and high heels tend to be perfect gentlemen. There *are* several cases, however, where transvestism has been a factor in the backgrounds of serial killers.

Early in their childhoods, both Charles **Manson** and Henry Lee **Lucas** were compelled to dress as girls. Manson, who endured the kind of brutalized **Upbringing** that seems guaranteed to produce extreme psychopathology, was constantly being shuttled between relatives while his wayward mother was off whoring or doing jail time. At six, he was shipped off to Virginia to live with an aunt and uncle. The latter proved to be a sadistic bully who was constantly deriding his little charge as a "sissy." To drive home the point, he imposed a vicious punishment, forcing young Charlie to attend the first day of school in a dress.

Lucas was subjected to the identical cruelty, only this time the perpetrator was his own hard-bitten mother, an insanely vicious woman who—among her countless other forms of abuse—curled her little boy's stringy blond hair into ringlets and sent him off to school in girl's clothes.

Clearly, neither Manson nor Lucas enjoyed being a girl. One legendary serial killer who *did* was Edward **Gein,** but he was less a transvestite than a thwarted transsexual. In his deranged efforts to turn himself into a woman, Gein attempted to fashion a suit made of skin flayed from the torsos of disinterred female corpses. Arrayed in this ghastly costume—a "mammary vest" and human-skin leggings, with a vulva affixed to his crotch—he would caper around his decaying farmhouse, pretending to be his own mother. Gein, of course, served as the real-life model for the cross-dressing Norman Bates, as well as for Buffalo Bill, the malevolent female-wannabe of Thomas Harris's *The Silence of the Lambs.*

Dressed to Kill

Michael Caine plays a New York City psychiatrist who turns out to be (surprise!) nuttier than a twelve-ounce jar of Jif in this 1980 Hitchcockian homage, directed with typical flair by Brian De Palma. Its most memorable scene—in which Angie Dickinson gets sliced to shreds in an elevator car by a cross-dressing killer—carries a real wallop (though it doesn't match the brilliance of its source, the renowned shower scene in *Psycho*). All in all, *Dressed to Kill* is an outstanding cinematic example of the transvestite serial-killer genre.

TRIAD

Although it's impossible to predict if a young person will grow up to be a serial killer, there are three childhood symptoms that criminologists regard as major danger signals. They are:

1. *Enuresis* (more commonly known as bed-wetting). Lots of children wet their beds. But this behavior may be a sign of deeper pathology when it persists beyond the age of twelve. (More than 60 percent of serial killers were still wetting their beds as adolescents.)

2. *Fire-starting.* Children like to play with matches because they are intrigued by the bright, colorful, flickering flames. But budding serial killers carry this interest to a frightening extreme. Their fascination with fire is an early manifestation of their fondness for spectacular destruction. Ottis Toole—the cretinous sidekick of Henry Lee **Lucas**—burned down a neighborhood house when he was six. Teenage thrill killer George Adorno was even younger when he first displayed his pyromaniac tendencies, setting fire to his own sister when he was only four. The incorrigible Carl **Panzram** was thrown into a reformatory when he was eleven. A few months later, he torched the place, causing damage to the tune of $100,000.

3. *Sadistic activity.* Before they are big enough to inflict harm on other human beings, future serial killers get their kicks from tormenting small creatures. See **Animal Torture.**

The word *triad* simply means any group of three. When criminologists use it in relation to serial killers, they are referring to this particular set of symptoms. Of course, even when a child exhibits all three—prolonged bed-wetting, fire-starting, and sadistic cruelty to animals—there is no guarantee that he will turn out to be a serial killer.

Still, it's a *really* bad sign.

TRIGGERS

A distinguishing characteristic of serial murder is the so-called **Cooling-off Period.** Weeks, months, even years can lapse between a killer's crimes. All the while, however, his hunger for blood is building inside him, his fantasies of torture and death are growing more urgent by the day. Suddenly, something pushes him over the edge from morbid daydream to murderous action, driving him to fulfill his lethal fantasies on living victims. Criminologists call that "something" a *triggering factor.*

Preventing serial murder might be easier if there were some way to identify the specific triggers that cause psychos to kill. Unfortunately, no such means exist. Almost anything can ignite a serial killer. Sometimes, it's the way a victim looks. Ed **Gein**'s homicidal mania was inspired by matronly women, while David **Berkowitz** vented his psychotic fury on pretty young women with long brown hair.

Cases like these make a certain amount of psychoanalytic sense, since the triggers can be seen as symbolic stand-ins for hated figures from the killer's past. (In Gein's case, it was his monstrous mama; in Berkowitz's, the various girls who had rejected him since childhood.) But—as is true of so many aspects of serial murder—the triggers that set these creatures off are sometimes beyond rational comprehension. One maniac butchered his victims after receiving instructions from UFO aliens, while German lust murderer Heinrich Pommerencke was inspired to commit serial slaughter by a scene in Cecil B. DeMille's *The Ten Commandments.*

The wholly unpredictable nature of these triggering factors is one of the scariest things about serial killers. One young woman may be murdered because she tries to run away. Another may be slain for the very opposite reason. By agreeing to perform whatever sex acts her abductor wants, she threatens his sense of control. Perceiving her desperate offer as an attempt to take charge of the situation, he grows enraged and kills her.

In short, there's just no way of telling what will send a serial killer into a sudden homicidal rage. One evening in late December 1981, a sociopath named David Bullock went to the apartment of an acquaintance named Herbert Morales. Morales was very proud of his Christmas tree, which he had taken great pains to decorate. While Bullock was there, Morales began adjusting some of the ornaments.

As Bullock later explained to police, Morales "started messing with the Christmas tree, telling me how nice the Christmas tree was. So I shot him."

> "He started messing with the Christmas tree, telling me how nice the Christmas tree was. So I shot him."
>
> **DAVID BULLOCK,**
> *explaining why he murdered an acquaintance following a 1981 Christmas party*

TROPHIES

For serious students of serial murder, a standard reference book is Michael Newton's encyclopedic *Hunting Humans*. The title of this work is meant to convey the predatory nature of serial killers—the way they stalk and slay their victims, as though other people were nothing more than game animals to be butchered for pleasure.

But Newton's title is apt for another reason, too. Like big-game hunters who commemorate their feats by bringing home a trophy of the kill—a set of antlers, a stuffed head, or a prize pelt—the serial killer often does the same thing, removing an item from his victim and preserving it as a precious keepsake.

Sometimes, these objects are completely mundane—a piece of costume jewelry, a cheap wristwatch, a family snapshot, or some other personal effect with little or no apparent value. But the object clearly has great value to the serial killer, or else he wouldn't run the risk of being caught with such an incriminating piece of evidence in his possession. Depending on what this value is, these items are classified by the **FBI** as either "souvenirs" or "trophies." "Souvenirs" are defined as items that are used to fuel the fantasies of a serial killer, whereas "trophies" are objects that are saved as proof of his skill.

For all intents and purposes, however, there really isn't much difference between the two. Ultimately, they both serve the same purpose for a serial killer, filling him with a sense of his own power and allowing him to relive his crimes in fantasy as he contemplates his morbid treasures. In short, these items are essentially *fetish objects* that provide intense, perverted pleasure to their collectors.

The proof of this perversity lies in the nature of many of these trophies. While some are commonplace, others are clearly sexual. A female victim's underwear is a particular favorite among lust murderers, with high heels and nylon stockings running a close second.

The most hideous trophies of all, of course, are human body parts. Serial killers have been known to collect everything from fingernail clippings to entire bodies. British sex killer John Reginald Christie kept three complete corpses in his kitchen cupboard, while Jeffrey **Dahmer**'s extensive collection included painted skulls, refrigerated heads, and male genital organs stored in a lobster pot.

The most infamous of all collectors of human trophies was the Wisconsin ghoul, Ed **Gein**, who turned his ramshackle farmhouse into a kind of museum of unnatural history, full of carefully preserved human artifacts. Among his ghastly treasures were chair seats made of human flesh, soup bowls fashioned from skulls, a nipple belt, and a box full of preserved vulvas. Perhaps most shocking of all were the items found in his bedroom: a collection of female faces, skinned from their skulls, tanned, stuffed, and mounted on the wall—exactly like prize hunting trophies.

TYPES

The exact **definition** of serial murder remains a matter of debate in criminological circles. In the view of some experts, serial killing, in the strict sense of the term, is essentially synonymous with sadistic lust murder. Other authorities, however, take a broader view of the matter and believe that there are different types of serial killers. According to these specialists, serial killers can be divided into the following four categories:

1. *Visionary* killers. Most serial killers are psychopaths—i.e., intelligent but utterly amoral human beings characterized by a complete lack of conscience or empathy. Visionary killers, by contrast, are *psychotics*—people whose minds are gripped by bizarre delusions and hallucinations. David "Son of Sam" **Berkowitz,** for example, claimed that he was obeying a demon who transmitted his orders through a neighbor's pet dog. Herbert Mullin, who killed thirteen people in the early 1970s, was a paranoid schizophrenic who heard "telepathic voices" commanding him to kill in order to avert a natural disaster, a catastrophic earthquake that would destroy California.

2. *Mission-oriented* serial killers see themselves as avenging crusaders, ridding society of "undesirables"—harlots, homosexuals, "foreigners," etc. In the late 1970s, for example, a Hitler-worshipping thug named Joe Franklin embarked on a one-man war against interracial couples, killing thirteen people before he was stopped.

3. *Hedonistic* serial killers have no motive beyond their own pleasure. They kill because it feels good. Inflicting death is the ultimate high for them, a source of intense, even sexual, pleasure.

4. *Power seekers.* The primary motive of these killers is the urgent need to assert their supremacy over a helpless victim, to compensate for their own deep-seated feelings of worthlessness by completely dominating another human being.

The problem with these categories is that there is often so much overlap between the different types that the whole system breaks down. For example, a missionary killer who targets prostitutes may well be responding to "divine" voices commanding him to clean the streets of whores. And the pleasure that a hedonistic killer gets from binding and torturing a teenage girl might derive from the complete power he is exerting over his victim.

> "Satan gets into people and makes them do things they don't want to."
>
> **HERBERT MULLIN,**
> *"visionary" serial killer*

UNSOLVED

Serial killers are the scariest of all criminals not simply because they do such appalling things. What also makes them really frightening is that—though capable of the most insanely violent acts—they are not raving lunatics. On the contrary, the typical serial killer is a man with an above-average **IQ,** exceptional cunning, and an uncanny ability to appear as boringly normal as the next guy. As a result, serial killers often go undetected for years. Indeed, some of them have been known to elude capture forever—leaving a trail of corpses in their wake but no real clues to their own identities.

The classic example of this phenomenon, of course, is **Jack the Ripper,** though there have been other, less renowned serial killers whose identities remain unknown. No arrest was ever made, for instance, in the case of the night-prowling butcher known as the "Axeman of New Orleans" (see **Axe Murderers**). Nor in the grisly string of "**Lovers' Lane**" homicides committed by the "Monster of Florence" (see **Foreigners**). And there have been plenty of even more obscure serial sex slayers who have gotten away with repeated murder, such as the psycho dubbed the "Colonial Parkway Killer," responsible for the deaths of four couples in Virginia in the late 1980s.

Why are some serial killers never caught? One possibility is that they simply decide to stop before they are arrested—in effect, to quit while they're ahead. But this seems unlikely, at least in the vast majority of cases. After all, homicidal maniacs are as addicted to death as alcoholics are to drink, and since there are no twelve-step recovery programs for lust murderers, it seems improbable that a compulsive killer would simply kick the habit on his own. A more plausible explanation is that some serial killers are *forced* to stop. They might find themselves locked up behind bars—either imprisoned for an unrelated crime or confined to a mental asylum. Or (like other mortals) they might die very suddenly, possibly at their own hands.

Suicide has been offered as a theory in the case of "Jack the Stripper," a serial killer of prostitutes who terrorized London in the mid-1960s. Though the case remains officially unsolved, many believe that the culprit was a security guard who took his own life (see **Rippers**). In the case of the mysterious "Toledo Slugger," another plausible explanation has been offered. In 1925 and 1926, a string of women were raped and bludgeoned to death by a shadowy assailant in Toledo, Ohio. In their zeal to find the culprit, the police rounded up every known "mental defective" they could get their hands on and shipped them off to state asylums. Since the Slugger's crimes came to an abrupt halt around this time, some people believe that the police managed to nab the killer in their citywide sweep.

Other cases, however, continue to pose enduring—and tantalizing—puzzles. Another Ohio maniac—the "Cleveland Torso Killer" (aka the "Mad Butcher of Kingsbury Run")—is a case in point. During a four-year span in the 1930s, this bloodthirsty maniac chopped up a dozen people, leaving body parts strewn around the city. Nevertheless, in spite of an all-out effort by law officials, led by no less an eminence than Eliot Ness, the former Untouchable who was serving as Cleveland's director of public safety), the "Mad Butcher" eluded arrest. In the spring of 1938, his atrocities came to a sudden, mysterious halt. To this day no one knows who he was. Suspects range from a mentally unbalanced premed student to a Bohemian immigrant to a psychopathic hobo. Perhaps the most unsettling theory of all was put forth by a Cleveland detective who believed that the torso slayings stopped because the culprit pulled up stakes and headed west to California—where he committed the infamous "Black Dahlia" homicide.

Cracking a legendary unsolved murder case is a challenge that some crime enthusiasts find impossible to resist. Every publishing season seems to bring another book, claiming to be the ultimate solution to one of these real-life whodunits. In the past few years alone, the American public has been treated to a former Los Angeles police officer fingering his own father as the "Black Dahlia" killer (Steve Hodel's *Black Dahlia Avenger*); a veteran true-crime writer naming the original "**Zodiac**" (Robert Graysmith's *Zodiac Unmasked*); and a bestselling mystery author announcing, with great fanfare, that she had finally figured out who Jack the Ripper was (Patricia Cornwell's *Portrait of a Killer*). Whether these books will truly prove to be the last word on their respective subjects only time will tell, though there is reason to believe that these cases (especially Saucy Jack's) will continue to generate new "ultimate solutions" far into the future.

Occasionally, of course, a long-unsolved serial-murder case really will come to a sudden, unexpected resolution—not, however, as the result of the ingenious theorizings of a bestselling writer but through the apprehension of the perpetrator after years of persistent police investigation. In December 2001, for example—twenty years after he committed his first atrocity—the infamous "Green River Killer" was finally brought to justice. A few years later, another notorious case that had frustrated investigators for decades—the "**BTK**" killings in Wichita, Kansas, came to a gratifying conclusion with the arrest of a suspect, Dennis Rader.

========= **Unsolved No More** =========

Time is not, as a rule, on the side of homicide investigators. With every passing year, the trail gets colder and the chances of finding the killer diminish. When whole decades go by, those chances fade to just about zero.

In at least one case, however, the reverse turned out to be true. The passage of time—and, more specifically, the technology that developed during that period—made it possible to identify one of the most notorious and elusive serial sex slayers in modern American history.

In the early 1980s, a mysterious psychokiller murdered dozens of young women, mostly prostitutes and runaways, dumping many of them along the Green River of Kings County, Washington—a signature pattern that earned him his homicidal nickname, the "Green River Killer." Most of his victims were strangled. In some cases, they had been raped after death.

Not only were the local police unable to identify the culprit, they had a hard time keeping track of how many people he killed, largely because he was so adept at squirreling the bodies away in the Kings County country-side. By 1984, when the murders seemed to stop, the authorities put the number of victims at twenty-four. Five years later, after finding more decaying remains, their best bet was forty-nine.

The police might not have had many conclusive leads, but there was one thing they didn't lack: possible suspects. Altogether, they compiled a list of some 1,300 names. One of them was a truck painter, Gary Ridgeway, who had been seen with a few of the victims. He also had a problem keeping his hands off women's throats. He had once tried to throttle a prostitute and another time tried the same with his wife. The police suspected him enough to request that he take a lie detector test. Ridgeway agreed and passed the test not once but twice. He was off the hook, at least for the next fifteen years or so.

From some of the corpses, investigators were able to collect semen samples, but they were minuscule—too small for 1980s forensic science to produce any useful results. By 2001, however, the situation had changed. Enhanced technology now made it possible to analyze such small samples, and the semen found on three of the victims matched the DNA in the saliva taken from Ridgeway.

In November 2001, police arrested the fifty-two-year-old painter, nearly twenty years after the last known victim had been murdered. In order to escape the death penalty, he agreed to cooperate, supplying the police with information about other murders that they were not aware of, one of them committed as late as 1996. At his trial, he confessed to forty-eight killings, but there might have been more—perhaps as many as sixty. The problem was, after so many years, Ridgeway had trouble remembering.

As he told investigators, "I killed so many women, I have a hard time keeping them straight."

UPBRINGING

It is common to describe an especially harsh, deprived childhood as "Dickensian"—but in the case of serial killers, that adjective is wildly inadequate.

Compared to the boyhoods of most serial killers, Oliver Twist's early years in a Victorian poorhouse seem like an extended vacation at Disneyland.

Albert "Boston Strangler" **DeSalvo** was raised by a monstrous father who liked to bring whores home with him, screw them in front of the kids, then beat his wife savagely when she complained. One of DeSalvo's most vivid childhood memories was of watching his father knock out all of his mother's teeth, then break her fingers one by one as she lay sprawled beneath the kitchen sink. DeSalvo himself not only received regular, vicious thrashings with a lead pipe but, along with his two sisters, was sold into slavery. An acquaintance of the senior DeSalvo paid nine dollars for the three children, who were shipped off to Maine and forced to work as farm laborers.

Henry Lee **Lucas** was raised in unimaginable squalor by a brutal, alcoholic prostitute who compelled her paraplegic husband to watch her have sex with her tricks. Henry was forced to watch, too—generally while dressed up in the little girl's clothing his mother made him wear. She also beat him mercilessly with objects ranging from broomsticks to two-by-fours and took pleasure in killing his pets.

Little Charlie **Manson**'s mother was a bisexual alcoholic prostitute, who reportedly once traded her son for a pitcher of beer. After she was thrown into prison for armed robbery, Manson was taken in by a brutal uncle, who derided him as a sissy and sent him to school in a dress. In later years, he was placed in an institution where he was routinely beaten with a wooden paddle for bed-wetting.

Raised in a gothically grim orphanage, Albert **Fish** was schooled in sadism by a female teacher who disciplined disobedient boys and girls by stripping them naked and beating them in front of the other children. Sex murderer Joseph Kallinger—whose victims included his own son—was raised by adoptive parents who kept him in line with a hammer, a cat-o'-nine-tails, and constant threats of castration. Serial killer Hugh Morse was brought up by an insanely tyrannical grandmother, who once punished him for sneaking out to the movies by butchering his pet mice.

According to **FBI** findings, 42 percent of serial killers have suffered severe physical abuse as children, 43 percent were sexually molested, and a full 74 percent were subjected to ongoing psychological torture.

Of course, there are those who sneer at the notion that an unhappy childhood is the main cause of serial killing, pointing out that countless people who grow up in seriously dysfunctional households do not turn out to be homicidal maniacs. These critics also refer to monsters like Jeffrey **Dahmer** and Ted **Bundy,** who appear to have come from more or less normal, middle-class backgrounds. And indeed, childhood snapshots of little Ted, dressed up in a cowboy suit or posing beside a snowman, would not look out of place in Ozzie and Harriet's family album.

It's undoubtedly true that other factors are involved in the making of serial killers (see **Causes**). Still, "negative parenting" (as the sociologists quaintly call it) is invariably present in their backgrounds. (There are indications that Dahmer and Bundy were both victims of sexual abuse by relatives.) Brutalized in childhood, the serial killer grows up full of a murderous rage that is turned against all of humanity. He can know pleasure only by administering pain. He can feel alive only when he is inflicting death.

> "I hated all my life. I hated everybody. When I first grew up and can remember, I was dressed as a girl by mother. And I stayed that way for two or three years. And after that I was treated like what I call the dog of the family. I was beaten. I was made to do things that no human bein' would want to do."
>
> **HENRY LEE LUCAS**

V

Joseph Vacher

One of the scariest things about serial killers is how normal they can seem. Ted **Bundy** looked like a frat boy, Jeffrey **Dahmer** like a computer nerd, and John Wayne **Gacy** like the president of the local Rotary Club. Frenchman Joseph Vacher (1869–1897) was different. In his case, appearances weren't deceiving at all. He had the kind of face that could give children nightmares. And his actions were consistent with his looks.

A repulsively seedy tramp with a palsied face and an eye that leaked a steady stream of pus, Vacher was born into a poor peasant family, the last of fifteen children. He committed his first known crime—the attempted rape of a young boy—when he was nineteen. Two years later, he was conscripted into the army, and he cut his own throat with a razor when he failed to win promotion to corporal. Several years later, he tried suicide again when a young woman he coveted spurned his advances. Vacher shot her three times with a pistol, then turned the gun on himself and fired point-blank into his own face.

The woman survived. So did Vacher, though half his face was now permanently paralyzed and his right eye was reduced to a raw, suppurating hole. After a year in an insane asylum, he was discharged as "cured." Equipping himself with a few basic necessities (maps, an umbrella, a cudgel, several butcher knives, and a cleaver), he tramped around the countryside for three and a half years. Stopping at a farmhouse whenever he grew hungry, he would pound on the door and demand food from the owner, who was usually happy to oblige just to get rid of the hideous tramp.

But Vacher was possessed by other, infinitely more loathsome appetites. During the course of his wanderings, he set upon and slaughtered eleven people of both sexes, assaulting them in a demonic frenzy—stabbing, strangling, mutilating, biting, disembowelling. Most of his victims, male as well as female, were raped after death.

The "French Ripper," as the shadowy killer began to be called, was finally apprehended in August 1897. At his trial, he argued that he was not mentally competent. His mind, he claimed, had been twisted as an eight-year-old boy when he was bitten by a mad dog. The court was not convinced. On New Year's Eve, 1898, the twenty-nine-year-old Vacher was sent to the guillotine.

VAMPIRES

There's both good and bad news about vampires. The good news is that they don't exist, at least not the kind found in old Bela Lugosi movies. There are plenty of things to worry about in life, but being attacked in your bedroom by a four-hundred-year-old Transylvanian demon isn't one of them.

The bad news about vampires is that some sexual psychopaths derive intense satisfaction from drinking human blood and will resort to serial murder to satisfy this monstrous craving. Deviants like these don't sleep in coffins or turn themselves into bats, but in one crucial respect, they are infinitely scarier than Bram Stoker's Dracula or the sexy bloodsuckers of Anne Rice's novels. These ravenous fiends are for real.

One of the most infamous real-life vampires was the Italian lust murderer Vincenz Verzeni. From an early age, Verzeni took exquisite delight in strangulation. At twelve, he discovered that he got tremendous pleasure from wringing the necks of chickens. By the time he reached late adolescence, he had progressed from poultry to women. At first, he simply throttled his victims until he achieved orgasm. Once he climaxed, he would let his victims live. In his early twenties, however, Verzeni's perversion took a horrific turn. In 1871, he pounced on a fourteen-year-old girl, dragged her to a field, and choked her to death. Then—in a sadistic frenzy—he chewed at her thigh and sucked her blood, ripped out her intestines, tore out her genitals, and removed a chunk of her calf, which he carried away with him, intending to roast and eat it. Eight months later, he savaged another young woman, garroting her with a leather thong, then biting open her neck and gorging on her blood. Verzeni was arrested after attacking his own nineteen-year-old cousin, who managed to fight him off, then immediately reported him to the police.

In the late 1940s, British serial slayer John George Haigh murdered half a dozen people to get his hands on their money, then dissolved their remains in his basement acid vat. At his 1949 trial, the notorious "Acid-Bath Murderer" insisted that before disposing of each body, he had tapped the victim's jugular, drawn off a glassful of blood, and quaffed it. Though Haigh's vampiric claims were viewed by many as a clumsy attempt to cop an insanity plea, it seems fairly certain that at the very least he was afflicted with a severe case of *hematomania*—a lifelong obsession with blood.

One of the weirdest cases of vampirism was that of Florencio Fernandez, a twenty-five-year-old Argentine stonemason who, in 1960, slipped through the windows of fifteen sleeping women and attacked them in their beds—pinioning their arms, biting into their throats, and drinking their blood. Like the Nicolas Cage character in the 1989 cult movie *Vampire's Kiss,* Fernandez apparently suffered from a serious vampiric delusion. He lived in a cave, prowled the night in a black Dracula-like cloak, and spent the daylight hours sunk in a comalike sleep.

Like Dracula's zoophagous servant, Renfield, young Richard Chase loved to drink the blood of animals—rabbits, cats, dogs. In 1978, however, he progressed to infinitely more monstrous crimes. During a four-day spree, he broke into several homes, killed and butchered the inhabitants (including a pregnant woman and a twenty-two-month-old infant), and wallowed in their gore. After his arrest, he confessed to drinking the blood of his victims. Chase—who was dubbed the "Vampire of Sacramento"—served as the real-life model for the unspeakable killer in the 1992 movie *Rampage,* a thought-provoking (and occasionally harrowing) film directed by William Friedkin of *Exorcist* fame.

For more on the world of real-life blood sucking killers, readers should

Richard Chase; from
Murderers! trading card set
(Courtesy of Roger Worsham)

check out the book *True Vampires* (Feral Press, 2003) by Sondra London (a writer who has earned some notoriety herself for her romantic attachment to not one but two infamous lust murderers, Gerard the "Butcher of Blind Creek" Schaefer and Danny the "Gainesville Ripper" Rollings). London's book is not just a comprehensive survey of its macabre subject; it also features handsome illustrations by one of the crazies she covers: Nico Claux, aka the "Vampire of Paris," who satisfied his unholy urges by desecrating graves, plundering morgues, and robbing blood banks.

> "I had an unspeakable delight in strangling women, experiencing during the act erections and real sexual pleasure. The feeling of pleasure while strangling them was much greater than that which I experienced while masturbating. . . . It never occurred to me to touch or look at the genitals. It satisfied me to seize the women by the neck and suck their blood."
>
> **VINCENZ VERZENI**

Holland isn't exactly |
ing that one of the n
killer appears in the
Sluizer.

The movie foci
whose girlfriend (
a roadside rest :
friend must hav
uncertainty an

The villain of tн
history, a meek, soft-spoken iaι.
speakable form of torture. Portrayed with оι.
named Barnard Pierre Donnadieu, the killer ultimately ∪ι.
haunted young man what the vanished girl experienced. In a shatteːː.ɡ
(if somewhat implausible) conclusion, Hofman accepts the killer's proposition—leading to one of the most nightmarish endings ever put on film.
This is one of those small, understated European fright films that has
infinitely more impact than the typical Hollywood splatter fest.

Hollywood, in fact, produced a remake of *The Vanishing* in 1993, starring
Kiefer Sutherland and Jeff Bridges. Though directed again by Sluizer, this
second version falls completely flat. Stick to the original!

VICAP

See **FBI**.

WANNABES

Serial killers are driven to perpetrate their outrages by profound psychological compulsions, generally of a perverted sexual nature. As a result, they tend to commit their crimes in highly personal, ritualistic ways. They may bind a victim just so, torture him or her in a specific way, use a particular kind of weapon to inflict death, then leave the corpse arranged in a specific position. All these elements—which make up the killer's unique "signature"—are dictated by his sick individual needs. This is why there are so few serial-killer **Copycats.** Homicidal psychos, for the most part, aren't interested in emulating other killers; they are only out to gratify their own depraved personal needs.

There is one need, however, that is common to most serial killers. Largely because they are so hideously abused and humiliated as children, most of these psychos grow up feeling utterly worthless and impotent. To compensate for this sense of nothingness, they often develop a raging megalomania—an uncontrollable need to prove to the world (and to themselves) that they are superior, all-powerful beings. For some, this need manifests itself as an insane ambition to earn everlasting infamy, to have their names go down in the history books alongside those of the legendary criminals of the past. Killers like these are the psychopathic equivalent of celebrity wannabes.

The German lust murderer Peter **Kürten,** for example, sought to surpass the evil of his idol **Jack the Ripper** and become "the greatest criminal who ever lived." The highly questionable confessions of Henry Lee **Lucas**—who admitted to over three hundred murders—were apparently motivated by the same self-aggrandizing impulses. Dr. H. H. **Holmes,** the nineteenth-century "multi-murderer" sometimes described as America's first serial killer, possessed the same bizarre ambition. Taking perverse pride in his status as the country's preeminent criminal (or "arch-fiend," as the newspapers liked to call him), Holmes eagerly confessed to the murder of several dozen victims—many of whom subsequently turned out to be alive and well.

Indeed, so hungry are some serial killers for celebrity status that they grow actively incensed when their crimes are ignored or underestimated. When German sex killer Rudolph Pleil was charged with nine savage murders, he indignantly insisted that the actual number was twenty-eight. Only one thing mattered to Pleil—that he be universally acknowledged as *"der beste Totmacher,"* the world's "best death-maker."

Similarly, when the Wichita serial killer who called himself "**BTK**" didn't receive the kind of press coverage he thought he deserved, he fired off a peevish complaint to a local newspaper: "How many do I have to kill before I get my name in the paper or some national attention?"

Colin Ireland, a British psycho-killer who preyed on gay men, thought he knew the answer to that question. In the spring of 1993, he savagely murdered five random victims. The reason? Ireland was a wannabe whose demented dream was to be known as a serial killer. He had read in a book that to be so classified, a person had to slay a minimum of four. He threw in the last one for good measure.

WARTIME

There's an old Chinese saying: "In crisis there is opportunity." This pearl of proverbial wisdom is epitomized by certain serial killers, who have turned the greatest crisis of them all—global warfare—into an opportunity for wholesale murder.

If World War I had never occurred, a small-time French sociopath named Henri Landru might have lived out his days as nothing more than a petty crook. When the conflict broke out, however, Landru suddenly perceived a unique opportunity to exploit his nation's woes for his own personal profit. With France's male population decimated, the country was suddenly full of young, well-off widows. Landru set about preying on these vulnerable women, luring them through seductive matrimonial **Ads,** then wooing them, wedding them, and murdering them for their money (see **Bluebeards).**

Some twenty years later—during World War II—France's worst fears were realized when Hitler's troops occupied Paris, succeeding where the Kaiser's had failed. Parisian Jews desperately sought a way to escape the Nazi terror. Waiting to prey on them was another French psychopath, Dr. Marcel **Petiot.** Posing as a sympathetic Resistance agent who would help smuggle them out of the country, Petiot slowly killed the would-be refugees with lethal "vaccines," then looted their possessions.

At roughly the same time in London—as the German Luftwaffe bombarded the city night after night—an English airman named Gordon Cumming found a chance to unleash his long-simmering sadism. Taking advantage of the city's mandatory blackouts, he prowled the darkened streets and, in less than a week, savagely murdered four women (see **Rippers).**

The chaotic conditions of war allowed another notorious lust murderer—Bela Kiss of Hungary—not to commit his crimes but to escape punishment for them. Before the outbreak of World War I, Kiss had succeeded in slaying no fewer than twenty-three women without arousing suspicion. By the time his crimes were uncovered, he had already enlisted in the army and been killed in action. Or so it appeared. Only later did authorities surmise that Kiss had actually switched dog tags with a dying soldier, assumed the latter's identity, and vanished without a trace (see **Whereabouts Unknown).**

WEAPONS

Cinematic serial killers are artists of death, constantly searching for imaginative new ways to create carnage. In their homicidal hands, everything from a scythe to a staple gun becomes an instrument of mayhem, wielded with the virtuosity of a maestro.

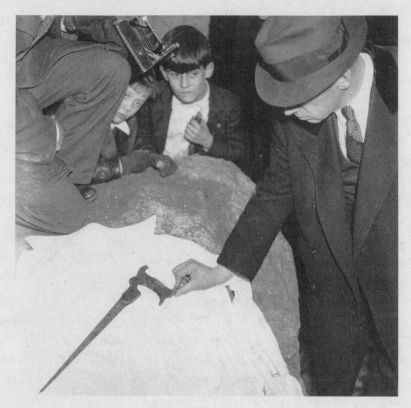

Investigators display the saw Fish used to dismember
Grace Budd's body

Fish's "Implements of Hell"; painting by Michael Rose

By contrast, real-life serial killers are much more conventional in their choice of weapons. What distinguishes them from ordinary killers is their preference for "manual" means of murder—stabbing, strangling, clubbing—over firearms. While the majority of American murders are committed with guns, serial killers favor the "hands-on" approach, which offers a more intense physical experience. When it comes to sick, sadistic pleasure, shooting people from a distance of twenty feet just can't compete with plunging a serrated hunting knife into their flesh.

Of course, there are notable exceptions. Ed **Gein** dispatched his victims with a bullet to the back of the skull. And before he began signing his letters "Son of Sam," David **Berkowitz**—the serial assassin who terrorized New York City in the late 1970s—was nicknamed after his favorite weapon: the ".44-Caliber Killer."

Whereabouts Unknown

The crimes perpetrated by serial killers are so appalling that when one of these creatures is on the loose, it sometimes seems as if a supernatural monster has risen from the underworld. Newspaper reporters trip all over themselves to come up with lurid, horror-movie monikers—the "Mad Beast," the "Vampire-Killer," the "Werewolf Slayer." So it's easy to feel a jolt of surprise when the monster is finally caught. The supernatural demon turns out to be a nondescript loser who looks about as threatening as a computer geek. The demon is reduced to pathetically human dimensions.

Unfortunately, some serial killers are never captured. In cases like these, the killer often continues to live on in popular fantasy as a kind of phantom or specter. Myths and folktales grow up around them. This is certainly true of the most famous of all serial killers, **Jack the Ripper.** But there are other well-known serial killers who vanished without a trace and whose fate continues to tease the imagination of crime buffs. The anonymous **Axe** murderer who butchered a string of derelicts in Cleveland during the mid-1930s is one of these cases. In spite of the concerted efforts of the Cleveland police—including the legendary Eliot Ness of *Untouchables* fame, who was running the department at the time—the "Cleveland Torso Killer" was never apprehended.

Like the Ripper, the "Cleveland Torso Killer" is a fascinating figure because he remains a total enigma. No one knows who he was or what became of him. There are other cases, however, where a killer's identity is not in question. The mystery has to do with the maniac's ultimate whereabouts.

Sifting through the ruins of the incinerated farmhouse belonging to notorious **Black Widow** killer Belle Gunness, searchers came upon a charred female body and assumed it was Gunness's remains. There was only one problem. The corpse had no head—so making a positive ID was a little tricky. Eventually, investigators concluded that the corpse was a substitute—a woman Gunness had murdered expressly for that purpose. In subsequent years, Gunness was allegedly sighted in different parts of the country, from New England to Los Angeles. But to this day, no one knows what really became of her.

A few years later, during World War I, officials in the Hungarian town of Czinkota discovered the bodies of twenty-three murdered women in and around the abandoned house of a retired tinsmith named Bela Kiss. Unfortunately, there seemed to be no way to punish the killer, since Kiss (who had enlisted in the army) had reportedly died in combat. Reports of his death, however, were greatly exaggerated. As it turned out, Kiss—while recuperating from his wounds in a military hospital—switched dog tags with a dying soldier and disappeared under the other man's name. From that point on, his trail vanished. Alleged sightings on both sides of the Atlantic—from Budapest to New York City—kept his legend alive.

Kiss's countryman Sylvestre Matuschka was one of the most bizarre serial killers of all time, a maniac who derived intense sexual pleasure from bombing railroad trains and listening to the dying shrieks of the passengers. Matuschka was actually convicted and imprisoned in the 1930s, but somehow he managed to get free during the turmoil of World War II. What happened to him next is anybody's guess. According to some crime historians, however, Matuschka was forced to join the Soviet army, which recognized his special talents and gave him a job for which he was uniquely qualified: explosives expert.

WOMEN

One of the most hotly debated questions among people who study violent crime is: Is there such a thing as a female serial killer? The simple answer is: Yes . . . and no. It all depends on how you define serial murder.

If you follow the **FBI**'s definition—three or more separate killings with an emotional cooling-off period between each homicide—then the answer is clearly affirmative. The annals of crime are full of fatal females who have knocked off large numbers of victims—**Black Widow** brides who dispatch a succession of hubbies; homicidal **Nurses** who administer death to dozens of patients; evil **Housekeepers** who dispose of entire families. Serial-killer encyclopedist Michael Newton has compiled a volume called *Bad Girls Do It!* that profiles nearly two hundred female multiple murderers—an assemblage almost imposing enough to confirm Rudyard Kipling's famous line, "The female of the species is more deadly than the male."

Of course, many specialists—Newton included—believe that true serial murder always involves another element, specified in the definition put forth by the National Institute of Justice in 1988: the presence of "sadistic, sexual overtones." Even when you add this ingredient, there's a sizable number of women who fit the bill, from "Lonely Hearts Killer" Martha Beck, to the British sex killer Rosemary West (accused of the grisly torture and murder of ten victims, including her own daughter), to Elizabeth Bathory, the notorious "Blood Countess" of sixteenth-century Romania, reputed to have slain as many as six hundred victims for her own erotic delectation.

The problem arises when you try to find a female criminal who matches the model of the modern-day serial killer epitomized by **Jack the Ripper**—the lone psychopathic lust murderer, coolly stalking and snaring his victims, then butchering and mutilating them in a sex-crazed frenzy. Here, the issue becomes much more tricky. Indeed, it is virtually impossible to find a single woman in the whole history of crime who fits this mold. (As culture critic Camille Paglia puts it with characteristic bluntness, "There is no female Jack the Ripper.") Beck and West, for example, were part of **Killer Couples.** And Bathory falls into the venerable—if thoroughly depraved—tradition of the evil **Aristocrat,** exemplified by monsters like Caligula and Gilles de Rais.

There is a solution to this puzzle. If you think of serial homicide as fundamentally a sex crime (as the NIJ definition suggests), it follows that female serial killers will differ from their male counterparts in roughly the same way that the erotic nature of women differs from that of men. Just as male sexuality is phallic-penetrative, promiscuous, and fairly undiscriminating, a typical male serial killer will butcher whatever random stranger he can get his hands on. The average female serial killer, by contrast, generally needs to have a relationship with someone before she'll kill that person. She derives her excitement not from violating a stranger's body with a penetrating implement but from a grotesque travesty of tenderness and intimacy: serving poisoned food to a husband, for example, or smothering a child to death. Jane **Toppan,** a Victorian poisoner who climbed into bed with her many victims and achieved orgasm while embracing them during their death throes, exemplifies this pattern.

Keep in mind, too, that—though their crimes are less grisly—female psycho-killers are no less sadistic than their male counterparts. On the contrary, it can be argued that—for all the postmortem butchery they were subjected to—the streetwalkers slain by Jack the Ripper died a swifter and more merciful death than the victims of madwomen like Nurse Toppan, who were made to suffer the prolonged agonies of slow poisoning.

The single, if arguable, exception to this rule is Aileen **Wuornos,** the one-time Florida hooker who slew a string of male pickups between December 1989 and the following November. Some observers viewed Wuornos as a classic serial murderer—a cold-blooded predator who killed for the sheer joy of it, like David "Son of Sam" **Berkowitz.** Certain experts even worried that Wuornos represented the start of a frightening trend: the first of a new breed of female serial killers that would soon be terrorizing America.

Those fears proved to be unjustified. Wuornos appears to have been an isolated case. Indeed, not everyone regards her as a serial killer in the classic sense but as a pathetic, lost soul: a brutalized woman whose rage at the world—and the male sex in particular—exploded in an outburst of horrific violence.

Aileen Wuornos

Some people regard her as "the first female serial killer in history"—a cold-blooded predator who stalked and murdered a string of victims over an extended period of time. Others (herself included) claim that she only killed in

Aileen Wuornos; from
Bloody Visions trading cards

self-defense, when threatened with violence and rape. Whichever of these
views is correct, one thing is certain. Between December 1989 and the
following November, seven middle-aged male motorists, driving the highways of central Florida, stopped to pick up Aileen "Lee" Wuornos and
ended up dead.

Virtually from the day of her birth in 1956, Wuornos's life was a nonstop
nightmare of deprivation and violence, abandonment and abuse. She was
the child of a teenage couple whose marriage had ended before she was
born. Her father would eventually hang himself in jail after being arrested
on child-molestation charges. One day when Aileen was only six months
old, her mother left the infant girl and her brother with a babysitter, then
telephoned to say she wouldn't be coming home. Aileen was taken in by her
grandparents but kicked out of their house when she was thirteen after
giving birth to an illegitimate child (the consequence, she claimed, of rape).
By the time she was fourteen, she was living a desperately brutalized life—
sleeping in an abandoned car, hustling for drinks, drugs, and an occasional
meal. At twenty, she married a seventy-year-old man, but their union lasted
only a month (according to her account, she abandoned him because he
beat her with a cane; according to his, he sued for divorce after she beat
him up to get his car keys). Two years later, she attempted suicide by shooting herself in the stomach. After recuperating, she robbed a convenience

store at gunpoint, was promptly arrested, and spent thirteen months in prison. Other arrests—for check forgery and auto theft—followed.

In 1986, Wuornos met the love of her life—a lesbian named Tyria Moore—at a Daytona gay bar. Even after their sexual passion cooled, the two remained inseparable for the next four years. During that time, Wuornos's rage and resentment toward men grew increasingly violent. She continued to hustle. Now, however, she carried a .22-caliber gun in her handbag when she worked the truck stops and roadhouses.

On November 30, 1989, Wuornos took a ride with a fifty-one-year-old electronics repair shop owner named Richard Mallory. The next day, his abandoned car was found in a stretch of secluded woods, along with his wallet, a half-empty vodka bottle, and a torn package of condoms. Twelve days later, Mallory's bullet-riddled corpse was uncovered in a junkyard. Six more nearly identical killings followed.

After Wuornos and Moore were spotted driving one of the victims' cars, Florida police were able to pick up their trail. Wuornos was arrested in a seedy biker bar called The Last Resort. Once in custody, she confessed to all seven killings, though she claimed she was acting in self-defense. Tried for the murder of Richard Mallory, she insisted that she had shot him after he choked and tortured her, raped her anally, and threatened to kill her. The jury was unpersuaded. Wuornos was convicted and sentenced to death. "I'm innocent," she shouted when the verdict was read. "I hope you get raped! Scumbags of America!" During a subsequent proceeding—at which Wuornos was given three more death sentences—she hurled similar obscenities at the prosecuting attorney: "I hope your wife and children get raped in the ass!"

As Wuornos sat on death row, she appeared to grow increasingly unbalanced. Even while proclaiming her innocence, she sent a letter to the Florida Supreme Court, declaring, "I'm one who seriously hates human life and would kill again." She fired her attorneys, stopped her appeals, and eagerly awaited her execution. She was put to death by lethal injection in October 2002. Her last words seemed to confirm the opinion of some observers that, by the end of her lamentable life, Wuornos had gone completely mad: "I'll be back like *Independence Day* with Jesus, like the movie, big mothership and all. I'll be back."

2003 was a big year for Aileen Wuc
previous October, when her long-de
fourteen months after she was kil
shockingly violent life story was i
claimed movies: Nick Broomfield
Serial Killer, and Patty Jenkins's
Theron.

On the face of it (as it were), casting Theron—one of
orously beautiful women on the planet—as the coarse-featured, case-
hardened Wuornos made about as much sense as deciding that Brad
Pitt would be perfect in the role of Quasimodo. Aided, however, by a
brilliant makeup job, Theron completely transformed herself into the
swaggering, foul-mouthed man-hater, winning a well-deserved Oscar for
her performance.

To get an idea of just how uncannily convincing she is in the role, viewers can compare her to the actual Wuornos in Broomfield's powerful docu
mentary, a follow-up to his equally fine 1993 film, *Aileen Wuornos: The
Selling of a Serial Killer.*

THE A TO Z

316

vacated his flat at 10
diately noticed a f
ing its source t
inside, and d
a conceal
under
bac

THE WRONG MAN

There's only one thing worse than being arrested, convicted, and imprisoned for a crime you didn't commit: being executed for it. And when the
crime in question is serial murder, the outrage is compounded. Not only is
an innocent man put to death, but the real culprit remains at large and continues to get away with murder.

Unfortunately, cases like this have occurred from time to time. One of
the most egregious was that of Timothy Evans, a dim-witted English truck
driver convicted of the brutal murder of his wife and baby daughter in 1950.
The chief prosecution witness against Evans was his downstairs neighbor—
a quiet, eminently respectable gentleman named John Reginald Christie.
Three years after Evans was hanged at London's Pentonville Prison, Christie

Rillington Place. The tenants who replaced him imme-
...oul odor emanating from somewhere in the kitchen. Trac-
...o a hollow section of wall, they tore off the wallpaper, peered
...iscovered the decomposed remains of three women shoved into
...ed cupboard. Another body—that of Christie's wife—was found
...the floorboards, and two more female corpses were unearthed in the
...yard. Altogether, the quiet little man had committed eight murders—
...our of them following Evans's execution. Christie himself was hanged in
July 1953. Another thirteen years would pass before the British government
finally admitted it had made an error in Evans's case and granted him a
posthumous pardon.

Fatal mistakes of this kind can happen anywhere, of course. But they are
particularly common in totalitarian nations, where "justice" is meted out
with alarming speed. During the 1930s and early 1940s, Nazi authorities periodically picked up and executed suspected deviants for a series of lust
murders taking place in the town of Kupenick, just east of Berlin. The real
culprit, however—a sociopath named Bruno Ludke—wasn't identified until
1943, by which time he had, according to his own admission, committed an
astonishing eighty-five murders.

A similar story took place in the former USSR. In 1978, the savaged
corpse of a teenage girl was found in a forest outside the industrial city Ros-
tov-on-Don. The Soviet police quickly arrested and executed a known sex
offender. Unfortunately, they shot the wrong man. By the time they identified the right one—Andrei **Chikatilo,** the "Mad Beast of Rostov"—he had
butchered more than fifty women and children.

The Milquetoast Murderer

The story of John Reginald Christie and his fall-guy neighbor, Timothy
Evans—one of the most sensational cases in the annals of modern British
crime—is told with understated power in Richard Fleischer's absorbing
1970 film, *10 Rillington Place.* Shot on location at the actual murder house
(which was torn down the following year to make way for a parking garage),
the movie achieves its genuinely creepy power by presenting the sensa-

tional facts of the case in a subdued, low-key manner, consistent with the apparent drabness of the killer himself.

Richard Attenborough—who went on to achieve fame as the Oscar-winning director of *Gandhi* and other high-prestige pictures—turns in a striking performance as the homicidal Milquetoast who raped and murdered eight women over a thirteen-year span, storing their corpses in and around his flat at the infamous address. Equally good are John Hurt as the pathetically dim-witted Evans and Judy Geeson as his wife, Beryl. Highly recommended for those who enjoy subdued, tasteful psycho films. If you're looking for hardcore gore—forget about it.

X CHROMOSOME

During the 1960s, some scientists tried to establish a link between violence and excessive masculinity. According to their research, the presence of an extra Y (or male) chromosome made a man more prone to violent crime (see **Y Chromosome**).

Nowadays, this theory isn't given much credence. Interestingly, however, there *has* been a documented case of a serial killer suffering from the opposite defect. Bobby Joe Long, who murdered ten women in the 1970s, had an extra X (or female) chromosome in each cell of his body. As a result, his glands produced an inordinate amount of the female hormone estrogen, causing him to grow breasts during puberty.

His humiliation over this condition may well have contributed to his mental imbalance—though it was certainly not his only problem. Wildly accident prone, Long suffered a string of grievous **Head Injuries** throughout his life. And like so many serial killers, he was also subjected to what sociologists like to call "negative parenting." Among other things, his mother slept in bed with him until he was thirteen.

XEROX

Contrary to popular belief, most serial killers are happy to commit their crimes in utter obscurity. They enjoy living in the shadows, where they can pursue their unspeakable pleasures without drawing attention to their identities.

Other serial killers, however, are the opposite. They are publicity hounds. Their perverted pleasure is reinforced by playing mind games with the police and the media. This often takes the form of written taunts—a phenomenon that dates at least as far back as the **Jack the Ripper** case. Sending such letters is the psycho-killer's way of thumbing his nose at his pursuers, of displaying his supposed superiority. "Catch me if you can," these messages seem to jeer.

Of course, with advances in modern forensic science, sending an original letter runs its risks—the stationery, for example, might be traced back to the store where it was sold, and from there to the purchaser. One way to get around this problem is to send a copy. That's exactly what happened in the case of the self-styled **BTK** Strangler—though this precaution actually ended up giving police an intriguing lead in the case.

As he terrorized the city of Wichita by binding, torturing, and killing at least seven victims, BTK kept up a steady one-way correspondence with the media. On February 10, 1978, he sent a letter to a local TV station in which he claimed to have murdered seven victims and petulantly asked, "How many do I have to kill before I get my name in the paper or some national attention?" The letter, however, was not an original but a Xerox.

In the fall of 1984, a member of the task force set up to identify the elusive serial killer took this piece of evidence to the Xerox company headquarters in Syracuse, New York. Technicians there determined that it was a fifth-generation copy, making it impossible to trace. They were, however, able to establish exactly *where* the killer made his copy. The Xerox machine was located at the Wichita State University library. Unfortunately, without any other leads, the police couldn't use this information to narrow down the number of suspects any further.

The investigation continued to spin its wheels until 2003 when the BTK Strangler decided to contact the media once again. Included in his new set of correspondence were other Xeroxed items: photocopies of a woman's driver's license along with copies of photos of her dead body. The killer had been fond of taking mementoes from the scenes of his crimes, so it wasn't surprising that he had held on to this woman's license. What *was* surprising was the identity of the woman. Vicki Wegerle had been found murdered in 1986, nine years after the last known BTK killing. Until they received this package, the police had no idea that Wegerle was another one of the Strangler's victims.

When they finally made an arrest in the case the following year, they had another murder to add to killer's résumé of terror.

The Xerox company also figured in the case of the worst episode of **Mass Murder** in Hawaiian history. On November 2, 1999, a disgruntled forty-one-year-old copy machine repairman named Bryan Uyesugi went on a rampage at his workplace, slaughtering seven of his fellow Xerox employees with a semi-automatic handgun. Despite defense efforts to portray him as mentally incompetent—the old "tormented by demons" ploy—Uyesugi was found guilty and sentenced to life without parole. His appalling act has earned him everlasting infamy in the annals of Hawaiian crime as the "Xerox Killer."

X-Rated

According to the experts from the **FBI**'s Behavioral Science Unit, perhaps as many as 80 percent of serial killers display a fondness for hardcore pornography, particularly movies and books featuring violent, sadomasochistic sex. Of course, this isn't exactly the world's most startling finding. Indeed, it would be far more surprising to learn that *Horton Hears a Who* was Henry Lee **Lucas**'s favorite book or that Jeffrey **Dahmer** was a big fan of the Nancy Drew series.

Still, various moral crusaders have used this statistic to help bolster their argument that pornography—along with other types of transgressive entertainment (like "slasher" movies and "death metal" rock)—is a leading cause of sexual homicide. Social scientists remain divided on this issue. For every psychologist who insists that there is a direct, causal link between X-rated entertainment and violent crime, there are others who argue the opposite—that material that depicts graphic sex and violence may actually help defuse aggressive impulses.

In short, the relationship between media violence and real-life crime remains extremely murky. It is worth noting, however, that, for as long as there has been such a thing as popular culture, it has been blamed for everything from juvenile delinquency to multiple murder.

A hundred years before porn videos and splatter movies, the favorite target of social reformers was the genre known as "dime novels"—cheap little paperbacks relating the lurid adventures of bloodthirsty bad men, cutthroat pirates, and two-fisted detectives. Writing in the late 1800s, Dr. Elizabeth Blackwell—America's first female physician—warned that "the dangers arising from such vicious literature cannot be overestimated by parents." The appalling case of the Boston child-fiend, Jesse Pomeroy, seemed to bear out Blackwell's claim. The grotesque-looking Pomeroy began torturing younger children when he was eleven. He graduated to murder at fourteen, savaging a ten-year-old girl and a four-year-old boy. After his arrest, outraged moralists blamed his crimes on the corrupting influence of dime novels like *Desperate Dan, the Dastard* and *The Pirates of the Pecos.* Unfortunately, their argument was somewhat undermined by the fact that Pomeroy had apparently never read a book in his life.

In our own times, other forms of pop entertainment have been attacked for their presumably pernicious influence. In the 1950s, horror comics were condemned as a major cause of juvenile delinquency. More recently, America's rising crime rate has been blamed on everything from *Friday the 13th* movies to gangsta rap.

In truth, it is very hard to establish a straightforward link between media images and human behavior, particularly when it comes to serial killers, whose minds work in such bizarre ways. The notorious 1930s cannibal-killer, Albert **Fish,** found certain passages in the Bible wildly arousing. Charles **Manson**'s murderous fantasies were inspired by one of the most benign works of popular art ever created—the Beatles' *White Album.*

German sex murderer Heinrich Pommerencke—known as the "Beast of the Black Forest"—is another case in point. One night in February 1959, Pommerencke went to the movies, and after seeing a bunch of women cavorting on screen, he became convinced that all females deserved to die. Shortly afterward, he committed the first of four savage rape-murders.

The film that inspired this rampage? Cecil B. DeMille's *The Ten Commandments.*

Pornography Made Me Do It

The night before his execution, Ted **Bundy** gave his final interview to evangelist James Dobson. With death just hours away, Bundy—the slayer of anywhere from thirty to fifty young women—had a message for America: Beware of pornography. Bundy confessed that at an early age, he had become addicted to images of sexual violence and claimed that his exposure to brutal pornography had turned him into a sex killer.

Antiporn crusaders embraced Bundy's statement. Here, they argued, was conclusive proof of everything they'd been claiming—pornography leads to ultimate evil.

There were a couple of problems with Bundy's statement, however. For one thing, he was born in 1946, which means that he grew up during the 1950s—an era when it was considerably harder to come by sadomasochistic porn than it is today. Back in the Eisenhower era, you couldn't just stroll into your neighborhood video shop and rent *Teenage Bondage Sluts* from the "Adults Only" section. If Bundy was really getting off on violent pornography back then, there must already have been something dark and twisted inside him that was driving him to go out and hunt for these images.

There is another serious problem with Bundy's admission, conveniently ignored by antiporn activists: Bundy was a psychopathic liar. For ten years, he had done everything possible to deny his guilt. Even when the jig was finally up, he found a way to shrug off responsibility for his atrocities by putting the blame on outside influences.

He wasn't responsible for his crimes. Pornography made him do it.

X RAYS

In the view of many crime buffs, the single most perverted killer in American history was the cannibalistic pedophile Albert **Fish.** Perhaps the most compelling evidence in support of this opinion were a series of X rays taken shortly after Fish's arrest for the kidnapping and murder of twelve-year-old Grace Budd.

Interviewed in his jail cell by two state-appointed psychiatrists who were trying to evaluate his sanity, Fish revealed that—as an act of contrition for killing the girl—he had purchased a pack of sewing needles and, using a thimble, had shoved five of them up behind his testicles so deeply that they had remained permanently embedded inside his body.

Though this story seemed too outrageous to believe, Fish was a degenerate of such extravagant proportions that the authorities decided to check it out. The old man was taken from prison to a nearby hospital, where his pelvic region was X-rayed by the hospital's chief radiologist.

One of the X rays of Albert Fish's pelvic region, showing more than two dozen needles shoved into his lower body
(*New York Daily News*)

As it turned out, Fish's incredible claim was actually an understatement. The X rays clearly revealed a number of sharp, thin objects scattered throughout the area of the old man's groin and lower abdomen. These objects—which resembled long, black splinters floating in the bright tissue around and between the hip bones—were unmistakably needles. Their location—around the rectum and bladder, just below the tip of the spine, and in the muscles of the groin—made it clear that they had been inserted into Fish's body from below, evidently through his perineum, the flesh between his anus and scrotum.

Unbelievable as it seemed, the old man had been telling the truth—or at least part of it. He had told the psychiatrists that he had punished himself by pushing five needles into his body. But when the physician counted the objects in the X rays, he came up with a significantly different figure. Lodged inside Fish's body were no fewer than twenty-seven needles! Among his dizzying array of masochistic pleasures, the wildly perverted old man had been sticking sewing needles into his own groin for years (see **Paraphilia**).

"These X rays are unique in the history of medical science."

DR. FREDERICK WERTHAM,
commenting on the X rays of Albert Fish's pelvic region

YARDS

A few years back, the satirical paper *The Onion* ran a pseudo-news story headlined "Neighbors Remember Serial Killer as Serial Killer." The article quoted (the entirely fictitious) Will Rowell of Dunedin, Florida, who recalled his neighbor, Eddie Lee Curtis, as "kind of a murderous, insane, serial killer-type of fellow. . . . He sort of kept to himself, killing nurses, having sex with their corpses, and then burying their bodies in his backyard."

As Homer Simpson might say, it's funny because it's true. While some suburban serial killers go to great lengths to dispose of their victims (Long Island psycho Joel Rifkin, for example, routinely drove all the way to New Jersey to get rid of the dismembered remains of the prostitutes he had lured to his home and then strangled), others are content simply to bury them in their own backyards.

Of the nine young women who met hideous deaths at the hands of the British **Killer Couple** Fred and Rose West, for example, a number—including their own seventeen-year-old daughter—ended up interred in the Wests' backyard garden.

Billy Mansfield, a refugee from a trailer park in Weeki Wachee, Florida, murdered twenty-nine-year-old Renee Salings shortly after relocating to Santa Cruz, California. A few months later, authorities in Florida dug up Mansfield's property back in Weeki Wachee and discovered the remains of four other women buried in his backyard.

Another Santa Cruz psychopath, Edmund **Kemper,** the "Coed Butcher," began using his yard for diabolical purposes at the tender age of nine, when he dug a hole in back of his house and buried the family cat alive. Years later, after graduating to sadistic sex murder, he fatally shot a nineteen-year-old student named Cynthia Schall, transported her body home in the trunk of his car, and kept it overnight in his closet. The following day, while his mother was at work, he dissected the corpse in the bathtub, then buried Schall's head in his backyard with her face turned toward his bedroom window. "Sometimes at night," he later confessed, "I talked to her, saying love things, the way you do to a girlfriend or wife."

Of course, planting corpses in your own backyard can be a risky business. In the early 1990s, for example, Herb Baumeister—a seemingly respectable Midwestern family man with a depraved double life—began trolling the gay hangouts of Indianapolis. Whenever his wife took the kids off for an overnight visit to Grandma, Herb would bring a male pickup back to his handsome suburban house, strangle the young man during sex, then dispose of the corpse in his wooded backyard.

All went smoothly until 1994, when one of Herb's sons, playing in the yard, stumbled upon the half-buried skeleton of a human being. Fortunately for Herb, his wife, Julie, had a highly developed capacity for denial. When she confronted Herb about this alarming find, he fed her a cock-and-bull story: the skeleton, he claimed, was just an old anatomical specimen he had inherited from his physician father and decided to discard. Julie chose to believe him.

Eventually—thanks to the efforts of a private investigator, hired by the mother of one of the missing young men—Baumeister was identified as a suspect. When the police searched his property, they turned up thousands of human bone fragments—jawbones, thighbones, fingers, ribs, vertebrae, all stripped clean by animals and the elements, some partly burned. Experts estimated that, altogether, the skeletal fragments constituted the remains of eleven victims.

By the time the digging was over, Baumeister himself was dead. Fleeing to Canada, he committed suicide in an Ontario park on the evening of July

3, 1996, shooting himself in the head with a .357 Magnum after eating a peanut butter sandwich.

Y Chromosome

Serial murder is such an overwhelmingly evil act that it's natural for people to wonder why. Why would a human being commit such a monstrous crime? There's a desperate need to find an explanation that would make sense of this incomprehensible horror. For at least a hundred years, scientists have been searching for a single, identifiable cause for criminal violence. In 1968, they finally came up with one. The answer to the question *Why?* turned out to be . . . *Y.*

More precisely, it turned out to be a *Y chromosome.* As everyone who's taken high school biology knows, there are two sex chromosomes, **X** (female) and Y (male). Every cell in the average man contains one of each. A few men, however, have an extra Y, or male, chromosome—a condition known as the XYY Syndrome. Once they made this discovery, scientists began theorizing that this extra dash of maleness made its possessor even more masculine—i.e., crude, aggressive, and violent—than normal.

Their theory seemed to be borne out by the case of Richard **Speck,** the notorious multiple murderer who, in 1966, slaughtered eight student nurses in their Chicago apartment. Speck, who was diagnosed as an XYY type, fit the image of a supercharged male brute to perfection. He was big, dumb, and savage, with a face ravaged by acne scars and a "Born to Raise Hell" tattoo proudly displayed on one arm. At his trial, his attorney argued that Speck wasn't responsible for his crimes because he was suffering from XYY Syndrome. In effect, Speck's tattoo was telling the truth—his extra male chromosome had made him bad from birth.

There was only one problem with this defense. Speck, it turned out, had been misdiagnosed. He was normal—at least from a chromosomal point of view.

Undaunted, proponents of the theory pointed out that there is an unusually high proportion of XYY types in the prison population. But these findings were shown to be skewed. The vast majority of men born with XYY Syndrome display no abnormally violent tendencies. By now, the theory has been largely discredited. As of this writing, serial murder remains what it has always been—an unfathomable evil. Or as the Bible puts it, a "mystery of iniquity."

The "Yorkshire Ripper"

Peter Sutcliffe; from
Bloody Visions **trading cards**

The five-year search for the homicidal maniac known as the "Yorkshire Ripper" was the biggest manhunt in British history. The police interviewed more than 200,000 people, took more than 30,000 statements, searched more than 20,000 homes. In the course of this mammoth investigation, a young truck driver named Peter Sutcliffe was called in for questioning no fewer than nine times—so often that his co-workers jokingly nicknamed him "**Jack the Ripper**." Each time, however, his interrogators swallowed Sutcliffe's alibi and let him go free.

On January 2, 1981, police discovered—almost accidentally—that Sutcliffe was, in fact, the killer. By then, thirteen women, ranging in age from sixteen to forty-seven, had been savagely murdered—bludgeoned, stabbed, and mutilated.

Sutcliffe led the kind of schizoid life so characteristic of serial killers. On the one hand, he was a reliable worker and devoted husband. On the other, he was a woman-hating sociopath whose crimes were motivated by intense sexual loathing. Sutcliffe himself claimed that his vendetta against **Prosti-tutes** began after a hooker cheated him of money. But the roots of his pathology clearly ran much deeper. As a teenager, he took a job as a mortuary attendant and enjoyed manipulating corpses as though they were ventriloquist dummies. He also spent hours at a local wax museum, transfixed by a display that showed the devastating effects of VD on the human body.

Sutcliffe began by assaulting prostitutes with homemade bludgeons— socks weighted with gravel or bricks. His first few victims survived these attacks. A twenty-eight-year-old hooker named Wilma McCann wasn't as lucky. On October 30, 1975, Sutcliffe smashed the back of her skull with a ball-peen hammer, then stabbed her fourteen times. Three months later, he killed again. Following this second homicide, Sutcliffe's murderous impulses seemed to subside. A year later, however, they erupted with a vengeance. In the fifteen months between February 1977 and May 1978, he killed seven more women, bludgeoning them first with his hammer, then savaging them with his knife. In some cases, he mutilated the genitalia. Most of these victims were streetwalkers, though one was a sixteen-year-old shop assistant who had been on her way home from a disco.

With all of northern England in a panic, police mounted an all-out hunt for the killer. They were sidetracked, however, by a tape recoording they received in June 1979, which purported to be from the Ripper. While police pursued this lead (which turned out to be a hoax), Sutcliffe continued to kill. By then, he was no longer restricting himself to prostitutes. Sutcliffe's final four victims were female college students and young working women.

His arrest came in January 1981 when a police officer on stakeout— Sergeant Robert Ring—spotted Sutcliffe in a car with a prostitute. A check of Sutcliffe's plates revealed that the car was stolen. Before being hauled down to the station house, Sutcliffe asked for permission to go behind some shrubbery and "pee." Sergeant Ring obliged.

The next morning, while Sutcliffe was still being questioned, a lightbulb went off in Ring's head. Rushing back to the spot where he'd arrested Sutcliffe, he searched behind the shrubbery and discovered a ball-peen hammer and a knife. Confronted with this evidence, Sutcliffe quickly confessed. He attempted to plead insanity, claiming that God's voice, emanating from a grave, had ordered him to kill. The court was not impressed. The "Yorkshire Ripper" was sentenced to life in prison.

Zealots

There are plenty of people around who blame our country's social ills—including our epidemic of violent crime—on the loss of old-fashioned religious values, as if the murder rate would miraculously decline if Americans spent fewer hours in front of the TV and more time studying the Bible. Unfortunately, there is a slight problem with this theory. Some of the most monstrous killers in American history were religious fanatics who could recite Scripture from memory and—when they weren't busy torturing children or mutilating corpses—loved to do nothing better than read the Good Book.

Albert **Fish,** the cannibalistic monster who spent a lifetime preying on little children, is a terrifying case in point. From his earliest years, Fish was fascinated by the Bible and at one point actually dreamed of becoming a minister. As he grew older, his religious interests blossomed into a full-fledged mania. Obsessed with the story of Abraham and Isaac, he became convinced that he, too, should sacrifice a young child—an atrocity he actually carried out on more than one occasion. From time to time, he heard strange, archaic-sounding words—*correcteth, delighteth, chastiseth*—that he interpreted as divine commandments to torment and kill. He would organize these words into quasi-biblical messages: "Blessed is the man who correcteth his son in whom he delighteth with stripes"; "Happy is he that taketh Thy little ones and dasheth their heads against the stones." Fish not only tortured and killed children in response to these delusions but subjected himself to a variety of masochistic torments in atonement for his sins. One of his favorite forms of self-mortification was to shove sewing needles so deeply into his own groin that they remained embedded around his bladder. For the hopelessly demented Fish, his ultimate crime—the murder, dismemberment, and cannibalization of a twelve-year-old girl—also had religious overtones. As he told the psychiatrist who examined him in prison, he associated the eating of the child's flesh and the drinking of her blood with the "idea of Holy Communion."

Fish's near contemporary Earle Leonard **Nelson** was another religious fanatic, who spent countless hours poring over passages from the Book of Revelations: "And the woman was arrayed in purple and scarlet color . . . having a golden cup in her hand full of abominations and filthiness of her fornication: and upon her forehead was a name written, MYSTERY, BABYLON THE GREAT, THE MOTHER OF HARLOTS AND ABOMINATIONS OF THE EARTH." Nelson's familiarity with the Bible was one of his most disarming features, allowing him to win the confidence of his landlady-victims, who never guessed that such a well-read and obviously devout young man was actually the infamous "Gorilla Murderer," the shadowy serial strangler responsible for nearly two dozen savage killings from coast to coast.

There have been plenty of other psychos who have committed their crimes in the name of religion, from self-ordained street preacher Benjamin Miller, who murdered a string of black prostitutes in the late 1960s as punishment for their sinful ways, to the homicidal hippie couple James and Susan Carson, who believed they were complying with the biblical injunction "Thou shalt not suffer a witch to live" (Exodus 22:18) when they murdered their victims.

Homicidal religious fanatics have been the subject of two memorable movies: the splendid 1955 thriller *Night of the Hunter* (in which Robert Mitchum does a terrifying turn as a sin-obsessed preacher) and the gruesomely baroque 1995 hit, *Se7en,* about a serial killer who arranges his victims in grotesque tableaux inspired by the Seven Deadly Sins: gluttony, lust, sloth, pride, anger, envy, and greed.

> "And I will cause them to eat the flesh of their sons and the flesh of their daughters, and they shall eat every one the flesh of his friend in the siege and straitness, wherewith their enemies, and they that seek their lives, shall straiten them."
>
> *Jeremiah 19:9 (Albert Fish's favorite passage of Scripture)*

ZEITGEIST

Anyone who makes a serious study of criminal history quickly discovers an intriguing, if depressing, fact: every period has produced many more cases of appalling murder than most people realize. To cite just one of countless examples, in 1895, a clean-cut medical student named Theo Durrant murdered and raped two young women in San Francisco and stashed their mutilated corpses in his neighborhood church. The Durrant case was a nationwide sensation—but who besides the most ardent crime buff has heard of it today?

This raises an interesting question: why do some heinous killers fade into instant obscurity, while others achieve an almost mythic status? Part of the answer certainly lies in the singularly horrific deeds of the latter. The legendary serial killers (Ed **Gein**, Albert **Fish**, Jeffrey **Dahmer**, etc.) have a larger-than-life quality. Their crimes seem less pathological than supernatural—the doings of demons and ghouls. But there is another factor, too. Certain criminals exert a powerful fascination because they seem to embody the darkest impulses and obsessions of their day—all that is most reprehensible about any given age. As much as any hero or celebrity, they personify the spirit of the time—what the Germans call the zeitgeist.

> "To parallel such a career one must go back to past ages and to the time of the Borgias or the Brinvilliers, and even these were not such human monsters as Holmes seems to have been. He is a prodigy of wickedness, a human demon, a being so unthinkable that no novelist would dare to invent such a character. The story, too, tends to illustrate the end of the century."
>
> *From an 1896 newspaper article on H. H. Holmes*

The nineteenth-century "multi-murderer" Dr. H. H. **Holmes** is a classic example. A debonair ladies' man with a deadly allure, Holmes seemed like the living incarnation of the fairy-tale monster **Bluebeard,** killing and dismembering a string of nubile young women in the murky depths of his "Horror Castle." At the same time, he was the terrifying epitome of all the excesses of the Gilded Age, a money-mad psychopath whose murders were motivated as much by greed as by blood lust.

In the 1930s—the era when the Lindbergh baby was kidnapped—Albert Fish represented every parent's worst nightmare, a fiendishly cunning child snatcher in the guise of a kindly old man. While the case of Edward Gein had the timeless horror of a "Hänsel and Gretel"-type fairy tale (the seemingly innocuous, out-of-the-way dwelling that turns out to be the abode of an ogre), his crimes also reflected the prevailing cultural pathology of postwar America, a time and place marked by extreme sexual hypocrisy, when the realities of erotic behavior were masked by an official culture of prudery.

Charles Starkweather—the sociopathic James Dean-wannabe who slaughtered eleven people during a three-week killing spree—embodied another quintessentially 1950s phenomenon: the wildly antisocial "juvenile delinquent" with a grudge against grown-up society. During the 1960s, Charles **Manson**—the sex-and-drug-crazed demon-hippie—was the nightmare realization of "straight" society's darkest fears, while Ted **Bundy** seemed to embody all that was most perilous about the 1970s me generation's swinging-singles scene: the danger of finding yourself with the wrong pickup and ending up in a very nasty one-night stand.

Bret Easton Ellis's much-reviled book *American Psycho* actually plays very cleverly with the notion of the serial killer as symbol of the zeitgeist. Its sociopathic Yuppie protagonist, Patrick Bateson, is meant to be a metaphor for the greediness of the 1980s Reagan era. His only concern is the fulfillment of his own appetites, and he regards other people as nothing more than highly disposable commodities to be used for his own pleasure.

Zodiac

Zodiac; from
Murderers! **trading card set**
(Courtesy of Roger Worsham)

California in the late 1960s was a hotbed of hippiedom—the site of the Summer of Love, the birthplace of the "be-in," the land where visitors were advised to wear flowers in their hair. At the same time, it was home to some of the most notorious psychos of the late twentieth century. Charles **Manson** and his blood-crazed "family" slaughtered seven people in Los Angeles in 1969. A year later, a hippie named John Linley Frazier wiped out a household of five in the Northern California town of Santa Cruz. Perhaps even more unnerving was the night-prowling gunman known only as "Zodiac," who terrorized San Francisco during a nine-month spree that began in December 1968. Before he was finished, five people were dead and two more desperately wounded.

His motive? "I like killing people because it's so much fun," he explained in an anonymous letter.

The first to die was a teenage couple, shot dead in a **Lovers' Lane.** Six months later, he gunned down another young couple, killing the young woman with nine blasts from a 9mm pistol (the young man, shot four times, survived). Forty minutes later—in what would be the first in a series of chilling communications from the killer—the police received an anonymous phone call from a gruff-voiced man: "If you will go one mile east on Columbus Parkway to a public park, you will find the kids in a brown car. They have been shot with a 9mm Luger. I also killed those kids last year. Good-bye."

While panic spread through the area, the killer began sending **Letters** to local newspapers, signed with the astrological symbol of the zodiac. Each letter contained a line of cipher. Decoded by a local high school teacher, the cryptic lines formed a single message that explained the killer's motivations: "I will be reborn in Paradise, and then all that I have killed will become my slaves. I will not give you my name because you will try to slow or stop my collecting of slaves for my afterlife."

Two months later, Zodiac (as he was now called) set out to collect some more slaves. Wearing a black hood with eye slits and the zodiac symbol painted on it in white, the killer accosted a young couple at gunpoint, bound them with rope, then attacked them with a hunting knife. The young man survived with five wounds in the back, but the girl—stabbed fourteen times—died.

His last known victim was a San Francisco cab driver who was shot once in the back of the head. Before fleeing the crime scene, the killer tore off parts of the victim's shirt. Shortly afterward, the editor of the *San Francisco Chronicle* received an envelope. Inside was a swatch of the cab driver's shirt and a letter from Zodiac in which he promised to "wipe out a school bus some morning." Fortunately he never made good on this threat. Nor—as far as anyone knows—did Zodiac ever kill again.

The classic Clint Eastwood movie *Dirty Harry* (1971) is a gripping fictionalized account of the hunt for the Zodiac killer, with Andy Robinson turning in an unforgettable performance as the unspeakable psychocreep. Needless to say, the movie has a much more satisfying ending—with Clint blasting the psycho into well-deserved oblivion—than real life supplied. In actuality, Zodiac simply vanished.

There have been many theories about his identity, but one has gotten more traction than others. In his 2002 book, *Zodiac Unmasked,* author Robert Graysmith claims that the killer was a convicted child molester and all-around misfit named Arthur Leigh Allen, who died in 1992.

Others, however, point out that neither Allen's fingerprints nor his handwriting match the evidence left behind by the murderer. In the end, Zodiac's identity remains one of the great **Unsolved** mysteries of modern crime.

ZOMBIES

Joyce Carol Oates's harrowing 1995 novel *Zombie* deals with a psychopath named Quentin P———, who is obsessed with the idea of creating a zombie who will become his personal slave. To that end, he performs a series of makeshift lobotomies on various half-drugged victims by sticking an ice pick under their eyelids and up into their brains. All he succeeds in doing, however, is killing them—though a few of them manage to survive for a brief period (see **Recommended Reading**).

Reviewing Oates's novel in the *New York Times Book Review,* one prominent critic interpreted this story as an "allegory" about "what American society itself is capable of." The character's "efforts to create zombies," this critic wrote, are "derived from the irreversible psychosurgical procedures performed during the 1940s and 1950s on thousands of unfortunate Americans judged to be psychotic, dangerous or incompetent."

> "A true ZOMBIE would be mine forever.
> He would obey every command & whim.
> Saying 'Yes, Master' & 'No, Master.' He would kneel
> before me lifting his eyes to me saying, 'I love you,
> Master. There is no one but you, Master.' "
>
> *From* Zombie *by Joyce Carol Oates*

While this is an ingenious theory, it ignores a crucial fact: Quentin P———'s zombie obsession derives not from the psychosurgical practices of the 1940s but from the far more recent atrocities of Jeffrey **Dahmer,** the obvious inspiration for Oates's novel. In addition to his many other unspeakable acts, Dahmer performed a number of do-it-yourself lobotomies in an effort to turn his victims into passive sex slaves whom he could violate at will.

Unlike Oates's fictional monster, Dahmer did not rely on an ice pick. Instead, after drugging his victim, he would drill a hole in the young man's head and inject muriatic acid into the brain with a hypodermic syringe. Most of the victims died instantly, though one actually remained alive and ambulatory for two days after being injected.

ZOOPHILIA

Zoophilia is the technical term for bestiality: sex with animals. Peter **Kürten** and Henry Lee **Lucas** are among the degenerates known to have engaged in this perversion as teenagers. Budding serial killers often combine bestiality with **Animal Torture,** as a kind of rehearsal for their later acts of lust murder. As a youth, for example, Kürten enjoyed slitting the throats of animals—pigs, sheeps, goats, dogs—while having sex with them.

Of course, zoophilia is only one of a shocking range of perversions that serial killers routinely indulge in. For more on the subject, see **Paraphilias.**

ZULU

While the majority of U. S. serial killers are white—mirroring our country's racial demographics—the situation is different in other parts of the world. South Africa, for example, has produced a striking number of serial murderers in recent decades, nearly all of them blacks from KwaZulu-Natal, or the Zulu Kingdom.

The most notorious is Morris Sithole. Abandoned by his widowed mother at an early age, Sithole was sent to an orphanage in KwaZulu-Natal, where he suffered harsh mistreatment at the hands of his supposed caretakers. Released from prison after doing time on a rape conviction, he embarked on a murder spree that left more than three dozen women dead between January and October 1995—throttled, strangled with their own underwear, or killed with a garrote. Following his capture, Sithole freely acknowledged his hatred of women, explaining that he was teaching his victims "a very good lesson" by killing them. His reign of terror earned him a combined prison sentence of more than 2,400 years.

Though they didn't match Sithole's body count, three other black serial killers from the KwaZulu-Natal province—Samuel Bongani Mfeka, Sipho Agmatir Thwala, and David Selepe—also raped and strangled an alarming number of victims during the 1990s. (See **Race and Racism.**)

Index